D0386293

The Security of Buildings

And you all know, security
is mortals' chiefest enemy

Macbeth
Act III Scene V

The Security of Buildings

Grahame Underwood DipArch RIBA

The Architectural Press: London

First published in 1984 by the
Architectural Press Limited,
9 Queen Anne's Gate, London SW1H 9BY

© Group 4 Total Security Limited 1984

British Library Cataloguing in Publication Data

Underwood, Grahame
    The security of buildings.
    1. Burglary protection
    I. Title
    690   TH9705

ISBN 0–85139–613–5

All rights reserved. No part of this publication may
be reproduced, stored in a retrieval system, or
transmitted, in any form or by any means,
electronic, mechanical, photocopying, recording or
otherwise, without the prior permission of the
publishers. Such permission, if granted, is subject
to a fee depending on the nature of the use.

Set in 10/13 pt Linotron Baskerville
by Phoenix Photosetting, Chatham

Printed and bound in Great Britain by
Biddles Ltd, Guildford and King's Lynn

Lay not up for yourselves treasures upon earth
where moth and rust doth corrupt, and where
theives break through and steal

St Matthew 6:19

The rain it raineth on the just
    And also on the unjust fella:
But chiefly on the just because
    The unjust steals the just's umbrella

Baron Bowen

Contents

Acknowledgements

I must thank all those members of Group 4 Total Security Ltd and Securitas International Products Ltd who gave me their time and assistance in the preparation of this book. I was able to develop a great respect for the professional skills of the security industry and I hope that I have been able to do justice to them.

Grahame Underwood

Birmingham 1984

Foreword

It was with considerable pleasure that I received the request to write a few words as the Foreword to this well worth while and in my mind overdue book on security, particularly as it affects architects and builders.

Throughout the world, losses and injury through crime have reached enormous and outrageous proportions. There is no doubt that crime is a threat to us all and the police are finding it increasingly difficult to fight alone the battle against the criminal. It is ever more important for all members of the public in all professions to assist the police in every way possible in the war against crime. In the particular context of this book, we must also think about the losses which amount to millions of pounds and are due to vandalism and fire.

I regret to say that in the past some architects and builders have been very loath to consider security. I have long felt that the architect should consider at the planning stage the security of a building, whether it be a large factory, office block or simple dwelling unit. That is not only the obvious time to do so but also the cheapest in the long term. I would like to see architects specifying the grade of hardware that is necessary to give cost-effective security. I know that some architects indeed do this, but builders are often unwilling to put in a good lock instead of a poor one if it costs more money. This is particularly so during a time of economic difficulty; I can well understand it but it is a very false economy.

Burglars are greedy people. They want as much property as they can get. They do not like hard work. Confronted with a good lock, a good safe or an alarm system, the burglar is likely to move on to an easier target. Time is of the essence: he must enter the premises quickly, steal and depart just as quickly. If we can hold up his endeavours so much the better: security is buying time.

Vandalism is an increasing and very worrying problem; much of it, particularly on building sites, is facilitated by design features which attract the vandal: low roofs, walls offering easy access, breakable light fittings, and so on. Precautions against vandalism must always be considered in advance by architects and builders and all these points have been covered by the author.

Security is concerned with preventing losses from crime, vandalism, fire, flooding, accident and waste.

Finally, to all architects and builders, I would say 'please plan for *your* prosperity and *our* protection.'

J. Philip-Sorensen

Chairman and Managing Director Group 4 Total Security, Limited

Introduction

1 Background

The purpose of this book is to bring together the many aspects of building design which are affected by considerations of security, both in its physical and its operational sense. Much is written about fire safety, functional requirements and the spaces necessary in various building types. The references for technical matters of weathering, insulation and the like are legion, and these aspects are also regulated by law and practice so that an overall standard is not difficult to achieve. For security, there is no such regulation and the available references are sparse. Much of the published data originates in the USA, and inevitably there is a strong US flavour to it which arises from the different patterns of American crime and society. In the main American data is not immediately applicable in Great Britain.

Security is important to many organisations and on a more personal basis to many individuals. And yet there is no stage of the building design or construction processes at which it is formally considered.

None of the professionals involved in the design of buildings—be they architects or engineers—have any instruction in security included in their education; a few schools include one or two informal lectures but these are exceptions. The concept of security is often misunderstood for this reason, and in any case is regarded as a low priority.

The police are the traditional authorities on security matters and crime prevention officers are maintained by all police forces to advise on the protection of property against crime. These officers experience opposite disadvantages to those suffered by architects, in that the police are taught little about the technology of building or the forces which operate to develop the design in a certain way. This disadvantage is shared to a large extent by the security industry.

It is therefore inevitable that communication is limited between the professionals in building and those in security, and that the view of each is too narrow. It is unfortunate that these circumstances have to some extent created two isolated groups, neither of which has any particular respect for the other. It is hoped that this book goes some way towards bridging the gap.

2 Society

The moral climate in society varies from time to time and carries with it a changing tolerance of crime. At one end of the scale, theft may be tolerated because its prevention, whilst quite possible, would cost more than the value of the losses, so an economic decision is taken. Shoplifting is a good example of this principle. On the other hand, it may be thought right to prevent theft or to detect the thief without necessarily measuring the cost directly against losses: this is a moral decision. In many cases the motives are mixed, but there should be a definition of the attitudes involved before a security system is designed, so that its purpose is clear and the direction of change can be predicted.

New attitudes to civil liberties are formed from time to time. The people of Ulster, for example, during their everyday activities tolerate searches of their persons and baggage on a scale which would be thought outrageous elsewhere; and for many years now airline passengers have submitted to stringent search without complaint.

3 Subjectivity

Security is an ancient need and rarely is it wholly related to a dispassionate assessment of risk. Both the requirement for security and the reaction to that which is provided are based on a subjective scale of emotions ranging from confidence to fear.

Neither are attacks on the security system always based on an accurate judgement of its resistance: just as an occupant may have a false perception of his security, so may a criminal.

For the purposes of this book, security may be defined as:

Confidence in the retention of belongings

Confidence in personal safety

4 Economics

Economic judgements and pressures are continually brought to bear on security measures; usually the pressure is applied at the immediate field level, setting the cost of defence against the loss; on a broader view, the level of policing and the cost of administration of justice are introduced, taking the cost of protection into the communal purse. Realistic costs are elusive. It has however, been said, that there should be an even wider study of the economics of security, particularly in a national period of economic recession. The business climate is a tenuous thing, and in an era when economic recovery is difficult, it must be nurtured.

The lack of secure environments for business and industry, most likely in older urban areas, presents a substantial obstacle to economic revitalisation, mainly because investment (old or new) is reduced by the dangers to person and property. A business cannot thrive if the employees cannot travel safely to work or park their vehicles with confidence, and feel that their workplace is not threatened by arson, vandalism or other crime. It cannot even survive if its base is insecure.

The types of business which exist in depressed urban areas tend to be small concerns which lack the scale, resources and expertise to influence the security of their locality: it is an economic matter and one which should properly be a major concern of the community.

An idea gaining some ground is that of the security grant. On the same principle as the grants made for insulation, money would be made available for individual premises so that the community as a whole need allocate fewer resources to policing. The idea is a long way from fruition.

5 Practicality

Whatever the solutions to the problems of security, be they physical or managerial, they must be designed for the practical world. It is relatively easy to lay down a policy and to install hardware, but if the system cannot be lived with day by day then it is doomed to fail. There is no doubt that the real skill in security design lies in the management of the practicalities.

6 The systems approach

It is important that security is seen as a whole, and both designed and operated as a system. The subsequent chapters try to maintain this approach, and mix considerations of policy and management with construction and hardware wherever appropriate.

The normal processes of management by objectives should be applied to the establishment of the system.

7 Decay

Throughout this book, reference is made repeatedly to the concept of *decay*. This is arguably the most serious threat to a security system and no apology is made for the repetition. Decay occurs when building fabric and hardware deteriorate and, far more frequently, when human frailties accumulate: there is no field in which familiarity more commonly breeds contempt than in security. It must be avoided and countered where possible but, most of all, it must be expected.

8 The brief

Any design requires a brief and the quality of the end product is determined to a large extent by the foundations laid in the brief. This principle holds equally good in the design of security and the same difficulties arise in practice over the generation of this brief. To begin with, who is the client? The building owner may well be a landlord—public or private—who has no interest whatsoever in the protection of the contents; and the occupier by the same token cannot control the building fabric to any great extent. Many buildings in the UK are constructed speculatively with no occupant in sight and so with little chance of meeting the specific security requirements of the eventual tenant.

Some organisations have considered their security on a corporate basis and a standard brief will probably be available for their buildings: banks are obvious examples and many local authorities also have standard requirements for their housing. It must however be said that the quality of these briefs varies enormously. Some are also outdated and inappropriate for the present day.

9 The future

In 1982, work began on the compilation of a new British Standard: the first to deal with security in any broad sense. Publication is intended in six parts, commencing in 1985. The first three will probably appear in 1985, 1987 and 1988 and will cover:

Dwellings

Offices and shops

Warehouses and distribution units

It has also been suggested that some security measures could be included in the Building Regulations. Problems of definition, standards and enforcement have so far prevented any serious progress in this direction.

10 This book

The structure of this book is simple: following a general consideration of the risks to be faced, the defences are set out element by element through the building and its environs. Chapter 5 is concerned with the growing anxiety about personal safety in the face of increasing violence. Chapters 6 and 7 cover the applications of physical devices to detect intruders and control access, together with their operational consequences. Vandalism is a special problem and is discussed in Chapter 8. Subsequent chapters are concerned with surveillance and monitoring, the quite separate criteria arising from safes and strongrooms, and the operation and maintenance of established installations.

1 Risk

1.1 The concept

1.1.1 The concept of risk is at the very heart of security. Attitudes to risks, however, are complex, and include such varied factors as chance, adventure, and simple ignorance. Risks may be miscalculated or misunderstood, but their study and assessment has long been a speciality of those involved in insurance, investment and horse racing. Many other professions manipulate risk in the course of their work, often without recognising that they do so. Car drivers are statistically at higher risk of personal injury and property damage during their time at the wheel than most of them are at any other time of their working or private life; and yet the major proportion of that risk is within their control and often fully understood.

1.2 The sources of risk

1.2.1 Know your enemy: in order to manipulate risks it is first of all necessary to define their source and try to understand their nature. In an organisation or business it is clear that there are two distinct branches of risk: first of all there are the business risks—those which arise from the normal course of operations and trading. These must be assumed to be completely within the expertise and control of the management: that is its main purpose. The second branch is formed by those risks which are outside that purpose and therefore unwelcome intrusions into the course of business. In addition, by their very nature, they may well be outside the competence of normal management. These risks can (and should) all be manipulated to a greater or lesser extent. They include those itemised in 1.2.2.

1.2.2 Personal safety
Death of an employee, customer, visitor, bystander or trespasser. The causes of this may not be limited to immediate hazards on the premises, but can include faulty products or advice, or can follow, years later, from some hazardous process.
Injury may be the lesser result of the hazard. There may also be criminal assaults to be considered.
Sickness may also arise from industrial processes or from less direct causes such as discomfort or fear of attack.

1

The burden of responsibility carried by an employer or a landlord in these matters is heavy; and rightly so. An injured person may look to civil action in the courts to obtain compensation, and to the many prosecutions which can be brought under the various Factories Acts and legislation concerning specific industrial processes and materials. Legislation of a more general nature includes:

> The Health and Safety at Work Act 1973
> The Occupiers Liability Act 1957
> The Defective Premises Act 1972

Employers also have a duty to protect those who may be thought specially vulnerable to criminal attack, such as employees who handle cash or valuable materials.

1.2.3 The physical effects of nature (acts of God)

Storm and flood damage can be disastrous, even in temperate climates, and the disruption to business can be equivalent to a fire. Suppliers, customers and employees in the area can also be affected.

Earthquake requires little comment, being not only an act of God but also *force majeure*!

Fire is preventable in the main, the obvious exception being a spread of flame from neighbouring property.

1.2.4 Technical events

Plant failure can be dangerous, damaging or both. The machinery itself may become dangerous when it malfunctions or it can cease to provide an essential safety function. On a lesser scale, damage may be caused to materials, products, data or other plant.

Safety device malfunction is common. It is damaging in that the devices are necessarily designed to fail safe, and therefore tend to shut down the system they control. The essence of a safety device is that it should be more reliable than the system to which it is fitted; the difficulties in achieving this are however so fundamental that the designer can rarely succeed. Devices which do not fail safe are highly dangerous.

Hazardous processes may be unavoidable and are often regarded as so—usually for historical reasons. By definition they are major sources of risk and the acceptability of this risk will vary with attitudes, technology and the development of alternatives.

Structural collapse may arise from bad design, bad construction or misuse. It may be minor and preceded by obvious signs of distress or it may be sudden and devastating.

Fire may be caused by the malfunction of a technical process, poor maintenance, arson or negligence. Many businesses find it impossible to recover from a major fire.

1.2.5 Social deviations from expected standards of conduct
Theft is a direct and deliberately caused loss. In legal terms, it must be accompanied by an intent permanently to deprive the owner of possession; the need to prove this intent has frustrated many prosecutions for theft and gives rise to inconsistencies over matters such as industrial espionage: the theft of confidential information which deprives the owner of a commercial asset but which is not in itself illegal if the information is still held. Nevertheless an owner knows very well what constitutes a loss to him and in security terms it is necessary to deter, detect and reduce the deliberate deprival of assets.

Thefts may be perpetrated by:

> Opportunists who may be watching for the holes in security or may be tempted by their presence
> Deliberate criminals who plan an attack on a security system.

The opportunist is by far the most common danger and the risk is not a simple one. First of all, it does not depend on the *value* of the goods to be taken, but rather on the coincidence of thief and absence of protection; thus the risk to any particular class of article is difficult to predict. Secondly, the risk will vary with time; that is to say as the level of security inevitably rises and falls in operation, so does the risk of opportunist theft, fig 1.1.

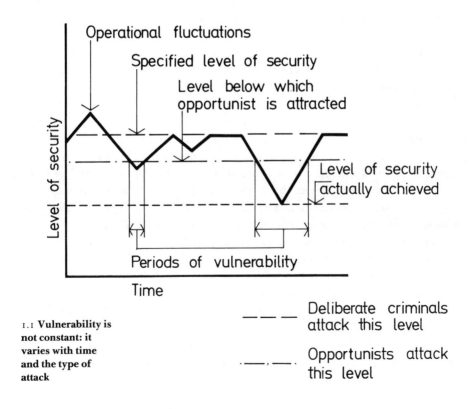

1.1 Vulnerability is not constant: it varies with time and the type of attack

The deliberate criminal, on the other hand, will expend skill, time and effort on planning an assault on a particular target. In effect, he is pitting his own assessment of risk against that of the property owner. He has the advantage that the initiative in these matters is always with the attacker. Although the risk from the deliberate criminal will be greater, it will be simpler than that from the opportunist and more amenable to manage: it does vary with the value of the goods for example, and it is not so vulnerable to sudden drops in the level of security. The degree of pre-planning involved will tend to mean that assaults are made on the normal level of security. It has been known for attacks on super-risks such as bullion vaults to take several years in their planning and execution.

Western society has been described as a mass thieving society and there is little cause to believe this is a temporary phenomenon. Other societies vary greatly in their attitude to property and theft, from the Marxist view that 'property *is* theft' to the Saudi Arabian extreme of ritual amputation for those found guilty even of minor thefts. Coveting thy neighbour's goods is a human characteristic and there is no doubt that the prevention of theft is the major function required of a security system.

The question of value must, of course, be taken into account under all headings of risk. The assessment of the risk of a theft in value terms is however difficult to make. First of all there is a value to the owner: this may be real, as in the case of money or gems; it may be sentimental, as with heirlooms or national treasures; artificial as with rarities, or the item may only have value if no one else possesses it, as with confidential information.

On the other hand, the value to the thief is unlikely to correspond with these considerations. It will depend upon the portability of the item concerned and the ease of its disposal, as well as the price obtained for it.

Fraud is a paper loss which does not involve the physical removal of goods. New technology has brought with it new opportunities for crime, particularly in fields where money and data are handled impersonally and may be transferred illegally following the discovery of authorisation codes for computers. Fraud of any kind is usually regarded as being outside the competence of the traditional security system: the losses are detected by accountants and the risks are managed by experts in accountancy or data handling. This situation may well change as computer technology becomes more familiar and is more readily manipulated by deliberate criminals rather than by technical opportunists.

Arson may be deliberate, or incidental to some other activity such as vandalism or burglary. In the latter case it may be used to conceal a theft. One third of the fire losses in the UK (approximately £100 million) are attributed to vandalism. Arson for its own sake may be carried out for reasons varying from simple mischief to a malicious grudge: there may be a psychopathic disorder involved.

Vandalism is a wasteful destruction of assets and is the special subject of chapter 8. There are many facets to the problem and it is not a simple risk to assess.

Riot is a matter for society to face and not a risk which can or should be manipulated outside a political framework.

Terrorism is a risk which deserves special study and reference should be made to chapter 5. Terrorist targets may be people or property, though the attacks are usually so violent that personal safety is an overriding concern. The targets may be selective or random: the risk arising from random targeting is almost unmanageable.

Negligence is included here as a risk arising from social deviations as, by definition and precedent, it is not expected of a reasonable person. The risk is a matter of degree but can be manipulated: at the simplest level, supervision and checking will reduce its occurrence, whereas it may be more constructive or effective to attack it at source and remove the opportunity or motivation.

War risk is excluded from consideration as the framework of society is likely to change to a degree which makes assessment prevention or control impossible.

1.3 The consequences of disaster

1.3.1 In any assessment of risk, the possibility of failure must be a major consideration. The laws of probability apply to a greater or lesser extent and fires, for example, may be mathematically as predictable as the weather. The hundred year wind is commonly used in structural calculation to produce a level of stability which will resist the maximum wind likely during any period of one hundred years. It is not foolproof because the thousand year wind may occur during the same period; but it is reasonable, and so it is with other risks.

The measure of the reasonable risk must take account of the consequences of the mischance. Clearly a mishap which causes a major pollution, as occurred at Seveso in Italy, deserves a different kind of attention from the chance of a motor accident following traffic light failure. Nevertheless, there is a great temptation for authorities to grade risks according to the resources which need to be set against them, rather than against any real assessment of their value.

By their nature, the catastrophic events which affect an organisation—fire, explosion and the like—are rare. There is a tendency therefore to overlook the realistic consequence of such an event, and the graph in fig 1.2 shows a typical operation pattern surrounding a catastrophe. It can be seen that recovery is unlikely to be complete, in that the position predictable before the event is on a higher level than that following 'full' recovery. The secondary and knock-on effects are rarely appreciated and it is instructive to examine those cases in which a full post-mortem has been held. One case, in the USA, was documented as follows.

A bomb explosion took place in a factory at 3.20am. It was presumed malicious, but because of the timing there were no deaths or injuries. The damage to property was assessed at £42 100. Some eighteen months later, this sum was compared with the actual costs of the event to the organisation: see table 1.1 overleaf.

Table 1.1. Assessment of actual costs consequent on bomb explosion

	£
Employees leaving through fear (44) and recruiting costs	26 000
Production time lost	45 000
Overtime to maintain deliveries	25 500
Extra management time	48 100
Pacification programme	8 150
Temporary staff	14 250
Next wage claim (estimated)	50 000
Increased security costs (1 year)	34 600
Uninsured property	11 200
Time lost on day following explosion	39 000
Special reports	4 400
Training replacement staff	37 500
New employee errors (scrap and reworking)	20 000
Total	£363 700

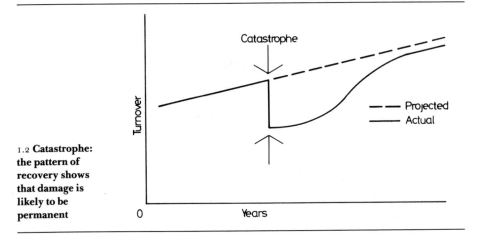

1.2 **Catastrophe: the pattern of recovery shows that damage is likely to be permanent**

On that assessment, the eventual costs to the company were nearly nine times the initial simple damage.

Members of the independent profession of loss adjusters are employed in such cases but can seldom look far beyond the primary consequences of the event.

1.4 Statistics of crime

1.4.1 Definitions

It may be useful at this point to include some rough definitions of the offences set out in the Theft Act 1968.

Theft. The dishonest appropriation of another's property with the intention permanently to deprive the owner of it.

Burglary. Entering a building as a trespasser with the intention of committing theft, rape, grievous bodily harm or unlawful damage. If committed while in possession of a weapon or explosive the offence becomes aggravated burglary and the maximum penalty is life imprisonment.

Robbery. The use or threat of force to a person before or at the time of a theft.

1.4.2 The criminal risks to be considered vary from year to year following gradual trends generated by society. The statistics are highly sensitive from a political point of view and so comparisons over a period of time are not always easy because of reclassifications of crimes and revised methods of counting. There is also a considerable lag in publication of the figures.

A number of points can be highlighted in the statistics for England and Wales over recent years:

1.4.3 Volume of offences

In 1982 there were approximately 3.25 million notifiable offences: an increase of about 10 per cent over the previous year. The number is the highest ever and the increase compares with an annual average increase of about 5 per cent from 1970–1979. The clear-up rate by police was lower than 50 per cent. 586000 offenders were found guilty or cautioned in 1982.

1.4.4 Categories of offence

Notifiable offences are subdivided into the following categories:

Table 1.2. Categories of notifiable offence

Offence	1981	Clear-up per cent	1982	Clear-up per cent
Burglary	723000	30	811000	29
Criminal damage	387000	27	418000	26
Fraud/forgery	107000	70	123000	69
Violence against the person	100000	75	109000	76
Sexual offences	19000	73	20000	71
Robbery	20000	25	23000	22
Theft and handling stolen goods	1603000	38	1756000	37
Other	4000	88	4000	83

It can be seen that the clear-up rate has dropped in almost every category. The proportion of each crime within the whole remains fairly static with the exception of a slight increase in burglary.

1.4.5 Burglary

The incidence of burglary deserves further examination in the context of building security:

Table 1.3. Incidence of burglary in various premises

	1981	1982	Clear-up: 1982
Burglary in dwellings	349792	407088	107073
Burglary in other premises	368689	398302	124609
Going equipped for burglary	4837	5197	5139

Table 1.4. Losses due to burglary

1982	£
Total losses in dwellings	159 265 000
Total losses in other premises	118 722 000
Recovered in dwellings	7 009 000
Recovered in other premises	12 463 000

1.4.6 Shoplifting

Shoplifting offences were officially responsible for an estimated loss of £7 643 000 in 1982, though this figure is regarded with some scepticism. There were 242 304 reported offences and the average loss was £32.

1.4.7 Criminal damage

The figures for criminal damage are difficult to compile for a number of reasons given in chapter 8, but those recorded were:

Table 1.5. Offences involving criminal damage over £20

1980	*1981*	*1982*
191 843	217 187	243 728

In 1982, 62 266 offences were cleared up.

1.4.8 Ages of offenders

The ages of offenders found guilty or cautioned for notifiable offences in 1982 were categorised as follows:

Table 1.6. Percentage of offences by age of offender

Age of offender	*10–14*	*14–17*	*17–21*	*21+*
All offences	10	20	24	46
Violence against the person	4	17	28	51
Burglary	12	27	30	32
Theft and handling	14	22	22	43
Criminal damage	14	21	30	35
Robbery	7	17	33	43

1.4.9 Firearms

The use of firearms in offences is also increasing, as shown in Table 1.7.

Table 1.7. Firearm use

All offences							
1975	*1976*	*1977*	*1978*	*1979*	*1980*	*1981*	*1982*
3 850	4 632	5 302	5 672	6 547	6 587	8 067	8 400
	+20.3%	+14.5%	+7.0%	+15.4%	+0.6%	+22.5%	+4.1%

The types of firearms used are also relevant, and are given in Table 1.8.

Table 1.8. Types of firearm used

Weapon	1981	1982	Percentage change
Air weapon	5629	5337	−5.2
Shotgun	846	1068	+26.2
Pistol	1114	1538	+38.1
Rifle	81	65	−19.8
Imitation	206	183	−11.2
Supposed	159	180	+13.2
Other	29	32	−9.4
Total	8067	8400	+411

1.4.10 Variations between regions

It is clear that in some areas of England and Wales serious crime is more prevalent than in others. Roughly (but not wholly) there is a relationship between the density of urban populations and the frequency of crime. Table 1.9 sets out the areas at most risk.

Table 1.9. Notifiable offences per 100 000 population, classified by police force area: (1982)

8000+
Northumbria, Merseyside, Greater Manchester, Nottinghamshire, London (Met & City), West Midlands

7000–7999
Cleveland, West Yorks, Humberside

6000–6999
Durham, Bedfordshire, South Wales

5000–5999
Lancashire, South Yorks, Derbyshire, Cambridgeshire, Northants, Gwent, Thames Valley, Avon/Somerset, Hampshire

Less than 5000
Cumbria, Cheshire, Norfolk, Warwickshire, Wiltshire, Sussex, North Yorkshire, Lincolnshire, Dyfed-Powys, Suffolk, Kent, North Wales, Staffordshire, West Mercia, Gloucestershire, Devon and Cornwall, Surrey, Hertfordshire, Essex, Dorset

1.5 Risk management

1.5.1 The scale of risk and the consequences of disaster have grown with the general growth of trade and industry, together with more complex technology. The profession of risk manager has emerged because of the needs arising from this growth, and the expertise involved is an amalgam of security, actuarial skills and systems analysis.

Risk management is concerned with the conservation of resources. The traditional insurance assessor appraises the risks, decides direct action necessary to reduce them and then accepts their transfer in return for a payment. The insurance company is there to provide certainty in uncertain situations. Unfortunately, however, the result can often fall short of certainty because the efficacy of the process depends on the perception and valuation of risk by both the policyholder and the insurer. These may differ and both may be wrong.

Risk management is a deliberate attempt to overcome these problems: it is a defensive strategy designed around the concept of sudden losses such as those arising from the risks set out in section 1.2. It covers the whole activity of an organisation and is not concerned solely with security, fire or the like. There must be a homeopathic approach to risk management; that is to say the whole body of the organisation must be examined and treated, rather than the more obvious symptoms of any one isolated weakness. The risks themselves may be handled in several ways, as described below and illustrated in fig 1.3.

1.5.2   Avoidance
A particular activity or process may be stopped. Of course, this is absurd if it is the main purpose of the organisation, but secondary activities may well be ceased if the risk becomes unacceptable. Periodic reassessments will be necessary to reveal what these risks are.

1.5.3   Transfer
Make someone else take the risk. In the case of hazardous processes for example, these can be subcontracted to a specialist who is able to take the necessary precautions more economically and competently. The handling and transfer of cash is incidental to most businesses and can be carried out most effectively by a security company.

The risk can also be transferred to an insurance company, and indeed this is the most common arrangement. It should be remembered however that considerable business disruption can still occur even when the primary risk is carried by someone else. The example in section 1.3.1 illustrates the degree to which such disruption may be present.

Conditions of sale will also play a part in the transfer of risk: these differ considerably from one country to another and are continually having to change in the atmosphere of consumer legislation. Heavy contingent liabilities may arise in this way, as a reverse transfer of risk from a purchaser back to the supplier, and in addition, these liabilities may be uninsurable.

The transfer of risk is not always a deliberate process and may well take place by default, especially when various security measures are applied piecemeal to an organisation and the weak points are plugged one by one.

A grave danger arises from the development of high security, and that is the transfer of risks from property to people: as goods become more surely protected, then the criminal will look to threats for his gains. This risk varies from the simple demand for the keys of the safe against a threat of violence to the more prolonged

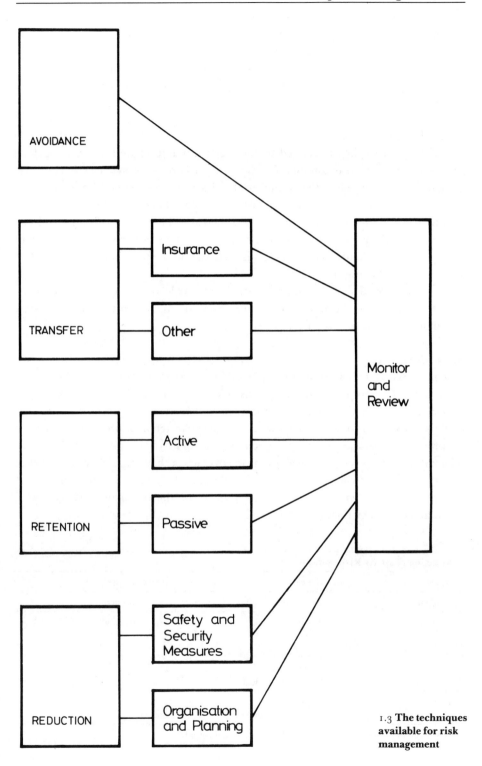

1.3 **The techniques available for risk management**

and organised affairs of kidnap and hostage. While these are not common dangers in the UK at present, they do exist and in other countries they are traditional components of the pattern of crime. The higher the degree of security imposed, the more likely it is that this risk will be transferred. Certainly therefore, the consequences of such a transfer must be part of the planning process for higher security.

1.5.4 Retention

The risk may be held and carried by the organisation itself, and this may be done in whole or in part. It is common for large organisations to practice self-insurance, or active retention, when the spread of the risk is considered sufficient to reduce any single event to less than a catastrophe. The danger in this procedure is inflation, and if such large risks are carried they must be re-assessed periodically so that none of them rises beyond the critical level. This is particularly important where part of the total (in fixed terms) is insured and the remainder rises out of all proportion to the original sum.

The other means of retaining a risk is by neglect, where it has not been appreciated or has been ignored. This retention by default is unfortunately common and is known as passive retention.

1.5.5 Reduction

The principle of reduction can be applied either to an event or to its consequences, or to both. The event can be made less likely to occur, and should it do so the effects can be minimised by, for example, early detection.

This reduction can be effected either by the introduction of physical barriers or by procedures, and depends very much on education and planning for the event. The nature of the events themselves means that when they occur an atmosphere of crisis is generated, which hinders effective planning to reduce the consequences. A purposeful scheme will therefore include proven contingency plans to be activated when an emergency does occur.

Selection chart 1.1 Risk management		
Action	*Comments*	*Appropriate use*
Avoidance	Not always possible	Secondary activities
Transfer	Sound principle Can occur by default	Subcontracting Insurance
Retention	Constant reassessment necessary Can occur by default	Large organisations Self insurance
Reduction	Applied to event or consequences	Prevention Salvage

NB A combination of the above remedies is usual and is quite appropriate.

Fire, flood and explosion are major events, and material losses may well be enormous. Contingency plans should provide for the rapid salvage of goods to prevent total loss, and this can be highly effective. In fact, in London, Glasgow, and Liverpool, the major insurance companies maintain special salvage corps with the appropriate vehicles and equipment to act in such circumstances.

1.6 Buildings

1.6.1 It is obvious that various types of premises and the different activities they house give rise to many kinds of risk. Those worth particular mention are listed below, with brief descriptions of the problems involved. The remedies are described in chapters 2, 3 and 4.

1.6.2 Banks, post offices, building societies
Typical risks: Theft
Robbery with violence
Armed robbery
Burglary
It is mainly cash which is at risk, and attempts may be made while it is in transit, in use, or secured for the night. Post offices and sub-post offices also have items of value such as stamps and pension books, which are not always put in a safe at night. Otherwise the risks are traditional and well known, so their management is relatively straightforward. Opportunist theft is less common by outsiders but the risk remains for staff.

1.6.3 Shops
Typical risks: Theft of goods
Theft of cash
Burglary
Vandalism
Fire
The theft of goods from retail displays is a major problem for shops and may be carried out by opportunists or by deliberate criminals. Goods may also be lost during delivery or stockholding. Cash may be stolen from tills, safes, employees' handbags, or less directly by frauds at the point of sale.

Burglary is popular, and location and access are critical matters. A typical high street lock-up shop with deserted rear service area is a high risk. Certain shops such as jewellers or camera shops also carry a risk of break-in during normal hours as a smash and grab raid.

Vandalism is a risk in the larger shops and department stores, and goods and displays may be damaged.

Fire can arise from various causes. Not only are there the normal occupied building risks, but there are also hazards introduced by the customer. Most of these are concerned with smoking materials and their disposal but others exist, such as electrical goods on demonstration, which a customer can switch on or damage.

1.6.4   Industrial premises
Typical risks: Personal safety
Burglary
Theft of goods
Theft of cash
Vandalism
Plant failure
Fire
Industrial espionage

Personal safety is at risk from hazardous processes and materials and this is totally dependent on the details of manufacture.

Burglary is obvious and the risk will vary with the type of manufacture: stores and components may be more attractive than finished products. The risk will also peak if wages are held overnight. Goods may be stolen by employees, visitors or others such as delivery drivers. The risk is widespread, predictable and continuous in much the same way as theft from retail premises, though clearly it is less of a problem in a steel mill than in a camera factory.

Cash for wages is at risk in transit, while being made up into pay packets and while being kept on the premises pending distribution. Thefts may be violent, as direct attacks on vehicles or wages rooms, or may be fraudulent, as with any other kind of cash handling.

Vandalism in industrial premises can take place externally as with other building types, or internally, in which case the building occupants are usually the culprits. The damage caused varies from the usual minor graffitti to the more sinister sabotage of plant and machinery; the latter may arise from industrial disputes.

Plant failure is a risk and, depending on the nature of the manufacturing process can cause injury, loss of production or further damage to other machinery or even the surrounding neighbourhood.

Fire is of special concern and many industrial processes by their nature carry with them a fire hazard. This risk can easily change with the development of the processes themselves and the introduction of new materials. A regular re-assessment is necessary.

Industrial espionage matters little to many businesses, but to others the preservation of confidentiality is crucial to their trade. Critical information can relate directly to the products made, to their method of production, or more simply to levels of pricing and tender.

Risks will also vary in different areas of the premises themselves, and some industries such as the pharmaceutical houses have obvious areas of high risk where controlled drugs are kept. Others have risks which are less apparent at first sight, such as electronics factories which store gold for use in connexions.

1.6.5 Warehouses
Typical risks: Burglary

Theft of goods

Fire

These are simple and obvious risks but are different in scale because of the concentration of goods and historical precedent.

1.6.6 Offices
Typical risks: Walk-in theft

Petty theft

Fraud

Espionage

The walk-in theft is commonest in large urban offices where a strange face is unlikely to be challenged. The usual targets are handbags, wallets from jackets and minor equipment such as calculators, but it is not unknown for larger items like typewriters to be taken.

Petty theft by employees is often tolerated by the management in forms such as taking stationery for use at home or free use of photocopying machines. Substantial values can be involved over a period however, and the situation can get out of hand.

Frauds are matters of accountancy and whilst most are concerned with the technicalities of the business and its paperwork, many involve unauthorised access to filing or computer areas.

Espionage has been mentioned under the heading of industrial premises, but offices are no less vulnerable.

1.6.7 Housing
Typical risks: Burglary

Vandalism

Robbery with violence

Burglary is the obvious risk, though in its loosest terms the risk also includes the walk-in daytime thief. The level of risk depends in part on the value of the contents as perceived by the criminal, and this perceived value is also influenced by more general factors such as the character of the neighbourhood. Much domestic burglary is opportunist.

Vandalism is more common in concentrated public housing and unusual in isolated private houses except where it occurs in connection with burglary. The damage caused in either case can cause a great deal of misery. Reference should be made to chapter 8.

Violent robbery in the form of mugging is increasing in the public and semi-public areas of housing estates. The effects of this increase, irrespective of its proportions, are to create fear and anxiety among some of the occupants, particularly the elderly.

It can be seen that most of the risks arising in connection with housing are to a great extent subjectively valued; this is to be expected where personal possessions, home and family are involved. It is difficult in such circumstances to assess the risks accurately, and indeed it may be a fruitless task, as the home occupier is quite likely to overrule any recommendations made and modify them to suit his own perception of the risk.

1.6.8 Schools

Typical risks: Vandalism
              Burglary
              Arson

Vandalism is the biggest risk. Schools are traditional targets for vandals both inside and outside school hours, and they are occupied by the age group most connected with the overall problem of vandalism. Location is an important factor, taken with the historical patterns of damage observed.

Schools are usually burgled for their equipment, such as laboratory instruments or typewriters, and although the values are not often very large, the risk is increased because the thief does not expect to find it very difficult to break in, and he is often given safety by the location and layout of the school.

Arson can coincide with an attack by vandals outside school hours, where the school is broken into by a group and the damage escalates from minor to major. Fires can also be caused quite deliberately as single actions, and in such cases where a culprit has been identified he has usually been found to be a pupil of the school.

1.6.9 Colleges and universities

Typical risks: Walk-in theft
              Vandalism
              Burglary
              Personal attack
              Drug offences

These are large institutions, with a changing population of both students and staff. It is very easy for an outsider to look plausible enough to wander anywhere on the campus without being challenged and so the walk-in thief has few problems in raiding students' quarters, changing rooms, laboratories or stores. Legitimate occupants may also be tempted, of course.

Vandalism is common and although it is predictable where public property is involved, there is also the risk of the more cold-blooded type of vandalism in universities, such as that arising from sit-ins or carried out as part of some demonstrative action. This is a difficult risk to manage as the reaction provoked becomes firmly connected with the motives involved in the original damage.

Burglary of student quarters may take place, as in other housing developments. Other target areas will be those with valuable equipment and materials.

There is a risk of assault, particularly around the residential areas, where the hazards are greater for female students.

Drug offences are traditionally held to be common in universities, but vary greatly from one place to another and from time to time. The real risks to security arise from the secondary effects of any hard drug usage, that is to say the presence of organised suppliers and the probability of criminal behaviour among the users.

1.6.10 Hospitals

According to official figures issued by the Department of Health and Social Security, crime in hospitals in the UK rose in 1979 by 60 per cent over the previous year; particular note was taken of the increases in vandalism and violence. The DHSS also estimated that annual losses amounted to £7 million. These figures are open to doubt, however, and various sources within the security industry have stated that the losses are far higher: figures of £45m to £90m are quoted.

Typical risks: Walk-in theft
  Pilferage
  Vandalism
  Personal attack
  Drug offences

There is, traditionally, little restriction on access to hospitals and most areas are open to the walk-in thief (especially if he wears a white coat). There are rich pickings: wallets and purses, equipment, instruments and stores. The stranger is unlikely to be challenged, especially in the larger hospitals, and if confronted, he is 'lost' or 'looking for a job'. In addition, the staff residential quarters can suffer in the same way as described for universities.

Hospitals are full of articles which are attractive to the pilferer, and once outside the stores there is little stock control. Apart from general items of stationery in the offices and food in the kitchens, there are medicines, dressings, linen, instruments, lamps and household equipment in plenty.

As with pilferage, the problems of vandalism increase with the size of the hospital; the bigger the institution, the less damage is thought to be caused by a single act. There are traditional targets: toilets, lifts, fire equipment and telephones; and there are some peculiar to hospitals such as medical equipment and trolleys, with which games are played.

Nurses are under risk of assault. They may be expected to be circulating at all hours of the day and night, so that there is a continual attraction for social deviants who wish to molest or assault them. The risk is present in the hospital grounds, in working departments, and most of all, in and around the nurses' accommodation.

Casualty departments frequently deal with patients or their companions who are emotionally charged, shocked or drunk, and there is another obvious risk of assault which is well known to hospital staff. One London hospital has an average of 4 assaults per night.

Drug offences are clear risks because of the necessary proliferation of narcotic controlled drugs on the premises. Though by law (Misuse of Drugs [Safe Custody] Regulations 1973) such drugs must be kept in special stores and cupboards constructed to an official design, there are weaknesses and the cupboards themselves are not capable of resisting a deliberate attack. There are some related risks such as the theft of prescription pads which may be secondary targets.

1.6.11 Hotels

Typical risks: Theft
  Pilferage
  Violent robbery
  Fraud
  Prostitution
  Fire
  Terrorism

In security terms, hotels present a most complex set of risks, owing to the nature of their business and operations. There is a constantly changing population of guests, many of whom are itinerant, and in the UK at least, there is a tradition throughout the industry of frequent changes of staff. Hotels also try to attract a multitude of casual customers to the restaurants, shops, exhibitions and conferences. None of these factors contribute to the feasibility of a security plan and all carry their own risks.

Theft is rife. Hotel property is stolen from bedrooms by some guests as a matter of course; guests' property is stolen by staff, intruders and other guests. Motels where there is vehicular access directly outside the bedrooms, are particularly at risk, and it has been known for whole rooms to be stripped, including the fitted carpets! Cash in tills is at risk, as are the contents of unattended bars.

Pilferage is the running sore of theft. It is to be expected where there are goods being distributed and sold and items at risk are:
  Alcohol and tobacco
  Food
  Linen

Most pilferage is carried out by staff, but they may be in connivance with delivery drivers, dustmen or other outsiders.

Violent crime is a serious problem when it occurs. A large hotel may have considerable amounts of cash on the premises, often in the reception area, which are an obvious attraction for the armed or violent criminal. This is not as likely, however, as the mugging of a guest in his room or the car park, or attacks on cash in transit. There is also the danger of violence from a disturbed or intoxicated guest. In one well-known case in the USA, a guest ran amok with a gun and shot over twenty people including the hotel security officer before being overcome. That is of course an extreme case, but when it is considered that later, in court, the hotel was held responsible and became liable for heavy damages, it is clear that the risk cannot be ignored.

Fraud is another continuing problem in hotels in its various forms. It is perpetrated by guests, other visitors and staff. The opportunities are numerous and it is not unusual for both staff and guests to stay in a hotel for the purpose of exploiting them. The main vulnerable areas are:

> Walk-outs by guests without payment
> Free use of rooms with staff connivance
> Credit card and cheque fraud
> Staff 'padding' bar stocks with their own bottles
> Fraudulent inventory checks
> Overcharging customers and short change
> Dishonest food purchase and connivance with suppliers
> Guests alleging false losses

Prostitution is a common security problem, especially in city hotels. The risk takes a practical form as well as a moral one, due to the high probability that the women involved are either thieves themselves or will entice their clients into circumstances where they can be robbed by accomplices. Prostitutes can be expected to try hard to enter the hotel and have even been known to climb up drainpipes to gain entry.

Fires can be caused by guests (typically by smoking in bed) or may arise from the kitchens, laundry, storerooms, or many pieces of equipment and wiring. There is a high fire risk, therefore, and this is combined with a high life risk connected with the large number of sleeping occupants. The measures taken by law in the UK to prevent, detect and fight fires whilst providing safe escape routes are generally of a high standard commensurate with the risks. As with many fire safety measures, however, the means of escape will create problems of security.

Hotels are common terrorist targets. They are also used from time to time as operational bases, from which plans to attack other targets are formulated and put into action. There have been several explosions in hotel bedrooms which have been the result of the assembly of bombs. The hotels themselves are easy targets for placement of explosives.

1.6.12 Airports

Typical risks: Theft
                       Retail offences
                       Customs and immigration offences
                       Terrorism

There is much crime committed in international airports, and many have their own police forces. The population is large and constantly changing; many people will be passing through on a once-only basis; huge quantities of goods pass through outside the control of their owners; and many of the passengers carry substantial amounts of cash.

Theft is present in many forms and there are few items which are not at risk. The problem is so severe at London Heathrow, for example, that it has earned the nickname Thiefrow. Some of the more significant areas of theft are listed below.

Baggage may be stolen or rifled; this may occur after check-in, in the hold of the aircraft, during loading or unloading, during recovery handling, on the carousel or after the passenger has reclaimed it

Freight may be stolen by connivance with delivery drivers or from cargo holding areas

Shoplifting is common amid the bustle

Pickpockets operate among passengers and are sometimes organised into gangs. It is not unknown for these gangs to appear on the air side of the building, having flown in and steal from embarking passengers before leaving themselves without even having technically entered the country.

Because of the multitude of shops, bars and restaurants operating in airports the risks of theft and fraud are common and are similar to those already described under the heading of shops and hotels.

Customs and immigration offences are fiscal and political risks, both of which vary enormously according to the legislation current in the country concerned. They are not security risks in the normal sense but both have to be controlled by the provision of secure areas and access control.

Airports are favourite targets for terrorists; their attacks vary from the direct military-style assault on terminal buildings to the placing of bombs in buildings and aircraft, and hijacking. The direct assault is catastrophic, as was seen at Rome and Lod. Bombs and the threat of them disrupt the whole operation of the airport at best, and the possibility of them being introduced onto aircraft is obviously a great danger to life. Hijacking is a relatively new crime but is clearly with us to stay.

1.6.13 Computer centres

Typical risks: Vandalism

            Fraud

            Fire

            Industrial espionage

            Terrorism

Computer centres are vulnerable either as buildings in their own right, or as parts of a whole. The equipment is expensive and sensitive to damage mechanically, electrically, and environmentally. The data held are necessarily extensive and their loss can rarely be tolerated within the normal workings of an organisation.

Vandalism is not an offence which is usually associated with computers, although it is growing and in the USA is not unusual at all. Physical damage is caused by intruders but the system can also be damaged by tampering with programmes or data so that either the system will not operate or false information is given out. This sort of tampering can be difficult to identify.

Computers which deal with accounts are open to sophisticated tampering, giving rise to all sorts of fraud. The simplest is probably the introduction of a false input form which instructs money to be paid out, and in offices these forms are often freely available to the walk-in thief. One of the most famous frauds arose from the UK banks' custom of disregarding all ½p amounts; An enterprising criminal inserted an instruction into the programme so that these many half pence were transferred into his account instead of being discarded, and he rapidly built up a substantial sum. The appearance that no one was losing from the crime gave it a false attraction.

Fire must be taken seriously. The risk of occurrence is not especially high though relatively large amounts of electricity are used, but the consequences are serious enough to merit substantial precautions.

Espionage is the risk of confidential data being examined. This may sometimes be possible by telephone from a remote site, and in any case is likely to be undetectable.

The physical fragility of computers makes them attractive to terrorists for threats or attacks.

1.6.14 Military installations
Typical risks: Theft
                    Vandalism
                    Terrorism
                    Espionage

Military installations are not free from civilian risks and the likelihood of theft and vandalism remains, though it will probably be lower. The pilferage of equipment from offices and supplies from bars and kitchens is likely. General military equipment including tools and vehicles is also at risk.

Terrorist attack is expected; either the installation itself may be a primary target for damage, or the purpose may be to steal weapons and ammunition. Espionage is an obvious risk, but as, by definition, secret information is involved, it is unlikely that the risk will be disregarded in an overall risk management programme.

1.6.15 Building sites
Typical risks: Theft
                    Vandalism
                    Pilferage
                    Wastage

By their nature, building sites are temporary arrangements. Many are disorganised and sites have always been habitual targets for theft and vandalism. Security is difficult to achieve and it is not surprising that building site losses from theft, vandalism and their consequences are estimated to be about £360 million each year: some 3 per cent of the industry's turnover.

Few individual losses are large: which does not encourage the introduction of planned security systems. The problem has been described as a running sore.

Consec, the security advisory group of the NFBTE, approaches the situation on a broader front and uses the term loss prevention, which includes aspects such as the reduction of wastage and weather damage as well as criminal loss and damage: wastage of materials by careless handling and storage is known to be substantial but no reliable assessments are available.

Materials and components are continually stolen by employees, subcontractors and visitors during the day and by intruders at night. The opportunities for fraudulent delivery and collusion are numerous. Theft of cash from site offices or during wages distribution is not unusual. Items of plant may also be stolen, and it has been known for large items of earth moving machinery to be taken from civil engineering works and immediately exported for sale.

The site attracts both the vandal, who finds a good hunting ground, and the potential vandal, who uses the site as an adventure playground. In the latter category, probably comprising 10 year old boys, there may be difficulties in distinguishing damage from play. In a secondary school in the north of England, a sample survey of 500 boys was carried out and it was found that 40 per cent had caused damage on a building site at least once in the previous six months. Reference should be made to chapter 8.

Checklist 1
Risk

Define the risks arising under

      Personal safety
      Nature
      Technical operations
      Social deviations

Assess the consequences of a disaster

Consider the management of risks by

      Avoidance
      Transfer
      Retention
      Reduction

2 The grounds

2.1 General

2.1.1 The design and construction of the site perimeter and the grounds within it form the first line of defence in the security plan.

In practice, except for high security premises, it is unusual for location or layout to be determined with security as an overriding factor, since there are too many other, more immediate forces shaping the decisions, such as:

Site availability
Transport access
Cost
Construction time
Functional efficiency
Appearance

In the case of existing premises where security is being upgraded or use changed, then the options of changing location or layout do not really exist. Nevertheless, much can be achieved by the application of a number of simple principles which increase security, often without compromising other considerations.

2.2 Location

2.2.1 The location of the site itself must be considered. The main risk to be taken into account is that of intruders, most of whom will make their attempts at night. Urban sites will suffer attacks from both the deliberate criminal and the opportunist; as a comparatively large number of people have legitimate reasons for being in the vicinity, the threshold at which suspicion is generated is also comparatively high. The character of the neighbourhood and its history of crime are important factors and will usually be well known.

Rural sites present a different kind of risk; opportunists are less common, but a degree of isolation will assist the deliberate criminal by allowing him time and privacy to complete his task. The opportunist is deterred by a fairly low level of security as long as it is maintained, and so on balance it is the rural site which requires the most physical hardening. The following specific matters arising from the location should be checked.

2.2.1 A perimeter on the railway is a high risk; it is traditionally so and this approach persists among criminals just as more legitimate traditions persist in other occupations. The railway is unlit, access to it is easy, and more importantly, an excellent escape route is available, fig 2.1.

2.1 **Location of premises: typical factors affecting vulnerability**

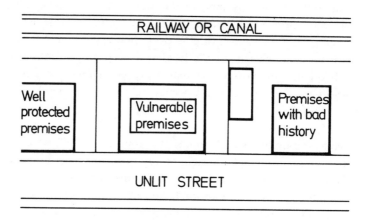

2.2.2 Canal and water frontages are often difficult to protect; it may for example be necessary to maintain open access for wharfage. It should also be remembered that the possibility of access may well change dramatically should the water freeze over or dry up.

2.2.3 A building site adjoining will create many opportunities for access to the grounds and these will constantly be changing throughout the construction period, as cranes, scaffolding and plant appear and disappear. Construction may take some years and should not be seen as a temporary risk.

2.2.4 Neighbouring premises generally should be examined, and enquiries made as to their history of intrusion and the nature of their business. If the primary level of defence against the intruder is to provide enough deterrents to make him go next door, then it must be remembered that this principle can also work in reverse. There may also be a risk of intrusion from the adjoining premises themselves, either through the perimeter or via buildings adjoining the boundary. In the latter case, entry may be made at ground level, through windows or walls; at upper levels in the same way; over roofs, or through basements, cellars and undercrofts. It is also useful to discover the previous ownership and use of the adjoining premises as there is a recurrent pattern to crime, and future repetitions are always possible.

2.3 Layout

2.3.1 The layout within the site boundary is not usually determined by the requirements of security. Proposed layouts are submitted to the town planning authority for general amenity, appearance, and the suitability of the development; they are submitted to the highway authority for access, the environmental officer for noise, smoke and pollution; the building control officer regulates distances from boundaries, and the fire brigade approves internal roads for its appliances. The mass of regulations is complex and it is difficult to satisfy all the requirements at the same time. Nowhere amongst these negotiations is security mentioned and if it is not part of the client's brief to the design team, then it is unlikely that there will even be a quick trip to the local police crime prevention officer. It should be remembered in this context that many developments such as industrial estates, offices and housing are built speculatively and so there is likely never to be any true client brief.

2.3.2 Public footpaths should be routed around developments rather than through them, though if a right of way exists this may not be possible. At the least, there will be legal complexities and astonishing delays.

Footpaths often run through housing estates, especially if they are built to modern town planning principles, fig 2.2. These involve partial or total segregation of vehicles from pedestrians, a principle which has many advantages such as the

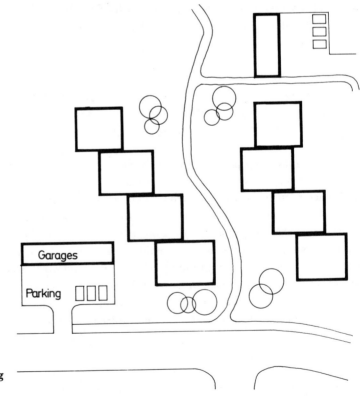

2.2 **Pedestrian and traffic circulation: communal routes through private areas and communal parking reduce security**

reduction of noise and increased safety for children at play. The inevitable consequence however is the creation of parking areas, garage blocks and heavily used paths to and from them. As a security principle this is poor because:

Strangers are more common and go unchallenged

Vehicles may often approach unseen

Garage contents are at risk

As a comparison, it is useful to imagine a potential burglar first sitting in a vehicle parked in a traditional residential street and then in a 20-bay communal parking area: it is clear that the degree of suspicion generated by the latter is negligible.

In a similar way, deck and balcony access to high density housing should be restricted to the minimum and the temptation to include a pedestrian street through the whole development must be resisted. It has been shown that the type and extent of communal access routes is a major factor in tenants' fears for their personal safety. Further reference should be made to chapter 8 on vandalism, in which the above principles are reinforced.

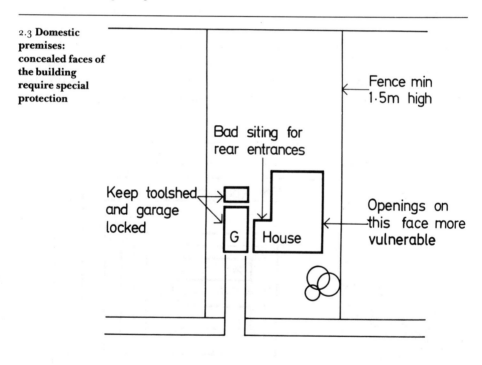

2.3 **Domestic premises: concealed faces of the building require special protection**

Fence min 1·5m high

Bad siting for rear entrances

Keep toolshed and garage locked

G   House

Openings on this face more vulnerable

2.3.3 Rear entrances to houses should be sited where they can be overseen by neighbours rather than be hidden by the building layout, fig 2.3. It is not realistic to expect fencing between gardens to provide real security, but it should certainly deter intruders from gaining access along a row of properties, particularly if they are carrying something. A height of 1.5m is sufficient for this purpose.

2.3.4   Garden tool sheds must be kept locked. This protects not only the contents but also helps to prevent the tools within from being used to break into the main premises. The most useful housebreaking tool is a spade: it can be used to great effect in the gaps in window and door frames.

2.3.5   Where separate garage blocks are provided, each car space should be lockable. It is common practice for public sector landlords to achieve this by installing wire mesh screens and doors. There is merit in this as the contents are on view, but there should be some supervision so that the dangers arising from the accumulation of rubbish or fuel for example are reduced. On the other hand, if the garage contents are not visible, the potential thief is presented with the risk that his crime will not be worthwhile, and on balance this is thought to be the preferable solution.

2.3.6   The layout of buildings inside a defined perimeter can also be considered with security in mind, fig 2.4. The first rule is to avoid placing buildings on the boundary itself, as they will be vulnerable and it is difficult to preserve the integrity of perimeter fencing or intruder detection systems. A clearance of 3 m is a desirable minimum. Secondly, the disposition of the buildings relative to outside observation should be examined, fig 2.5, and screening, partially enclosed courts and any areas should be eliminated which would allow an intruder to gain access in privacy.

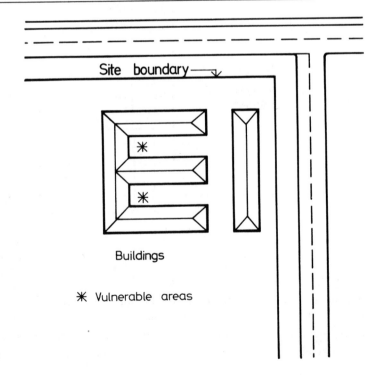

Site   boundary

Buildings

✳ Vulnerable   areas

2.4 **Layout of buildings on the site: bad security**

2.3.7 If the site is patrolled, there will be a base for the patrolmen. This post should not be located in a conspicuous position and in higher security installations should not be combined with the policing of the entrance. The ideal location is an anonymous one with a good view over the grounds. If it is thought that the site might be a terrorist target, then the security post must be sited in a protected position and communications to it must also be protected.

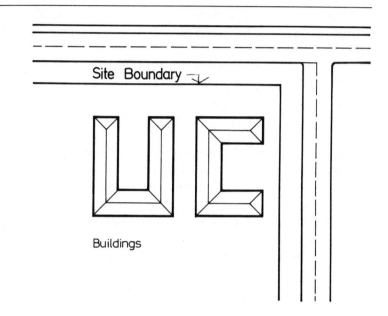

Site Boundary

Buildings

2.5 **Layout of buildings on the site: better**

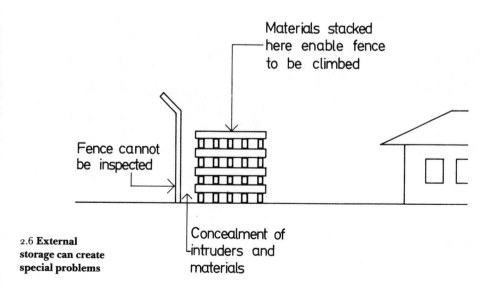

Materials stacked here enable fence to be climbed

Fence cannot be inspected

2.6 **External storage can create special problems**

Concealment of intruders and materials

2.3.8 External storage is frequently overlooked when making a security plan and this may be the result of unplanned development of open areas into stores. Here there are several dangers: storage of valuable materials or scrap should not be adjacent to the perimeter, fig 2.6; materials must not be stacked high enough by the perimeter to compromise the security of the fencing, or so close to the fencing that inspection for holes is inhibited; and finally, open air storage of gases and inflammables must be kept well away from the perimeter, preferably in the centre of the site. This latter requirement is often particularly difficult to satisfy. These sensitive areas should be fitted with intruder alarms and visited at night.

2.3.9 In a similar way, sensitive and vulnerable plant such as transformers should be sited well away from boundaries. This is most important if terrorist action is anticipated, as a minor amount of sabotage can cause disproportionate damage.

2.3.10 The most essential principle of layout where terrorism is likely is the restriction of vehicle access to the vicinity of the building. The amount of explosive which can be carried and planted by an individual pedestrian is minimal compared with that which can be installed in a vehicle. In addition, an isolated package will arouse more suspicion than a strange parked vehicle.

2.3.11 On commercial and industrial sites the positions of car parking facilities should be given special attention as there are many opportunities for pilferage which will only be possible if the pilfered articles can be readily secreted in a car: figs 2.7, 2.8. Car parks for employees should be totally separate from visitors' areas

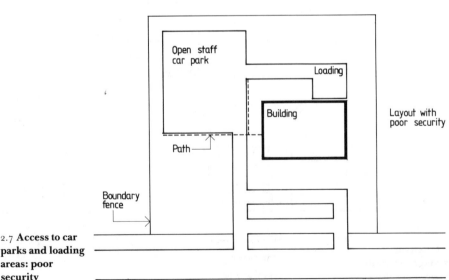

2.7 Access to car parks and loading areas: poor security

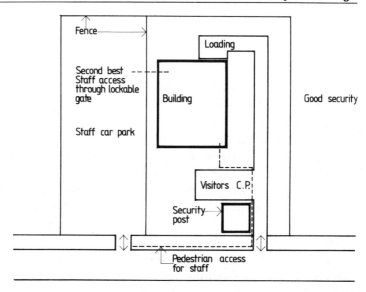

2.8 Access to car parks and loading areas: good security

and ideally should also be outside the main secure area and not near the buildings. Where this is not acceptable or feasible then a single pedestrian access (which can, if necessary, be policed) gives adequate but lesser security. There must be a lockable gate at the connecting point.

2.3.12 Adequate secure storage must be allowed for ladders and tools. These must not be allowed simply to stack in the open air, as they may be used to help intruders to break in to the premises.

2.4   Access

2.4.1 In many cases, access to the site itself is not restricted: for example, housing developments, schools and shopping precincts. The reasons differ in each case, but sometimes arise from the impracticality of providing a secure perimeter for access control and sometimes from the costs involved or from simple tradition. If access is to be restricted it should be allowed at as few points as possible: preferably one only. When planning access points the following categories must be taken into consideration.

> Vehicles
> Pedestrians
> Overtime access
> Building entry points

2.4.2 Vehicle access is significant where the main risk is theft from the premises, but matters little in the prevention of vandalism. Indeed, in the latter case, it may be better to allow free vehicle access to an unattended site so that police patrols may visit more easily. The potential for theft, however, varies greatly according to whether a vehicle is used in the act. A car or van may:

> Act as shelter for reconnaissance
> Break through gates or fences
> Ram or tow off doors and grilles
> Provide light and power
> Transport stolen goods
> Assist in escape

Automatic vehicle access systems are not to be regarded as part of a secure access control system, as they are subject to too much abuse.

Simple vehicle restriction for low risks out of hours is achieved by installing gates in the perimeter line. These are not manned and should be of a similar height to the boundary fencing. The hinges must be properly constructed and not of either the lift-off type or those with pins which can be driven through. If the gates are timber, the hinges should incorporate straps with bolts through the whole thickness of the wood and the top threads destroyed. The standard for security fencing (BS 1722: Part 10: 1972) states that single gates in chain link should not exceed 5 m in width; this dimension is generated by the presumption that gates are installed across roads, but as a secure physical barrier a gate of this size is on the limits of practicality.

If double gates are installed they should be fitted with secure drop bolts which, ideally, will assist in the support of the gate when it is open or closed. The bolts and gates should be secured by a padlock of the close shackled type: see chapter 7.

Hinged gates provide the simplest answer to the problem but there are disadvantages: power operation is relatively difficult and slow; those fitted with nosewheels require level ground over the area of the swing; and there is some obstruction of the entrance area when they are parked open, fig 2.9. Sliding gates are alternatives, especially where power operation is required. They also are slow and there are height restrictions, though they can be supplied without track where the ground is not level and there is less obstruction around the entrance, fig 2.10.

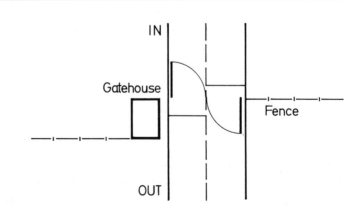

2.9 **Hinged gates occupy space on site**

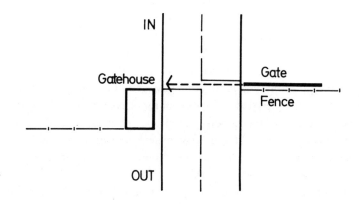

2.10 Sliding gates park away neatly

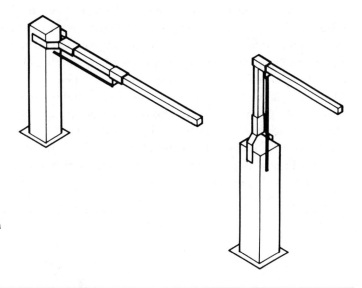

2.11 Lifting poles: a swan-neck version for restricted headroom

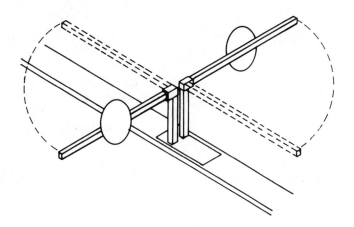

2.12 Slewing poles are useful deterrents

The point of weakest security with regard to gates is the management component: it is necessary to make sure that they are locked.

It may be decided that the perimeter should exclude vehicles alone, or that they should be controlled during the day, and there are several types of barrier suitable for this purpose apart from the two described above:

Lifting poles may be manual or powered. They only deter vehicles and are not suitable for long lengths (over 5 m) or for areas where high winds are likely. There are obvious height restrictions which prevent their use underneath obstructions or near cables or trees, though a swan neck version is available in short lengths to overcome this. They tend to be vulnerable to damage by vandals and irate motorists in automatic car parks.

Slewing poles also only act as deterrents but are usually manually operated. They are also prone to vandalism but there is no problem with restricted heights.

Rising chains are more resistant to vandal attack. Their availability is limited in the UK, and as the chain is more difficult to see, they are used with traffic lights. The chain falls into a drained slot in the road and the main disadvantage is the need for a mechanism at both sides of the road. Again, they are only deterrents but are not likely to be forced so casually as the pole types.

One-way plates (dragon's teeth) are useful traffic controls and effectively prevent light vehicle access from one direction, fig 2.13. They are maintenance-free, vandal-resistant, unpowered and automatic. Motorists are wary of them, so there is also an element of speed control. It has been suggested that they are a hazard to pedestrians however, and some authorities have refused to install them for that reason.

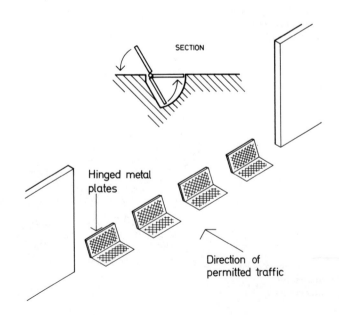

SECTION

Hinged metal plates

Direction of permitted traffic

2.13 **Dragon's tooth plates to allow vehicles to pass in one direction only**

Rising steps provide the most effective vehicle barrier and can be used where it is necessary to prevent the passage of all light and medium vehicles, fig 2.14. They are used with traffic lights and are highly vandal resistant, though some types do not have a reputation for reliability. They are powered and require a recess in the road surface, so they may not be usable in suspended slab construction.

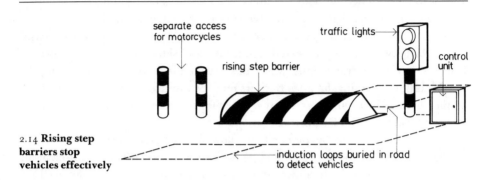

separate access for motorcycles

traffic lights

control unit

rising step barrier

2.14 Rising step barriers stop vehicles effectively

induction loops buried in road to detect vehicles

Selection chart 2.1 Access

Barrier	Advantages	Disadvantages	Use
Hinged gates	Simple Cheap Familiar	Power operation difficult Nosewheels need level ground	5 m max width openings
Sliding gates	Power operation easier Parking of gate	Slow Height restrictions	Wide openings on level ground
Lifting poles	Cheap Simple Power operation easy	Vehicles only Deterrent only Vulnerable to wind and vandalism	5 m max width openings
Slewing poles	Cheap Simple	Vehicles only Deterrent only Power operation difficult Vulnerable to vandalism	5 m max width openings, no height restrictions
Rising chains	Vandal resistant	Complicated More expensive Unfamiliar Vehicles only Deterrent only	Rare
One way plates	Cheap Simple Effective stop Speed control	Vehicles only Possible hazard to pedestrians Not controllable	Exits One-way systems
Rising step	Effective stop Robust	Ground level only Expensive Vehicles only Restricted width	Secure entrances Car parks Unattended locations

All the power operated barriers can be operated by switch from the premises, card or coin access controls, or sensors in the road surface: see chapter 7.

If vehicle access is to be controlled during occupied hours, the gate point at which authority is given should be manned and there should be a reasonable queuing area to allow for the anticipated traffic, so that there is time for proper control to be exercised without the pressure of vehicles obstructing the highway. The gatehouse should have a reasonable view of approaching traffic, fig 2.15.

Vehicle control is particularly important for terrorist targets, and in such cases some vehicles will have to be searched and the undersides inspected with mirrors. The layout of the entrance must allow this to take place without obstructing the flow of authorised traffic, fig 2.16. Barriers must be capable of stopping a vehicle. A simpler arrangement, in reverse, may be used for premises where it is necessary to check outgoing vehicles for pilferage (see para 5.3.2).

Vehicle control must be planned to allow for access by fire engines in an emergency. Whereas normal gate and padlock security presents little problem for the equipment carried on a fire appliance, rising step barriers may well be

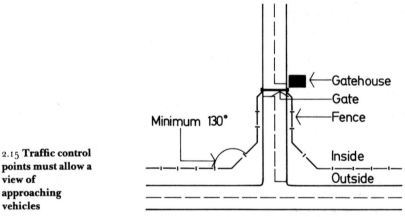

2.15 Traffic control points must allow a view of approaching vehicles

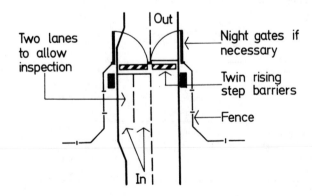

2.16 For higher risks, adequate space for inspection must be allowed

impassable and so, once again, there is a possible conflict between fire safety and security. For vehicle access to the buildings generally see chapter 3.

2.4.3 Pedestrians are excluded from a site by hinged gates constructed in the same manner as the perimeter fence, and by the fence itself. They are not excluded by the other vehicle barriers described above, though there may be some degree of control at a manned gatepost.

Turnstiles are ideal for pedestrian access control, fig 2.17. Supervision is not always necessary and the flow of traffic may be regulated or stopped. There are three basic modes of operation:

> Controlled entry, free exit
> Controlled entry, controlled exit
> Controlled entry, no exit

In addition, high security types with 45° leaves make it impossible for more than one person to pass through. Control may be exercised:

> By card systems
> By code numbers
> By personal verification

Details of the way in which these systems operate are set out in chapter 7 but it should be mentioned here that there are practical problems which arise from the installation of card and code number systems hardware on the public side of an unmanned perimeter gate, in that the equipment itself is liable to be damaged mischievously.

Controlled entry
free exit

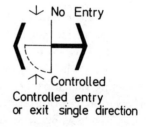

Controlled entry
or exit single direction

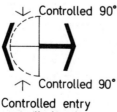

Controlled entry
controlled exit
double direction

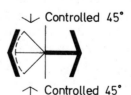

Controlled entry
controlled exit
high security 45° movement

2.17 **Turnstiles:**
modes of operation

If personal checks or searches are to be carried out, then there must be a firm policy for doing so and adequate facilities must be provided at the site entry point. If delays or queues are allowed to form, there will be pressure on the security personnel to reduce the checks and the system will begin to decay. Staff morale and industrial relations can also suffer where personal checks are necessary and the policy must allow for a demonstrably fair system to operate. This can be achieved either by a relentless rule that all are searched or by introducing some random factor: for example a turnstile counter or timer which designates every tenth person (say) to be stopped and searched.

2.4.4   The security plan must be decisive in the matter of overtime access to the site. It is commonplace in many organisations for individuals to work late on their own initiative or to have casual access to the site at night or weekends. In addition, there are those businesses, such as computer installations, which find it necessary to run a regular skeleton staff service at night. Three main risks arise:

Normal staff supervision is absent

Site security is delegated by default

The staff themselves may be at risk

The treatment of these risks is dealt with more fully in chapters 4 and 7.

2.4.5   The site access point should also bear some relationship to building entry points and loading bays in particular.

2.5   The perimeter

2.5.1   It is clear that the perimeter barrier is the first line of defence against intruders. In ancient times, natural features such as cliffs and rivers were used, or a moat might have been constructed round the property to some effect. The most common barrier however, was and still is, a fence or wall. There are many ways of constructing such a barrier and it is rarely possible or necessary to prevent intrusions over, under or through it. The aims are rather to deter the intruder by creating an obstacle which will take time to overcome, and to designate a zone for the detection of such an intrusion. The barrier may in fact be the only line of defence in open situations such as sports stadia, building sites and lorry parks. On the other hand, it may be quite impractical to provide a perimeter barrier at all, as for example in the case of housing developments.

It may not be possible to provide a consistent level of perimeter barrier around the site because of existing conditions such as street or water frontages, or neighbouring buildings on the boundary. These weaknesses should be taken into account and balanced by additional detection systems or surveillance. The requirements of the barrier will vary according to locality and between day and night. Where there are multiple tenancies, either of a building or of a site, then the security of the perimeter barrier must be discounted and additional measures taken at the building envelope.

For definition of the perimeter and for low risks, simple chain link fencing or vertical railings 1.5 m high will suffice. The barrier will be climbable, though this is more difficult if palisading with sharpened tops is used, but it will be difficult to carry things over and it will help to deter vandals.

For higher risks, BS 1722 parts 1–12 sets out the various types of fencing in common use and for security purposes and is a good standard to follow. As a general rule, the minimum height required is 2.4 m from the highest ground level.

There are differing views about the visual nature of the barrier. First of all there are considerations of amenity and the image presented to the world outside; secondly, however, there is the question of concealment as opposed to exposure. If the barrier is solid enough to conceal what is behind it, the criminal must accept the dual risk that he may immediately be detected by unseen devices or patrols, and that once within the site he may find further progress impossible or pointless. A transparent barrier, on the other hand, tends to be more flimsy but the criminal can be seen in his approach from inside, and once past the barrier is still exposed to view. It should be noted, however, that this principle only holds good at night if the site is illuminated. There is a balance between these two views and there are circumstances in which each will be valid.

If fencing is not physically strong, it must be monitored and alarmed (see chapter 6). In any case it must be inspected as a routine security matter, so that both natural deterioration and evidence of intrusion can be detected.

The barrier itself should be 2 m clear of buildings, roads, vehicles or stockpiles of materials, and trees within this distance should also be cleared. It is obvious that these requirements cannot always be satisfied but it must be appreciated that the level of security will fall as a result, figs 2.18–2.21.

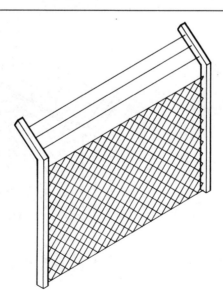

2.18 **A simple chain link security fence**

**2.19 Further
security at the top
to make bridging
more difficult**

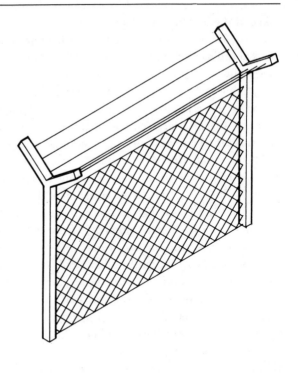

Coiled barbed wire

**2.20 Coiled barbed
wire increases the
resistance of the
fence, but gives it a
forbidding
appearance**

2.21 Vehicles can breach a fence, so extra protection may be necessary

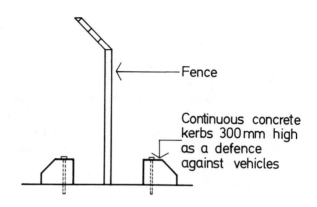

Fence

Continuous concrete kerbs 300 mm high as a defence against vehicles

Chain link fencing is relatively difficult to scale and can be made more so by the addition of three strands of barbed wire at the top on cranked posts. This adds some 0.5 m to the standard 2.4 m height. The wire should be cranked outwards but this is not always possible because of problems of intrusion into neighbouring property or over footways. In such cases, the cranks may be fitted inwards with minimal loss of security. Barbed tape is held by some to provide a more continuous deterrent but this is a matter of opinion. Further security at the top of the fence can be provided by double cranks forming a Y which can then be filled with coils of barbed wire if necessary. The fence should always be firmly anchored at its base. The weaknesses of this type of fencing are that it can be cut relatively easily and flattened by a moving vehicle; it can also be pulled down by spiked ropes.

If it is necessary to prevent vehicle penetration, then continuous concrete kerbs should be fitted each side of the fence, approximately 300 mm high.

Stronger physical barriers include brickwork, reinforced concrete panels and posts, and rolled steel palisades. These should also be 2.4 m high and may need

Selection chart 2.2 Perimeter barrier

Barrier	Advantages	Disadvantages	Use
Chain link 1.5 m high	Simple, cheap		Low risks
Chain link 2.4 m high	Simple, cheap Difficult to climb		Normal risks
Chain link 2.4 m high plus barbed wire 0.5 m	Simple, cheap Very difficult to climb	Unattractive	Medium and high risks
Solid barriers 2.4 m high plus spikes	Effective Visually more acceptable	Expensive	High risk

topping with a climbing deterrent such as barbed wire, spikes or rotating expanded metal mesh.

The height of the barrier may be increased where necessary, though there are then practical problems of stability, so that security is not automatically increased. Ball stop fencing, for example, is available up to 14m high without struts or bracing, but is not normally regarded as a security barrier.

Right angle bends allow the possibility of bridging across the corner and so should be avoided. The minimum angle permissible is 130°.

When terrorist attack is anticipated, vehicle barriers must be incorporated in the perimeter and it is also important to provide a visual screen against snipers.

2.6   Surveillance and lighting

2.6.1   Surveillance requires a high degree of human control in its operation. It is therefore subject to great variation from time to time and is one of the most expensive forms of security. Surveillance may be partial: that is, based on random and/or occasional visits to the site, or it may be continuous. In either case, it may be carried out by employees or under contract, and because of the problems of cost and quality control it is *essential* that the personnel involved are properly trained and supported in their job, otherwise the undertaking will be pointless. The simple presence of a man with a cap badge who is moonlighting from his regular daytime employment is irresponsible and will not do.

The professional security industry has suffered greatly from fringe operators whose competence and conduct has not been wholly satisfactory. It has been estimated that 150000 people are employed in the UK as security guards and the growth of such an army of surrogate policemen has quite properly been the cause of some public concern. The British Security Industry Association lays down a code of conduct in this respect for its members and this code includes, *inter alia*, the following principles:

  Guards are not to be used as substitutes for police or bailiffs

  Suspected criminals will not be pursued in public places

  Guards will not take part in the control of political or industrial meetings

  There will be no undercover or plain clothes work (except for store detectives)

  No weapons of any kind will be carried

  Dogs will be properly kept and controlled

If surveillance is continuous it is best carried out in a covert manner: the criminal should not be aware that he is being watched. If on the other hand the security presence is a visiting one, then advantage should be taken of the deterrent value of advertisements, so that security does not drop so far in between visits. Notices on gates and fences do have some limited effect.

Most intrusions take place at night and lighting is important both in deterrence and as an aid to surveillance. Darkness aids the criminal: it gives him concealment, confidence and more time to achieve his objective. Before considering the form of security lighting, the limitations of night vision should be understood. In clear weather with average daylight and against a contrasting background a man can be observed at a range of about 1 km; at night with a cloudy sky this range drops to about 25 m even after night vision has developed. The normal operation of the eye is set up for daylight and when the light level changes within this range the iris opens and closes accordingly so that the illumination on the retina at the back of the eye remains roughly constant. When the available light drops to night levels the operation of the eye changes gear and the internal chemistry alters to a low-light system. This is called the development of night vision and, typically, takes about 15–20 minutes of darkness before full efficiency is available. Unfortunately, reversal of this process is much more rapid: a few seconds of brighter light are enough to return the chemistry of the eye to its normal mode.

The quality of night vision is one of the reasons why foot patrols carrying torches are not particularly effective as they tend to look only in the area lit by their torch and are unable to observe very much in the darker areas. In addition, they advertise their whereabouts well in advance.

These limitations do not apply in general to remote surveillance by TV cameras. For descriptions of the systems available, see chapter 9.

When designing security lighting two reservations must be kept firmly in mind:

It must not assist the intruder

It must not handicap the security officer

It has been suggested that lighting could be installed together with an intruder alarm, so that it is only switched on when the alarm is activated. Alternatively, if left on all the time it could be arranged to throb or flash to disconcert the intruder. On balance it is felt that this does not help surveillance and adds complexity to the system and so is not normally recommended. Security lighting should be in continuous regular use every night from dusk until dawn.

For low risks it will be sufficient to provide general lighting for car parks and

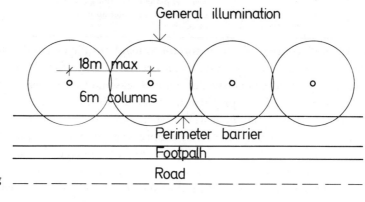

2.22 General perimeter lighting creates a zone for surveillance

outdoor storage areas together with individual illumination of building entrances – especially the back doors of both commercial and domestic premises, which are traditional entrances for the criminal. Where such individual areas are lit it is important that more than one fitting is used in each location, so that the absence of light is regarded with suspicion rather than as a simple lamp failure.

In areas of higher risk, general floodlighting of the grounds and/or perimeter lighting will be appropriate. Floodlights make a large area visible for immediate checking by eye or TV cameras. The level of illumination necessary will vary according to the surroundings: where there are no street lights or adjacent illuminated buildings a level of 5–15 lux is sufficient; where adjacent areas have their own lighting a comparable standard must be provided and the levels may have to be increased to 10–15 lux and 20–30 lux. Standard floodlighting equipment may be used with any of the common light sources but it is preferable to mount the fittings at a high level to reduce the incidence of vandalism. Table 2.1 gives more detailed guidance as to lighting intensities for average levels of security.

Table 2.1. Lighting intensities for security

Location		Lux
1. Building surfaces	Up to 2.4 m high	20
	To roof	10
2 Grounds near building	Parking	10
	Road	4
	Storage	2
	Footpath	2
3 General site area	Parking	10
	Road	4
	Storage	1
	Footpath	2
	Open	0.5
4 Perimeter	Pedestrian entrances	20
	Vehicular entrances	10
	Vertical plane to 1 m (for glare barrier)	2
	On fence line or water approach	1
	Open	0.5

Where it is particularly important to maintain the external lighting in cases of higher risk, the lighting system can be connected to the alarm system so that a signal is given if the lighting fails for any reason, or is tampered with.

Perimeter lighting is provided to illuminate the immediate area of the perimeter barrier itself, and may be installed where, for some reason, general lighting is not practical, or can be designed to confuse the intruder and put him at a further disadvantage. High intensity lights inside the perimeter and shining outwards will create sufficient glare to prevent him from seeing any detail beyond, and will destroy his night vision; at the same time he will feel more exposed and will indeed be more visible to observers inside the site.

2.23 **Directional perimeter lighting provides a more aggressive deterrent to intruders**

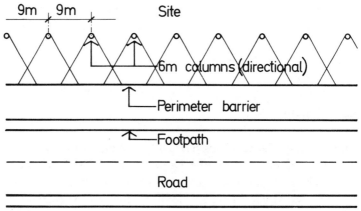

The usual method of providing illumination at the perimeter is with directional lighting from column-mounted floodlights inside the site. The levels should be relatively even, and if wide distribution fittings are used, column spacing should be no greater than 3 times the height of the column; if more directional fittings are used then this spacing is reduced to 1.5 times the column height.

It must be remembered that all external surveillance—be it personal or by camera—will be frustrated to a greater or lesser extent by fog, rain or snow, and that security will be reduced during this weather.

2.7 Vehicles, plant and equipment

2.7.1 The security of vehicles on an unattended site is most difficult. The most common risk is theft of or from a loaded goods vehicle and the most effective counter-measure is a management one: do not allow loaded goods vehicles to stand unattended. This however is not always possible; but it should be understood that available vehicle alarm systems are not tamperproof and neither are the various electrical and mechanical immobilisation devices. It is better in such cases to link vehicle removal with the building alarm system and details are given in chapter 6.

Vehicles used within the site for transport or mechanical handling can be used by the intruder: it has been known for a crane to be used to lift a safe through a rooflight onto a waiting vehicle. The more common risk is the simple use of force to break through or pull down sections of the building envelope to gain access. Immobilisation of vehicles and plant, though not infallible will provide a practical deterrent for this.

2.8 Spoiling and wastage

2.8.1 This is not a traditional area of security in that no criminal action is involved. It is however concerned with the protection of assets, and the losses to an organisation from spoiling and wastage of materials stored badly in external areas can be considerable. A security plan should consider the policy for protecting goods in such areas, and the routine inspection should include a report on the state of the protection. The absence of a tarpaulin, for example, should be a matter for surveillance.

2.9   Building sites

2.9.1   The special problems relating to building sites are set out in chapter 1. It is clear that in many cases the perimeter of the site cannot be secured at all: motorway sites, for example, spread for several miles, and some housing developments become partially occupied during construction.

The site itself will also change during construction as different materials and plant are brought along, and as access to the buildings themselves becomes more or less difficult. Thus both the target risk and the security available vary constantly.

In the case of theft there are often great difficulties in identifying the stolen property, and this can prevent its recovery, as well as allowing the criminal to go free. Many of the vulnerable articles are in manufacturers' packing without any serial numbers. Clearly, general building materials are difficult to mark, but every attempt should be made to label tools and plant in a durable way. This is not as easy as it may sound: larger items such as excavators have serial numbers which are relatively difficult to conceal, but the smaller power tools and hand tools are awkward, since paint wears off and stamped marks can damage tools or their insulation. The security advisory group of the National Federation of Building Trades Employers (Consec) maintains a lost and found register which helps; they also have a list of house colours of plant and machinery. One company (Camrex) which specialises in unusual coatings, offers an individually formulated paint which can be applied to plant. The formula will be allocated to one customer and can be subsequently identified

Different views are taken of insurance. Many contractors carry their own risk, or at least bear a substantial excess on their policies. Insurance companies are aware of the fluid situation on building sites and do not take much notice of any special security arrangements that are set up, so it is not usually possible to influence premiums to any great extent.

Handover of completed buildings must be clear and the responsibility formally defined. Although this responsibility may pass out of the hands of the builder in a phased manner over a period of time (on a housing scheme for example), the new building owner should be encouraged by the builder to maintain security so that, as far as possible, the whole site is equally secure.

Every effort should be made to reduce the likelihood of occupation by squatters.

Where possible, the site should be fenced. When this is not practical, there must be one or more compounds for the storage of materials, plant and for offices.

Fencing can be expensive and whatever type is selected should be capable of being re-used on other jobs. Chestnut palings 1.2 m high are effective when combined with stout posts up to 1.8 m (such as scaffold poles), with barbed wire stranded between. Chain link can also be used and is more effective, but tends to suffer during the job so that its re-use is uncertain. Alternatively, on urban sites or where a hoarding is required, 19 mm ply can be used 2.4 m high, again supported on stout posts or scaffold tubes. Gates must be of equivalent strength; and where risks are higher, especially around site huts and compounds, gates should be the equivalent of a 2.4 m high corrugated metal hoarding fixed to stout timber or scaffold poles. The top 300 mm can be coated with anti-climb (sticky) paint. Portable sections of interlocking weldmesh are also effective and are specially made for site compounds, where they may be altered as the job proceeds and re-used a number of times. Gates should be compatible with the fence construction and be fitted with padlocks. The use on the inside of the gate frame of welded staples which are accessible through a small hole is recommended: although the gate is more awkward to operate, it is extremely difficult to use hacksaws or a bolt cropper from the outside. Padlocks should never be left unlocked on the open gate.

Notices should be posted giving details of rewards offered for conviction of vandals or thieves. These should be properly signwritten in a business-like manner and the general view is that their effectiveness rises in proportion to their size. Some success has also been reported following the distribution of reward leaflets to individual households nearby.

Site huts must themselves be secure, preferably with screened windows and certainly with good quality padlocks, hasps and staples. Note that few site hut doors can be fitted with mortice locks and that rim locks not only provide poor security here, but depend too much on the strength and fit of the framed opening. Two-storey site huts are ideal: they use less space, the upper floor is inherently more secure and they provide a good view over the site area, so that both management and security supervision are improved. Site huts must always be inside the site compound and should not form part of the perimeter.

The police should be notified of the works. They should be told of the nature of the scheme, the presence of any special risks, and in particular the working hours. Police patrols who observe that there are personnel on site in the evening or at weekends should know whether they are authorised or intruders, and should be able to check their authority.

Plant and machinery should be immobilised and made secure. Very few machines are fitted with anti-theft devices and manufacturers have been criticised for this. It would seem simple, for example, to fit the steering locks which have proved fairly effective on cars. Bear in mind that, apart from the risk of theft, a modern machine can cause a lot of damage on a site in a short time and even the collapse of a trench can cost half a day's work. The responsible contractor will also try to prevent children from playing with his machines for fear of them being injured.

Large concentrations of plant (and fuel) will require more deliberate protection and should be driven into compounds overnight or at least at weekends. The plant compound should be fenced to 3 m, including barbed wire, and should be fitted with alarms. The machines should be immobilised.

Apart from major plant there will also be many valuable minor tools on the site, and some of these will be the property of subcontractors and individual workmen. Secure storage chests should be provided for these as necessary, plus lockers fitted with padlocks for other minor tools and personal clothing. Marking of tools should be positively encouraged.

Site storage areas should be defined rather than casual, and those areas for such valuable materials as non-ferrous metals should not be near the site perimeter or be protected solely by the perimeter fence.

Site storekeeping is a neglected business although a good storekeeper is good value for money. Apart from the obvious security control, the storekeeper will be able to reduce wastage and handling charges for restocked goods returned to suppliers. Accurate inventories of goods will detect thefts as well as avoiding excess ordering, and although inventories have traditionally been difficult to maintain, due partly to the nature of a building site, the availability of cheap micro-computers should provide an immense benefit even on moderately small sites.

Deliveries of valuable materials should be planned and phased so that the minimum quantities are floating at any time. There is a real risk of fraudulent deliveries, so a routine for checking, counting, and acknowledging goods received must be established.

The parking of private cars on the site should be strictly forbidden as a matter of principle. Checkers or timekeepers should control and record deliveries to the site, and there should be a published and enforced policy of random checks on vehicles leaving the site.

Lighting must be considered, and like fencing it may not be practicable on all sites. The provision of overall site lighting is a worthwhile deterrent, however, and should be included wherever possible, at least for compound areas; it may be possible to site these so that some illumination is given by street lights where no power is available. Site lighting may sometimes be combined for both security and winter working. As a matter of routine, however, all lights inside buildings should be switched off at night so that police or patrols can treat any that are seen with suspicion. Lights on rural sites in particular may be expensive to maintain because they can become popular targets for airguns.

Cash on site should be limited as far as possible and a proper safe (not a spare old one) should be fitted in the site offices. The criminal will assume that several hundred pounds is commonly held on site, and, in addition to the night risk, the site office may well be unoccupied during periods of the day. There are dangers surrounding the delivery and payment of wages on site, which may vary according to the amounts involved and the location of the site. Although the traditions of the industry do not make the problem easy to solve, the following principles should be observed.

> Encourage non-cash payment when possible (of at least part of wages)
>
> Split pay-days (say Thursday and Friday)
>
> Drive the security vehicle onto the site and where possible close the gates
>
> Pay employees directly from the vehicle so that cash is not left in bulk on site
>
> Take advice from local police

The contractor should also know and control the procedures used for payment by his subcontractors.

2.10 Trespass

2.10.1 There are some common misunderstandings concerning the matter of trespass. It is not a criminal offence in the UK and trespassers may not normally be arrested (there are exceptions, such as railway and military property). The sign Trespassers will be Prosecuted is a nonsense. Any damage which is incidental to the trespass is usually a civil matter and the culprit must be sued for damages. The police are reluctant to intervene in cases of trespass except to ensure that there is no breach of the peace.

In the case of squatters a court order may be obtained for their ejection and it may be necessary to follow this with a writ and enforcement of possession by bailiffs, except in the case of disorderly occupation where the police are empowered to act.

The occupier of land (or his agent) may use a reasonable degree of force in order to prevent a trespasser from entering, or to eject him. There is an overriding duty in law, however, to act with common humanity. None of the measures taken should cause harm or injure the intruder.

Checklist 2

Grounds

Consider location

  Urban
  Rural
  History
  Railway or canal
  Building site adjoining
  Neighbours

Principles of layout

  No public footpaths
  Restrict deck or balcony access
  Visible entrances
  Lockable garages
  Keep buildings clear of boundary
  Control external storage
  Restrict vehicle access for high security
  Separate employee parking
  Secure roof storage

Means of access

  Reduce points of access
  Consider vehicles and pedestrians separately
  Select appropriate gates and barriers

Perimeter barrier:

> Fencing height
> Visibility and surveillance
> Physical strength and monitoring
> Vehicle penetration

External lighting and surveillance:

> Patrols
> Point or area lighting
> Illumination level
> Perimeter lighting

Vehicles plant and building sites:

> Alarm system
> External storage protection
> Label tools
> Plant and storage compounds
> Notices
> Site hut security and location
> Police liaison
> Immobilise plant
> Fuel storage
> Site storekeeping management
> Delivery control
> Private parking prohibition
> Lighting
> Site cash and wages management
> Trespass or squatters

3 The building envelope

3.1   General

3.1.1   The external skin of the building must be regarded as a primary line of defence. It may have to be the first line of defence if there is no secure perimeter, and in any case its purpose is to house and protect the contents and occupants. This has always been so: if the first reason for constructing a shelter was protection from the elements, then security from attacks by predators must have been a very close second. The image of the predator is a useful one to have in mind when attempting to create a secure shell: the criminal is hungry and will seek out weak points: if he cannot find them, he will go elsewhere.

The building envelope is likely to be easier to secure than the perimeter and it may not always be possible to provide a perimeter barrier in situations such as street frontages, housing and multiple tenancies. In schools and other unattended sites the perimeter of the grounds should be defined as a statement of ownership but must be disregarded for security purposes.

Where multiple tenancies are anticipated in office blocks and the like, the boundaries of the tenancy effectively become the building envelope.

The main risk is the intruder, and the aim of the defensive measures must be to force the burglar to carry tools, to take time and to make noise in his attempt, so that he is exposed to risk.

Strength is the primary requirement in the building envelope and this strength must be provided to a realistic and consistent level over all the walls, roofs and floors, bearing in mind the locality, target value, and means of access. Of course, the building designer does not have a free hand in the design of the building envelope and the whole will be shaped by a number of other forces such as town planning legislation and building regulations.

3.1.2   The local town planning authority must be satisfied as to the general amenity value of the development, the siting, use and appearance of the building. The assessment of these factors is largely subjective and there is much room for negotiations, but it is likely that strong views will be held by the authority on:

> Materials used
> Glazing
> Points of access
> Roof type

It can readily be seen that all these matters are crucial to the physical strength of the external skin of the building. In addition, the character of any adjoining buildings must be taken into account, and in some instances a new building must copy the existing. Authorities are becoming more responsive to arguments based on security, however, on the grounds that the incidence of crime has a direct effect on the amenity of the area and is therefore a legitimate matter to be taken into consideration.

It should also be noted that where a building is listed as being of architectural or historic interest, or where it is in a conservation area, then planning permission may be required for any alterations to the external appearances or even to the interior.

3.1.3 After the appearance of the external skin has been agreed by the town planning authority, the method of construction of this skin may be decided and once again legislation applies to control the process. In the UK, one of three sets of regulations apply:

The Building Regulations

The Scottish Building Regulations

The London Building Acts and Constructional By-laws

The regulations are concerned with stability, public health, fire precautions and, lately, energy conservation. There is no mention of security. They differ greatly in details and are constantly changing but they are more rigid than the Town and Country Planning Acts and there is less room for negotiation. It is not necessary to go into the details of the regulations but it is useful to consider the main headings and their general effect upon security:

Walls and roofs must resist the weather and be suitably durable. Floors must resist rising moisture.

Structural stability of walls and foundations must be assured

The elements of structure must generally be incombustible

Walls must have fire resistance from the inside to prevent the spread of fire to other buildings

External walls with openings must not be placed on the boundary

Linings of external walls must not allow flame to spread

Roofs must resist fire from the outside

Escape routes must be provided for use at all times that the building is occupied

Thermal insulation to a standard is required for roofs and walls. This includes limits to glazed areas

Sound insulation is required between dwellings

External stairways must be designed to a standard

Windows to habitable rooms must be openable and of a minimum size for healthy ventilation and light (in London, offices are also included)

3.1.4   Services installations in modern buildings are complex. Openings may be needed in external walls for intake and extract grilles for air conditioning systems, and relatively large sections of the wall could have to be removable or openable for the replacement of major items of plant. There may be roof fans, housings and plant rooms which further perforate the envelope.

3.1.5   Lastly, there is the question of cost. As a very rough rule of thumb, strong constructions are more expensive than weak ones, heavy more than light, so there is likely to be a financial pressure moving the construction of the envelope towards the more lightweight penetrable assembly. This principle is helped along by the fact that the external skin is the most expensive element of the building fabric. Because the eventual tenant or use of the building may well not be known many new buildings, especially office blocks, industrial estates and housing, are built speculatively, and only after completion is a tenant considered. By this time, whatever other security measures may be applied, it is unlikely that much strengthening of the external skin will be possible, other than the openings of doors and windows.

3.1.6   Where a fairly high degree of security is required, the external line of the building must be as clean and unobstructed as possible. There should be no recessed or hidden entrances and no hand-holds for climbing. Rainwater pipes are common climbing routes; they should be located inside the building. Failing that, they should be shielded with a U-guard so that a handgrip is impossible, fitted with a spiked collar above head height or painted with non-drying anti-climb paint. The addition of a ring of barbed wire is not particularly effective.

3.1.7   Buildings are dynamic things: they need to grow and change according to the activities of their occupants and the fashions of the day. It is clearly necessary to consider and control the alterations to the building envelope with the same concern for security that was required for the initial design. The neglect of this principle is a common cause of decay in the security of buildings.

3.2   Walls

3.2.1   It is easy to jump straight to the vulnerable openings in walls—doors, windows, and grilles—without any real consideration of the construction of the wall itself. This is dangerous in the present day, as in the development of materials and methods of construction many new wall assemblies have been introduced.

The external wall may well vary from place to place around the building. In practice, any wall constructed in a workmanlike manner which fulfils its main purpose of weather protection will almost certainly provide security against casual criminals and opportunists without any further protection. It should also be sufficiently strong to protect low values against the more deliberate criminal and the vandal, though in the latter case the surface itself will be more or less vulnerable to defacement; if vandalism is likely then surfaces such as insitu concrete and facing brickwork are more difficult to repair or replace.

Where the target value rises, the efforts of the deliberate criminal will also rise, and the construction must be designed to provide physical strength. Table 3.1 gives a rough guide to the grade of resistance to attack provided by some common constructions.

Table 3.1. Walling: Grades of resistance to attack	
Grade 1	Reinforced concrete insitu 225 mm +
	Brickwork 325 mm
Grade 2	Reinforced concrete insitu 125 mm
	Brickwork 215 mm
Grade 3	Precast concrete
	Brickwork 103 mm
Grade 4	Solid concrete blockwork 75 mm
	Metal sheeting on metal studs
	Metal/grp/grc panel cladding
Grade 5	Hollow concrete blockwork 100 mm
	Glass bricks
	Curtain walling
Grade 6	Asbestos cement sheet
	Timber boarding
	Tile hanging
	Lath and plaster

3.2.2 Profiled asbestos cement sheet is particularly poor in this context: it can be shattered easily by impact and falls into large pieces, and it is usually fixed to a light steel frame so that the opening which appears following the breakage is large enough to provide ample access. It should also be remembered that breakages can occur innocently as a result of impact from manouevring vehicles or through children at play, and that such breakages will leave a weakness to be taken advantage of by the opportunist.

3.2.3 Timber and pvc boarding is easily removed with little noise or force. The practicalities of construction, however, usually cause the boards to be fixed to timber framing at relatively close centres. Whilst these by no means present impenetrable barriers to the intruder they act as a delay, taking time to overcome. A lining which is firmly fixed from the inside will add greatly to the defence, but nevertheless these claddings should not be used in concealed or unobserved locations at ground level.

3.2.4 Tile hanging can present problems as the tiles or slates themselves can almost be removed by hand, one at a time. As with boarded claddings, the minimal degree of security available must be provided wholly by the supporting structure and the inner skin.

3.2.5   Plastics are commonly used in modern buildings. Profiled lightweight plastic sheets should not be used as they are not substantial enough and can be broken or melted without great difficulty. Moulded panels constructed from glass reinforced plastics are usually tough enough to resist some physical attack, and if properly fixed will provide a reasonable degree of security; the fixings deserve special attention as there are common problems: clip-on panels can be unclipped for example, and some forms of gasketing can be unzipped.

3.2.6   Profiled sheet metal cladding is quite tough and will withstand moderate physical attacks but has two main disadvantages. First of all it is easily dented and subject to vandalism at ground level—damage which is difficult to repair—and secondly the fixings may be easily removed. Fixings at ground floor level should be blind or deformed to prevent removal and not the common power-tool applied screws; even so, their positions are obvious, and with a little more time and noise they can be drilled out.

3.2.7   If vehicles can approach the external wall they provide the means of applying considerable force easily and quickly; they may be used to ram the wall or to pull out sections of it. Construction should be limited to well-built brickwork or insitu concrete. Precast concrete may be used in most cases, especially where a barrier is included to prevent vehicle contact and, in high security circumstances, the inner skin should provide a second line of defence. Note, however, that a continuous barrier which is too close to the building will increase the danger from explosive attack. Firstly the charge may be concealed behind the barrier and secondly, the barrier itself can reflect and therefore reinforce the effect of the explosion. A gap of about 1.8 m should be left, fig 3.1.

3.1 **The protection of building exteriors against vehicles and explosives**

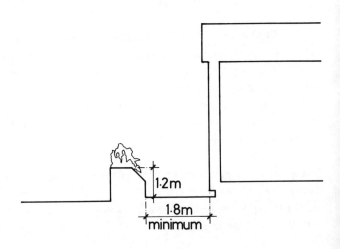

1·2m

1·8m
minimum

3.2.8 The resistance of a wall to terrorist attack is limited to minimising the effects of blast from explosives. The power of the blast will depend on the site layout and whether or not vehicles can approach closely. The following principles apply where attack is likely.

> Do not use materials which shatter such as asbestos cement, tiles, vitrolite or precast concrete.
>
> Remember that the glass infill in cladding or curtain walling can be as dangerous as the glass in the windows.
>
> Do not locate grilles or louvres so that explosives can be inserted.
>
> Walls should either be massive enough to withstand blast or flexible enough to absorb part of the energy. Well-fixed profile steel sheet is an example of the principle of flexibility, as used in a motorway crash barrier.

It should be realised that the power of modern explosives and the military weapons likely to be used by terrorists are beyond the experience of most building designers, and data is hard to come by. Concentrated explosions such as tamped charges, rocket attacks or underground explosions are the most dangerous: even if the wall is not penetrated, large fragments of the inner surface will be projected violently into the building. There are three main approaches to the wall construction necessary to defend against such an attack.

> Overall thickness. A single skin of reinforced concrete, which may well be in the region of 0.5—1 m thick will provide tough continuous protection.
>
> Double skins. Two thinner skins will give better protection against spalling of the inner surface for a single explosion. They are more difficult to construct and maintain however, and much of their protection may be lost after the outer skin is breached by a first charge.
>
> Lining. A steel lining can be provided on the inner face as specific protection against spalling. It can be used in conjunction with either single or double skins.

Expert advice should be sought as to the likely energy of explosions if such protection is required; crime prevention officers will be the first source of information. The behaviour of glass is dealt with more fully in section 3.4.

3.3   Entrances and exits

3.3.1 In this section, the location and construction of entrances and exits are considered with regard to providing physical barriers at these points. The *regulation* of entry is not covered, as it falls within the total planning concept of access control which is dealt with fully in chapter 7. For this reason, wherever locks are discussed in this section, only their physical strength and fixing are considered; all consideration of mechanism and keying is left to chapter 7.

The main function of an entrance is of course to let people in, and so, unlike other elements of the building, some deliberate action is required to change this function fundamentally to that of keeping people out. Doors are second only to windows as the most common means of illegal entry to buildings, and much attention is paid to their security, not always to good effect; sometimes they are raised disproportionately far above the level of defence of other parts of the building.

3.3.2 The number of entrances and exits should be kept to a minimum. It is easy to let this get out of hand during planning, particularly where building use is seen as flexible and allowance is made for free access to outdoor spaces. All these points of access must be managed however, and the practical security which can be achieved falls as the number of doors increases.

Irrespective of the number of doors provided, one must be designated as a final exit door with deliberate provision for opening from the outside; this designation also becomes important in the design of intruder alarm systems which are covered in chapter 6. Physical security for the other points of access then becomes a little easier to achieve.

Although one door may be intended as the sole final exit, other patterns of traffic may develop in the use of the building when the occupants find alternative routes more convenient, such as rear exits to car parking areas. This is a common source of security weakness and a security plan must be flexible enough to recognise such deviations from intent and be adapted to suit.

3.3.3 Entrances and exits should be placed where they do not reduce security. Exits and loading bays must not be adjacent to passing traffic routes and must not open from narrow alleys. Direct access to car parks should be avoided wherever possible so that pilferage is reduced; for the same reason, delivery doors must be closed when not in use. Loading areas themselves should be planned so that goods inward are clearly and physically separated from despatches.

Main entrance doors in public buildings such as museums, theatres, or department stores have a more complex function in the security plan. When the premises are closed they must provide whatever degree of security has been designated for the building envelope. When the building is open, the public must have free access in large numbers and, indeed, must be actively encouraged to enter with as little hindrance as possible. Although during this phase the doors themselves have little purpose, the entrance is the point at which:

   Tickets are sold and/or checked
   Admission may need to be refused
   Searches may be required of bags, cases
   Theft may be detected on exit from shops or libraries

3.3.4 The establishment of a locking routine is good management and the absence of a formal policy will create serious weaknesses in security which will be exploited by the opportunist criminal. Premises which close in a regular manner, such as shops, are easy to manage: the same person is nominated to lock up each night at the same time. Other buildings such as offices are more difficult, since occupants may leave over an extended period each day, which may stretch well into the evening; this trickle exit is likely to be entirely casual and two bad habits can develop:

> The last person to leave does not have a key and cannot secure the premises
> Alternatively, over a period of time, many people acquire keys, and a cumulative loss of security results, simply from the number of keys in circulation

It is clear therefore that in these circumstances it must be possible to secure the final exit without using a key. This presents problems, since devices which latch automatically do not give the same degree of security as those which are positively locked. The ideal solution is a key operated deadlock for the final exit, but if management routines are unable to overcome the risks of late exit set out above, then a latching device must also be fitted as a reserve.

3.3.5 One of the most difficult problems to solve is providing security while maintaining fire safety. There is an essential conflict between the requirements of the fire officer, who demands a number of exits which are freely usable at any time and those of the security officer, who demands minimum exits, each with positive control. The escape requirements are statutory and there is usually a more direct risk to personal safety, and so they take precedence. The conflict is usually resolved by a rather shaky combination of management and ironmongery; there is no doubt that major weaknesses in security can appear, and a high degree of security may not be possible in some buildings.

Multiple tenancies increase the problem. Not only are the tenants interdependent for fire prevention routines, but their times of occupancy will overlap and escape routes may even pass through spaces belonging to different tenants. The design of some shopping malls, for instance, relies for escape on access through the shops to the outer service area.

The fire exit doors themselves will often need to be double leaves because of the number of people in the building; the physical strength of a pair of doors will inevitably be lower than that of a single leaf.

In premises such as shops, warehouses and cash-and-carry markets the fire exits are liable to be used to remove goods illegally—they are well signposted and often discharge conveniently onto the car park. In other buildings they may be used, with collusion, as unauthorised entrances.

There are four basic complementary approaches to the overall problem:

> Management
> Detection
> Hardware
> Planning

Management. In some cases, given the approval of the authorities, fire exits may be made secure and impassable while the building is unoccupied. As there is a routine to be followed in unlocking the exits, it will sooner or later fail to operate and the consequent dangers are obvious. Indeed fatalities in fires are recorded as a result of locked escape doors. Discipline in locking routines must be rigid if this principle has to be considered. One method used, more or less successfully, is the padlock board: escape doors are padlocked at night, but during occupation all the padlocks are displayed on a numbered board mounted where it is immediately available for inspection. It is not possible, however, to provide high security with the use of padlocks.

Detection. The escape doors or the hardware attached may be connected to an alarm system and notices clearly posted to this effect on the doors themselves. Whilst this certainly deters people from using the exit casually as a short cut, the main drawback of the solution is that it literally allows the stable door to be locked after the horse has bolted: a determined thief may be quite prepared to race the response to the alarm. See also chapter 6.

Hardware. Escape hardware is generally poor in design and construction and has changed little over the years. The specification, fitting and door construction are all critical and must be given the most careful attention. There is a new British Standard for panic hardware and it is clear that, although security has not been ignored (there are tests for end-loading of bolts, for example) it has not been a prime consideration, and indeed security is not even mentioned as a performance requirement. Fire authorities will generally require this standard to be followed in the UK, however. External knobsets should not be used.

Planning. Good building planning can minimise the abuse of fire exits and enable a higher degree of security to be maintained. On the outside, the opening swing of the doors should ideally be protected by rails rather than be within a recess, figs 3.2, 3.3. This is not always possible but it does carry with it the advantage of increased floor area inside the building as well as observation of the exit. The door should not discharge into an alleyway. On the inside, the approach should also be clear, which is consistent with good fire planning. The exit should be sited so that

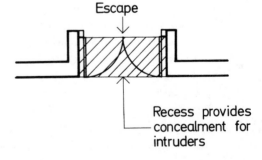

3.2 **Recessed escape doors provide concealment and an opportunity for refuse accumulation**

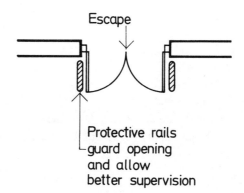

Escape

Protective rails
guard opening
and allow
better supervision

3.3 **A more secure solution is the protection of the opening by rails**

it is within constant view of the building occupants. In high security situations a lobby should be provided, with the alarm signal being given when either door is opened; in this way abuse is discouraged and the intruder must break two barriers, fig 3.4.

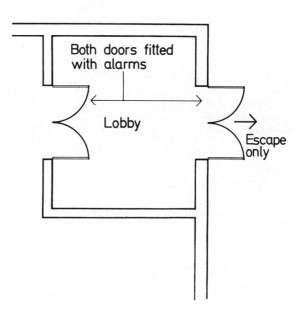

Both doors fitted with alarms

Lobby

Escape only

3.4 **Escape and security: a lobby discourages abuse and gives earlier warning of intruders**

3.3.6   It is useful to begin by considering the most common methods of attack on doors:

Jemmy, fig 3.5
Side loading (frame spreading), fig 3.6
Gap opening fig, 3.7
Lock removal, fig 3.8
Panel removal, fig 3.9
Ramming, fig 3.10
Pulling, fig 3.11

With these in mind, the construction of door and frame can be more effectively designed. The threat energy which can be applied to a single external door can be assumed to be as given in table 3.2.

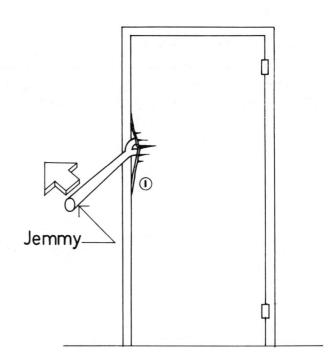

3.5 **Jemmy attack prises or breaks the door away from the frame**

Table 3.2. Energy applied to single external doors

Threat	Force (Nm)
Hammer	14
Kick	88
Ram	120
Shoulder	205

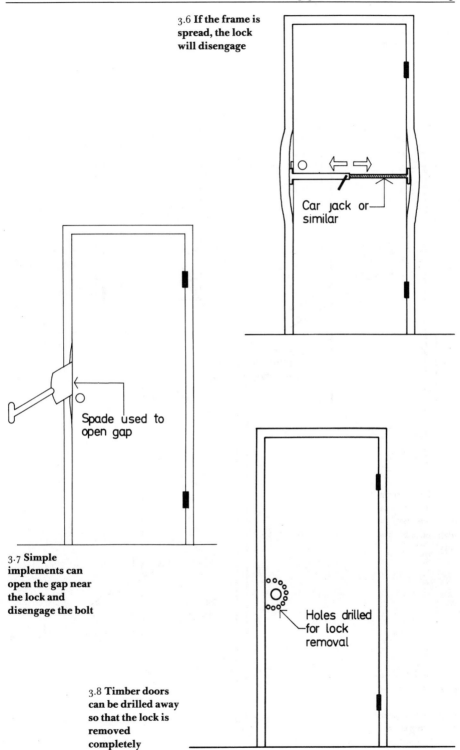

3.6 If the frame is spread, the lock will disengage

Car jack or similar

Spade used to open gap

3.7 Simple implements can open the gap near the lock and disengage the bolt

Holes drilled for lock removal

3.8 Timber doors can be drilled away so that the lock is removed completely

**3.9 Panelled doors
are vulnerable:
whole panels may
be removed**

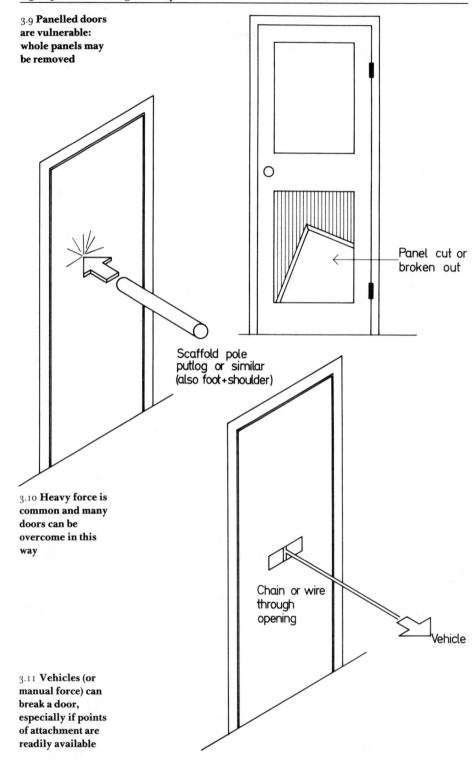

Panel cut or
broken out

Scaffold pole
putlog or similar
(also foot+shoulder)

**3.10 Heavy force is
common and many
doors can be
overcome in this
way**

Chain or wire
through
opening

Vehicle

**3.11 Vehicles (or
manual force) can
break a door,
especially if points
of attachment are
readily available**

A pipe wrench can exert a force of 375 Nm; it is ideal for the removal of locking knobsets, which are likely to fail at about 20 Nm, or a projecting cylinder requiring an average of 55 Nm. Cylinders can also be removed by an impacting puller: an average of only seven attempts is required. Some defence against crowbar attack can be achieved by incorporating soft edges to door and frame, so that any crushing will be local and not transfered along a length of the edge.

3.3.7 The balance of opinion maintains that security doors should always open outwards—that is, in the opposite direction to the attack—and that this principle should extend to any inner lobby doors. In practice, many external doors will be designated as primary or secondary escape routes and so be required to open outwards for safety. There are disadvantages, however, because the normal UK door will thus expose the knuckles of the hinges and there will be a gap at the opposite edge where the lock bolt can be attacked. Rebated doors such as those more commonly used elsewhere in Europe help to overcome the lock problem and the hinges can be protected by the use of hinge bolts or dog bolts, which engage as the door shuts, fig 3.12.

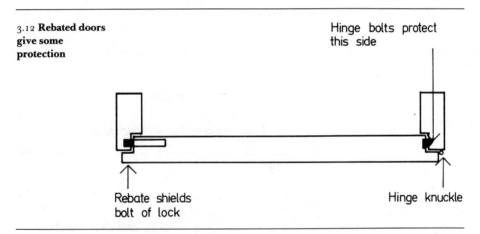

3.12 **Rebated doors give some protection**

Hinge bolts protect this side

Rebate shields bolt of lock

Hinge knuckle

A minor problem encountered with outward opening doors is the occasional vandalism of striking plates, where these are bent over mischievously, so deliberately holding the door shut.

Double doors are to be avoided if possible, as the meeting stile has no support from the frame. The stile should be rebated to protect any chain or panic bolt from attack and to make the use of a jemmy more difficult, fig 3.13.

Inward opening doors are supported only by the lock against a forceful assault, and with sufficient effort the lock can be broken out of a standard timber door. In addition, the frame itself is exposed, and if the lock is fitted in the centre as is normal, the frame can be spread by the use of car jacks until the bolt ceases to engage, fig 3.14, though this is not usually possible with a single door fitted between masonry reveals.

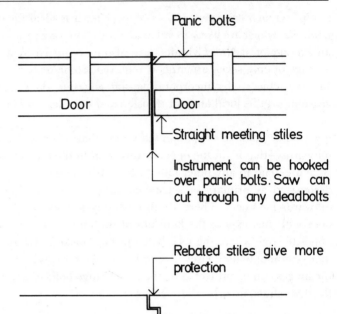

3.13 **The meeting stile of double doors is always a weakness. Rebates give some protection**

Panic bolts

Door   Door

Straight meeting stiles

Instrument can be hooked over panic bolts. Saw can cut through any deadbolts

Rebated stiles give more protection

INSIDE

Poor support for striking plate

Frame provides purchase for spreader

3.14 **Inward opening doors allow several methods of attack**

OUTSIDE

Ramming or pulling the door with a vehicle can be anticipated; the direct access to the door can be planned to deter vehicular approach, perhaps with steps or rails (making sure that no bearing for a jack is created), and if the surface of the door is imperforate it will be difficult to attach a tow.

Sliding doors are difficult to secure. They either hang from a top track or run on a bottom channel, and in either case they can usually be lifted off by the application of some force. There are operational difficulties arising from maintenance and dirt in the mechanism which do nothing to aid security; the support system is also susceptible to attention from vandals.

Roller shutters are frequently used for industrial entrances and they provide a reasonably practical answer to the functional requirements. There are several common problems which arise:

> Chain operated types should not be secured merely by locking the chain into a holder
>
> Power operated types should not rely only on being switched off for security
>
> The shutters should be protected from physical damage as they can be rendered inoperable by impact
>
> Wicket gates provide poor security and should not be included

3.3.8 Routine deliveries of mail and consumables create weaknesses in security management, particularly in multiple tenancies where the delivery man is given free access to the building interior: it is difficult to ensure that this access is limited to bona-fide visitors: see chapter 7. Postal delivery boxes help to overcome the problem and though they are widely used elsewhere in the world, their use in the UK has not traditionally been popular. There are several types available, in single or multiple units, which offer reasonable degrees of security. Some may usefully be combined with intercom and access control systems, fig 3.15.

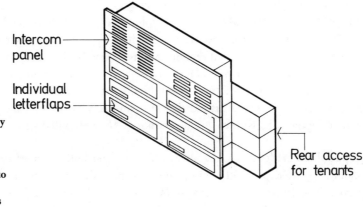

Intercom panel

Individual letterflaps

Rear access for tenants

3.15 **Postal delivery boxes are more common in Europe; they can add considerably to security in multiple tenancies**

3.3.9 There are no British Standards which cover the whole door and frame assembly with its fixing, and therefore several different aspects must be put together in order to establish the requisite grade of security. Some of the standards which do apply are:

> BS 459: Part 3: 1951 Fire-check flush doors
>
> Part 4: 1965 Matchboarded doors

BS CP 151: Part 1: 1957 Wooden doors
BS 5872: 1980: Locks and latches for doors in buildings
BS 3621: 1980: Thief resistant locks

In addition to these, the Association of Burglary Insurance Surveyors operates its own star grading system for locks. It is interesting to note that the security offered by locks intended for higher risks is not easily assessed as the methods of attack are so varied: even BS 3621: 1980 leaves the final approval to the opinion of a panel of locksmiths.

The requirements in the British Standards for construction for doors, doorsets and frames are relevant only to weather and fire resistance and security is incidental. Neither is there any consideration of security in the standards for any of the other items of ironmongery fitted to external doors, such as hinges and letterplates.

Door frame construction and fixing are vital matters: it may seem obvious that a frame must be well fixed within its structural opening but this fixing is rarely specified and its strength is seldom checked on site. The section of the frame should be strong enough to resist deflection when forced, and large enough to accept the hardware specified without producing an excessive local weakness. Firm guidance is difficult to give in general terms, but the specifier must regard the location, door construction and degree of security required. Certainly, where mortice locks are used, a timber frame section should not be less than 75 mm × 45 mm.

Frames should be fixed within their opening by screws at 300 mm maximum centres on three sides. The common practice of relying on galvanised steel straps built into brickwork is not entirely satisfactory; the straps can work loose and if any do not easily correspond with mortar joints they are likely to be discarded on site.

Timber frames within reveals are usually quite adequate; extruded aluminium frames are often thin-walled sections and not very rigid, so they must be reinforced with steel inserts; most manufacturers offer this as an optional extra. Aluminium framing systems are sometimes assembled by springing components together and are susceptible to being dismantled in a similar way. Steel frames will provide a higher degree of resistance, and even more if they are filled with a cement mortar.

3.3.10 Timber doors should always be solid; no hollow cored or panelled doors should be fitted. A solid timber door will provide adequate strength for normal risks if it is thick enough to maintain cover over the mortice lock. This, of course, depends on the body of the lock, but in practice a leaf 45 mm thick will be sufficient.

In other cases or when greater strength is necessary, a 16 g (1.60 mm) steel sheet can be fixed to the door; again, there is a difference of opinion and some authorities recommend fitting the sheet to the inside face, with only mushroom coachbolt heads showing on the outside, while others maintain that it is the lock which is to be protected and fit a whole or partial sheet to the outside face. On balance, external protection is favoured, as it is a more obvious deterrent.

Equivalent protection is offered by proprietary doors which incorporate a continuous steel sheet behind the decorative veneered face; they do not prevent attacks but merely repel them, as their strength is not obvious. Repairs can be expensive.

The next obvious step upwards is the sheet steel door and these do indeed provide additional security, provided the gauge of steel is adequate. There should be reinforcement within the door around the edge and at lockrail height. A disadvantage is the need to select ironmongery in advance so that the correct mortices can be included in the factory.

3.3.11 Glazing presents problems and there are often overriding reasons for its inclusion in external doors: matters of appearance may take precedence, illumination of lobby areas may be required, or there may be enough glazing in adjacent windows to make its omission in the door pointless. If glazing is included, the following principles should apply.

> There should be no glazing below lockrail height
> Glazing should be toughened or laminated glass
> Panels should be a minimum size, preferably with one dimension not exceeding 600 mm
> Glazing should be fixed with beads on the inside, screwed to the door
> The door must not be operable from the inside (this rules out the use of glazing in escape doors)

In some circumstances transparent plastic sheets are acceptable and they can certainly be highly resistant to routine vandalism. They are however more flexible than glass, and can sometimes be sprung out of the frame; thermoplastics can be melted by heat and thermosetting plastics can be burned out, though this does presume a level of attack which would also break toughened glass.

Other openings should also be examined as they will form points of weakness in the door. Louvres are highly susceptible to vandalism and careless impact damage and so should never be included in external doors. Letterplates can be used to gain access to the locking device, to steal mail, for vandals to post rubbish through, or to act as a useful anchor for towing the door off. It is surprising that there is no standard letterplate available which can be secured from the inside. Postal delivery boxes are alternatives: see 3.3.8.

3.3.12 The ironmongery specified must be equal to the general constructional resistance of the door and frame to attack. It is not a simple matter and is certainly not restricted to general statements about the number of levers in the locks.

First of all, the door must be hung and this may require either pivots or hinges. Pivots are used in connection with floor springs or concealed overhead closers mounted in the transom, and may be single or double acting. The most common use is on shopfronts and office entrances and although in these situations there are

3.16 **Pivots, such as those used with floor springs, allow attack**

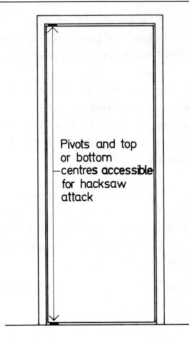

Pivots and top
or bottom
—centres accessible
for hacksaw
attack

likely to be easier ways of breaking in (such as through the glass), it must be appreciated that pivots are inherently insecure: sometimes the door may be lifted slightly to disengage the bottom pivot and in any case both top and bottom pivots are vulnerable to hacksaw attack.

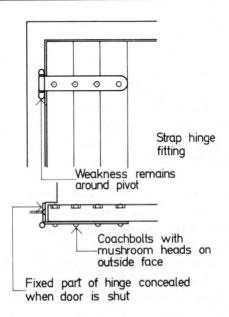

Strap hinge
fitting

Weakness remains
around pivot

Coachbolts with
—mushroom heads on
outside face

Fixed part of hinge concealed
when door is shut

3.17 **Strap hinges must be carefully detailed if any security is to be provided**

Hinges should always be butt hinges and not straps which can be unscrewed from the outside. Large timber doors which must be fitted with collinge type hinges should have them fixed with coachbolts with the mushroom head outside, though this is still not wholly satisfactory as the main weakness is, again, around the pivot. Butt hinges should be steel, stainless steel, brass or bronze and not plastics or aluminium. There should be at least three per door and the pin should not be removable. Even so, the knuckle will be exposed and higher security can be achieved by the use of hinge-bolts or dog bolts, which engage as the door shuts.

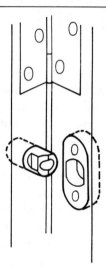

3.18 **Hinge bolts give protection when the door is shut even if the hinges are smashed**

The door closer *must* function where automatic latching is required on exit doors and those controlled by electric releases. Obviously operation must be reliable, and the correct specification is a good quality hydraulic surface mounted door closer on the inside face and incorporating adjustment for latching speed. It must be maintained in good working order.

Bolts are good: they are easily used and no parts appear on the outside of the door to be attacked. There are some points to be remembered, however. The usual bolt weakness is the staple and its fixing, and in many cases, the staple is only fixed to the frame by small woodscrews. Where double doors are used, the dead leaf should be bolted and here there are some practical difficulties: if a flush bolt is fitted to the rebated meeting edge it is awkward to detail but is protected when the doors are shut and is held by the strength of the door; if it is fitted to the inside face it is the strength of the small woodscrews which holds the door shut, and these may well be fixed into a weak part of the door structure. For reasons best known to builders however, the floor socket for the lower bolt is often lost or fitted badly so that security is reduced.

Traditional panic bolts are notoriously difficult to fit accurately to double doors and the mortised types should only be installed in the joinery shop. There is no provision for adjustment in the mechanism, and any warping in the doors can

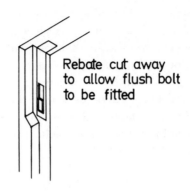

3.19 **Flush bolts are awkward to detail and fix properly especially if end-grain timber is to be avoided**

Rebate cut away to allow flush bolt to be fitted

make them difficult to secure. In addition, entrapped dirt in the frame at the water bar or in the sockets will affect their operation. Rebated pairs of doors require a double panic bolt and this is vulnerable to a looped wire inserted through a loose rebate and over the transverse bar, or similarly to string left hanging from the inside by collusion; in either case a downward pull will open the doors. The great strength of bolts, however, is their position at the corners of the door, where the frame is strongest and pressure is harder to apply.

The physical strength of the locking device receives much attention—not least from the intruder—and it is this device which suffers most from economic pressure; this is surprising, as good locks are unlikely to cost as much as door closers, and in fact represent such a miniscule proportion of the building cost that economies are ridiculous. Keying and mechanisms are dealt with in chapter 7 but considerations of strength are set out here.

There are two basic lock configurations: *rim locks* and *mortise locks*. Rim locks should not be used for external doors because the whole of their resistance to force is provided by screw fixings to the door and frame. In addition, the rim locks on the market tend towards the flimsier type of construction. Mortise locks are

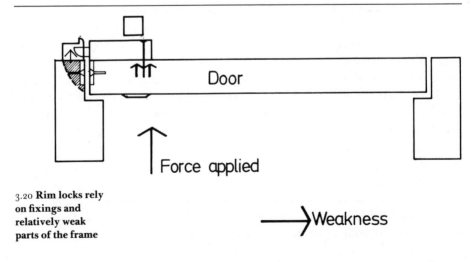

Door

Force applied

3.20 **Rim locks rely on fixings and relatively weak parts of the frame**

⟶Weakness

protected by the substance of the door (which must be adequate) and so are inherently stronger.

The cylinder rim night latch is the most common lock to be fitted to domestic front doors in the UK; it is NOT SUITABLE for this purpose. Mortised night latches are adequate for daytime use but at night or when unoccupied they should be reinforced by deadlocks.

Rim nightlatches can be overcome by a kick on the door which will either break the staple out or pull the lock fittings away. It is also possible for the springbolts on simpler nightlatches to be forced back into their cases by end pressure from flexible strips, fig 3.21. Outward opening types can be opened by passing a loop of wire around the back of the bolt.

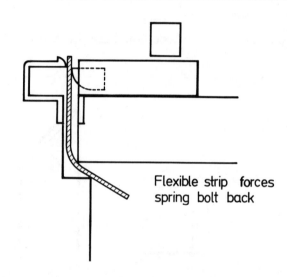

Flexible strip forces spring bolt back

3.21 **Simple rim locks can be overcome by flexible strips inserted in the gap**

If mortised nightlatches are used, the latchbolt must be protected from end pressure. Devices such as automatic deadlocking and anti-thrust bolts or slides may be incorporated to achieve this: they prevent the latchbolt from being pushed back into the case while it is engaged in the striking plate, fig 3.22. The device may not function if the latchbolt is prevented from extending fully into the striking plate by poor fitting or by dirt. At present, there is only one British-made mortise night latch incorporating such a mechanism.

Ordinary mortise locks should be constructed to BS 3261 which means that the cases will be hardened against drilling; the bolts will be hacksaw resistant and proof against substantial end-pressure, and there will be a length of bolt left within the case to give a lever arm to resist side force, fig 3.23. The striking plate will be boxed to protect the bolt; but beware of some models which rely on this protection too much, to the extent that the mechanism of the lock itself will not resist other attacks.

Slide

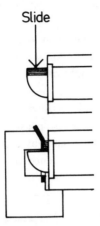

Slide held back by striker

3.22 **An anti-thrust mechanism locks the bolt in place against end-pressure**

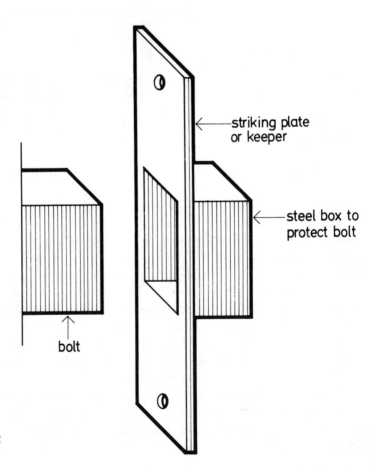

←striking plate or keeper

←steel box to protect bolt

bolt

3.23 **The extended bolt is protected against attack by a reinforced striking plate**

Lever mortise locks usually contain their mechanism within the case and are thus inherently more physically secure than cylinder mortise locks where the mechanism is partially exposed on the face of the door. Projecting cylinders can be wrenched round, shearing the locating pin, fig 3.24 while the cylinder plug itself can be drilled out, fig 3.25, thus allowing the mechanism to rotate, fig 3.26. This is balanced to some degree by the greater key security and convenience of the cylinder types.

Tubular latches with locking knobsets should never be used on external doors; the locking mechanism is inside the exposed knob which can be forcibly knocked off, leaving the door unsecured, fig 3.27.

3.24 **Projecting cylinders can be wrenched around**

3.25 **The plug can be drilled out**

3.26 **Tools can remove the exposed mechanism**

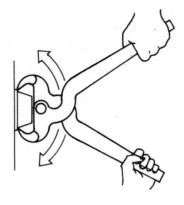

3.27 **Locking knobsets can be knocked off. They are not suitable for external doors**

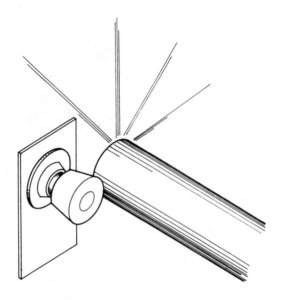

Where pairs of doors are used, an ordinary deadbolt will become ineffective if the bolts on the dead leaf are overcome; this can be remedied by using locks designed for sliding doors, which have hooked or clawed bolts to hold the doors together. Choice will be limited though, as few of these locks are designed to the higher constructional standards required.

Some deadlocks incorporate a double-throw bolt mechanism which extents the bolt further into the striker by a second turn of the key. This is a good principle in theory, but in practice there is a tendency for the key to be turned only once, and the lock may then be less secure than an ordinary single action lock.

The single deadlock has obvious weaknesses and there are locks available which operate on multiple bolts from a central mechanism. This is a convenient means of providing substantial physical strength but it does have the disadvantage that control is from a single mechanism, so that time is likely to be on the side of the criminal, fig 3.28. Although it is less convenient, and so relies more on management disciplines, two locks will be better than one because the criminal is presented with the problem of overcoming two separate mechanisms and the locks can be placed so as to spread most effectively the line of resistance to force. Some care will be necessary in the door's specification, to ensure that it is substantial enough to support locks in positions other than the normal lock rail zone.

3.28 Multiple bolts increase the physical resistance of the door to attack

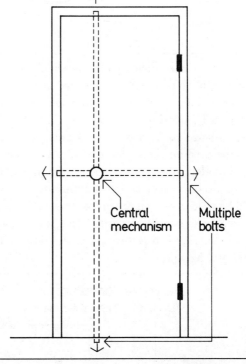

Central mechanism

Multiple bolts

Padlocks should only be used as a last resort and preferably on the inside of doors and in conjunction with swinging bars engaging in suitable slots in the frame, fig 3.29. If they are necessary on the outside, the following conditions must be imposed:

Always use the close-shackled type

Never use with chains

Ensure hasps and staples are substantial and their fittings protected

Padlocks should have: hardened shackles

anti-punch pivots

65 mm wide hardened steel body

750 g minimum weight

3.29 **A well designed, secure padlock incorporates protection to the shackle**

As a matter of management, padlocks should not be left open during normal working hours, but should either be locked onto the staple or removed altogether. Otherwise, the padlock may be lost, preventing locking, or changed by a thief for one of his own, for which he has a key.

Locking bars are used across pairs of doors in conjunction with padlocks. They should not be used on single doors as the staple can usually only be fixed to the frame with woodscrews and insufficient strength will be provided. The bars should be drop forgings or sheet steel with a minimum section of 55 × 6 mm and the hinge pin should be welded or countersunk to prevent it from being punched through. As before, coach bolts should be used for fixings through the doors. Special locking bars with the mechanism incorporated and designed to resist attack will provide higher security, fig 3.30.

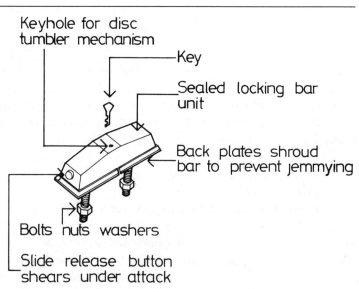

Keyhole for disc tumbler mechanism

Key

Sealed locking bar unit

Back plates shroud bar to prevent jemmying

Bolts nuts washers

Slide release button shears under attack

3.30 **Locking bars for double doors can be designed with attack taken into account**

3.3.13 Vandalism of entrances frequently affects security: there is the obvious use of force which breaches the door in the same way as a criminal attack, but there are also more indirect effects. In schools for example, panic hardware is often interfered with, and screws removed; the door then becomes either unusable as an escape or insecure. Vandals may also apply chewing gum to keyholes (or worse: superglue has been a recent innovation) so that the locks are inoperable.

3.4   Windows

3.4.1 Windows are common points of illegal entry and are the most vulnerable parts of the building envelope. If a window is designed to open and it is accessible to an intruder, then there is an obvious threat to security: not only is it physically weak, but sooner or later it will be left open when it should be shut.

More than half of all residential break-ins occur through rear windows, though it should not be assumed that all illegal entries are made during the hours when a building is empty: entry can be made at any time through an open or badly secured window and also by collusion with the occupants.

One of the reasons why windows are so popular with intruders is the common mismatch between the degree of security applied to doors and that for the windows, which often receive less attention and so provide an easier route.

3.4.2 Window security is not covered in the Agrément Board's method of assessment and testing. The only British Standards which are relevant (BS 5051 Part 1: 193, Part 2: 1979, BS 5357: 1976 and BS 5544: 1978) are restricted to defence against heavy physical attack by tools and firearms.

As with doors, there may well be a conflict between the needs of security and those of fire escape. Modern principles of fire safety rely on proper protected routes leading to escape doors, and windows are disregarded both as means of escape and rescue by the fire brigade. Nevertheless there are many middle-aged and older buildings where the windows are either designated as escapes or will inevitably become the only routes available. In two recent fires in the UK—one in a department store and one in a factory—lives were lost, and it is arguable that the barred windows on both premises contributed to the deaths; certainly they did not help either the occupants to escape or the fire brigade to gain access.

3.4.3 The location of the window is critical and the most vulnerable are:
Ground floor windows and below
First floor windows accessible by ladder or from the top of a vehicle
Other windows accessible from rooftops, walls or adjoining property
In such locations, the opening lights should have one dimension which does not exceed 125 mm. Although this should ideally refer to the light itself, some protection can be obtained by restricting to a similar dimension the amount by which the window can open. Care should be taken with the selection of opening

restrictors, as many types are not strong enough to hold the window against any degree of force and are only intended for the safety of children inside the building.

If a higher degree of protection is required then the window itself should be barred or reduced in size so that the glazed area does not exceed 125 mm in one direction or 500 cm^2 in total, and should preferably be mounted at high level. Of course the ultimate protection is achieved when there are no windows at all in the vulnerable areas, but this is usually acceptable only in situations of the highest security.

Sills and ledges may give a good foothold for access to a high level light which would otherwise be out of reach. A typical UK example is the traditional parapet/mansard detail which has several features favouring access, fig 3.31.

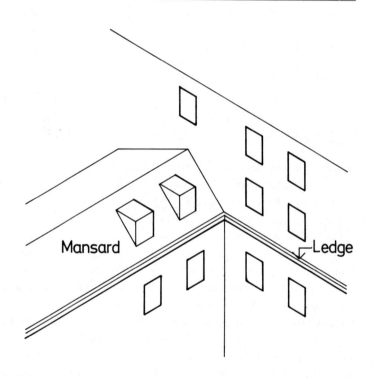

3.31 **Sills and ledges offer good footholds. These are not always apparent from an inspection of plans**

The above considerations of location and reduction in size become academic where shopfronts are concerned and there is a need for open attractive display; there are some notable exceptions, but in the main protection must be transferred to intruder detection systems and secondary barriers such as grilles: see 3.4.6. Incidentally, the construction of the shopfront often includes elements other than glass and doors: a common weakness is the insubstantial false soffit over the approach to the shop door, which is easily broken and probably not alarmed, fig 3.32.

3.32 A common weakness is the construction of shopfronts; alarm systems do not always compensate

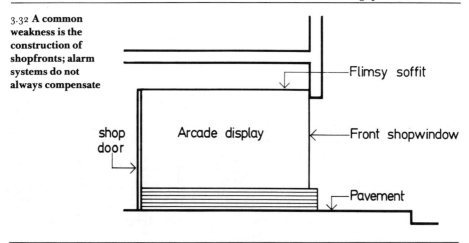

Flimsy soffit

shop door

Arcade display

Front shopwindow

Pavement

3.4.4 The opening mode of the window is another matter which affects its resistance to an intruder, and the different types require different means to secure them, fig 3.33. The opening modes in use are:

Louvred
Side hung
Top hung opening out
Bottom hung opening in
Horizontal and vertical pivots
Horizontal sliding
Vertical sliding
Dual action (turn-and-tilt)

Louvred windows have a poor reputation for security. Their mechanisms and construction are often flimsy, and with standard types entry can be made quietly and easily by removing the blades one by one; it may not even be necessary to cut the first blade. Some manufacturers have attempted to strengthen their windows by altering the design of the blade holder so that the glass is held positively. Nevertheless, such windows are subject to more attack because the vandal or intruder expects to succeed: that is to say, louvres with upgraded security are not easily distinguishable from the normal, vulnerable types.

Side hung casements, in metal or timber, are very common, especially on domestic and older buildings. In their standard form they rarely provide much security but it is not difficult to increase this to an adequate level. First of all, they should fit properly: years of paint, dirt and rust frequently prevent complete closure so that the windows are left unsecured. Windows of this type are usually supplied complete with their ironmongery, and the detailed specification of this is frequently overlooked in selecting the window. Hinges of the projecting (or easiclean) type can be smashed and so only standard butt hinges should be used. Casement stays do not provide enough fastening and some can be dislodged simply by rattling the frame. Locking casement stays are an improvement and are useful in locking the window partially open for night ventilation. It is not difficult to break them, however. Locking casement fasteners are also to be recommended, but the most effective security is obtained by the inclusion of separate mortised key-operated bolts, fig 3.34.

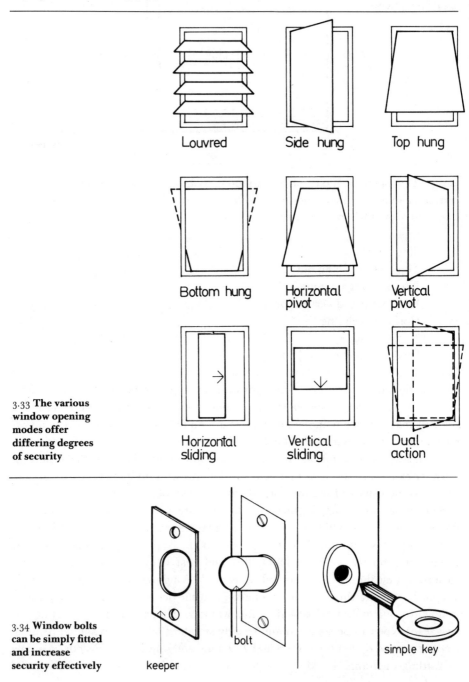

Louvred   Side hung   Top hung

Bottom hung   Horizontal pivot   Vertical pivot

Horizontal sliding   Vertical sliding   Dual action

3.33 **The various window opening modes offer differing degrees of security**

3.34 **Window bolts can be simply fitted and increase security effectively**   keeper   bolt   simple key

Selection chart 3.1. Window types

Type	Advantages	Disadvantages	Use
Louvred	Cheap ventilation Can be cleaned from inside	Flimsy Insecure	High level Small openings

Side hung
Top hung
Bottom hung
   opening in
	Simple, common
	Cheap
		Additional ironmongery
		   usually required for
		   security
		Cleaning difficult
		Ventilation only moderate
			General

Horizontal pivots **Vertical pivots**	Can be cleaned from inside	More expensive Weathering difficulties Ironmongery complicated	General
Horizontal sliding	Cheap Easy to secure Simple ironmongery No projections	Poor ventilation Poor weathering Cannot always be cleaned from inside	General
Vertical sliding	Good ventilation Good weathering No projections Easy to secure	Ironmongery difficult Cannot always be cleaned from inside	General Not large openings

The same considerations apply to top hung sashes and, in the main, to bottom hung vents, though these open inwards against a more permanent stay and are less vulnerable.

Horizontal and vertical pivots tend to be higher quality and fitted with more substantial ironmongery. Projecting and face-fixed pivots are vulnerable to force though, and advantage should be taken of one of the multi-point locking devices available, incorporating a lock in the operating handle. These will, incidentally, help to improve the thermal and sound performance of the window by ensuring a firm seal all round the perimeter.

Most sliding windows are easy to secure, though the simple catch fitted to vertical sliding sashes can be overcome by sliding a blade between the two frames and the screw-down or cam fastener is a minimum to prevent this. In addition, a locking projecting stop will provide good resistance to attack, and if fitted in the correct place will also allow safe night ventilation. Horizontal sliding windows are a little more difficult and aluminium types are not always provided with adequate fastenings; care should be taken, especially with the larger patio types, that the whole window cannot be lifted away from the fastening or even right out of the track.

The various dual-action types of window are supported by fairly complicated ironmongery and the geometry is such that each must be examined in detail to ascertain the need for additional protection.

3.4.5 Ordinary glass is obviously the weakest component of a window, figs 3.35, 3.36. It can be broken—with some noise—or it can be cut out more quietly. Pane size should be limited to 500 cm^2 as an ideal, though it is appreciated that there are many situations where this will not be acceptable. Glass should be fixed by glazing beads on the inside face.

3.35 **Simple tools can break glass in small areas**

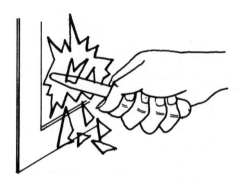

Spring loaded punch

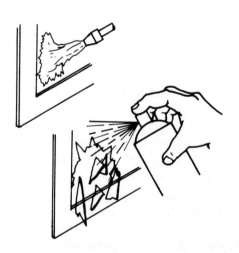

3.36 **Flame or evaporating sprays cause glass to break more quickly**

Thermal shock

Double glazing acts as some deterrent since two panes must be broken and, surprisingly, this often means a two-stage attack which will take more time. If the glass is broken, however, it will be relatively expensive to replace.

Wired glass is difficult to remove quickly by the traditional adhesive tape and glass cutter methods, and a hole of any size will take proportionately longer to create, needing some considerable force. When attacked by vandals the glass tends to stay in its frame, but this is not always an advantage: there is a tendency to neglect the replacement of cracked panes and this gives an air of abandonment which encourages further vandalism: see chapter 8.

Toughened glass is not always obvious and so attacks are not prevented. It does provide some degree of protection as it is quite difficult to break and considerable force is needed: even if a cutter is used this will usually cause the whole pane to fragment with a certain amount of noise.

Laminated glass is also extremely tough and is much more difficult to cut. As with toughened glass its presence is not obvious, though, and attacks will still occur. Both are considerably more expensive to replace than ordinary glass.

Plastics are often used in an attempt to increase the resistance of a window to both vandal and intruder attack. Acrylics and butyrates have proved unsuitable for a number of reasons and the most acceptable plastic material for glazing is polycarbonate; this has approximately 250 times the strength of glass and so provides excellent resistance to impact damage. In addition, the pieces do not form dangerous fragments when broken. Its use is limited by the following disadvantages:

It is relatively expensive compared with toughened glass

It is easily damaged by heat and a common form of attack by vandals with cigarette ends and lighters causes disfigurement

It is difficult for firemen to break in and for occupants to break out

Abrasion resistance is comparatively low, restricting cleaning methods and durability

Abrasion resistance can, in fact, be improved by the addition of a polymer coating and although it still remains lower than that of glass, manufacturers claim it is satisfactory and can be used in highly abrasive situations such as vehicle windscreens.

In very high security premises, glazed openings in vulnerable locations should be avoided, or at the very least should be constructed using a highly resistant medium such as glass blocks or anti-bandit glazing as set out in BS 5544: 1978, see chapter 4. Resistance to firearms (BS 5051: Part 1: 1973, Part 2: 1979 and BS 5357: 1976) is also described in that chapter. Deliberate attack by firearms from the outside through closed windows is not likely as the bullets are likely to be deflected by the glass, making the aim uncertain.

The possibility of terrorist action or other use of explosives makes window design a matter of great importance. Injuries caused by flying glass in such cases are often severe, dangerous and disfiguring. Though BS 5051 *Security glazing* gives performance standards for defence against firearms of various calibres, no reference is made to the effects of blast. *On no account* must anti-bandit glazing to BS 5544: 1978 be used as a defence against blast *or* firearms: it is designed to resist manual attack by pickaxe handles bars etc and its behaviour in other circumstances is likely to be unsafe.

Selection chart 3.2. Glazing types

Type	Advantages	Disadvantages	Use
Clear float glass	Clear view Simple Cheap Breakage noisy	Fragile Dangerous fragments	General 500 cm^2 max pane size for security
Double glazing	More time to break More noise	Expensive to replace Escape problematical	As above
Wired glass	More difficult to break	Expensive	Fire resistant glazing
Toughened glass	Safe fragments More resistant to attack	Expensive Escape difficult	General Larger panes Circulation areas
Laminated glass	Very tough Resistant to attack in various grades Fragmentation unlikely	Very expensive Escape difficult	General Larger panes Circulation areas Security glazing
Plastics (polycarbonate)	Very tough Resistant to attack in various grades Safe fragments	Damaged by heat Expensive Damaged by abrasion	Security glazing Vandal resistance

A reference to the precautions necessary to give protection to walls against high explosive (see 3.2.8) will demonstrate that windows of any kind would be inappropriate in such circumstances. There are some sensible minimum pre-cautions which can be taken against the most common improvised explosives and three basic approaches exist.

Avoid using glass. In theory plastics such as polycarbonates will give greater physical protection and produce less dangerous fragments. There is insufficient data to substantiate this.

Stop any glass from splintering. Toughened glass does not break into such sharp-edged pieces as ordinary glass but the high velocities of fragments caused by larger explosions are still dangerous. The application of special tough and tenacious films is claimed to be successful. It is important to leave a gap of about 10 mm around the edge of the glass so that a shear line is produced, enabling the pane to fail relatively safely in one large piece held together by the film. Application is a specialist job.

Catch the glass in flight. This is done by fitting special curtains to the inside of the opening. The curtains look like ordinary net but are, in fact, dense knit polyester to a minimum weight of 50 gm/m^2; they are hung over-length so that they billow out in a blast. The curtains should hang as close as possible to the glass with the extra lengths as shown in the table. Over-lengths should hang free if possible, or may be stowed in a sill box.

Max window height (sill/head) m	Curtain overlength m
2.4	1.0
2.7	1.1
3.3	1.5
3.9	2.0
4.5	2.2

Table 3.2. Curtain over-length to catch flying glass

3.4.6 If a window is considered vulnerable to intruders because of a combination of its location, size and construction, then additional protection should be fitted.

Although they are not traditional in the UK it is worth noting that the roller shutters commonly fitted to houses and other buildings elsewhere in Europe give a reasonable degree of protection against vandalism and opportunist criminals in addition to their other functions of controlling heat and light. They are fitted externally and allow safer night ventilation when combined with inward opening or sliding windows.

External grilles or portcullises are particularly suitable for shops and are fitted across a whole opening. They must be securely anchored down within their side channels and they are retracted by spring rollers during trading hours. They are vulnerable at the fastening, which depends on a padlock, and to attack by vehicles, which can drag them away by force. The door or window construction provides a second line of defence however, and the time and fuss necessary to overcome both obstacles may well provide sufficient deterrence.

Solid slatted metal shutters provide better protection and less of a purchase for two ropes and grapnels. They do have disadvantages in that goods do not remain on display after opening hours and it is more possible for thieves to enter the premises elsewhere and work in concealment.

Collapsible grilles may be fitted inside shop windows. The mesh size must be selected to protect the goods on display: a brick-size mesh may well protect TV sets but smaller items will require a much closer spacing. These grilles are not of high strength but cannot be attacked until a large hole has been made in the glass.

Shops usually operate a routine closing sequence which ensures that grilles are left in position at night, but other types of business often lack the management routines to accomplish this.

Single vulnerable windows should be protected by installing steel bars. These must be fitted to the inside because:

Access to them is more difficult for the intruder

They are more likely to be fitted to the solidest part of the masonry

They are less vulnerable to being dragged off by vehicles

The window is more easily cleaned

The grilles should be permanent and should be constructed from 20 mm diameter steel rods at 125 mm centres, fig 3.37. There should be a surrounding frame of 50 × 10 mm steel flat and if the bars span over 750 mm similar steel sections should be included at 500 mm maximum centres to prevent spreading. The whole should be manufactured as a unit and welded together: it should be fitted into the opening by fixings of equivalent section 75 mm deep into the masonry. On no account should the bars be fixed to the window frame by woodscrews. It may be possible, depending on details, to fit a barred grille which can be hinged and locked into place so that it can be removed for window cleaning: there will be some reduction in security.

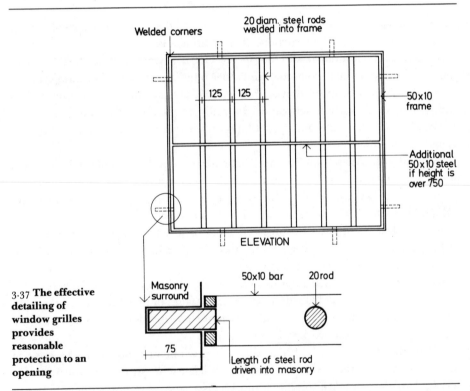

3.37 The effective detailing of window grilles provides reasonable protection to an opening

There is some pressure from various sources to outlaw barred windows as an unacceptable risk to life in the event of fire, as mentioned in seciton 3.4.2 above. It is difficult to evaluate this risk, as escape through windows (if indeed there are any) is problematical; though it is perhaps unkind to note that among those calling for the abolition of bars are some manufacturers of intruder detection equipment.

Internal shutters should be across the whole opening and should be made of

13 mm ply fixed on the inside, or 16 g (1.60 mm) steel sheet. These are more appropriate for unoccupied premises.

3.5   Roofs

3.5.1   Roofs themselves are relatively sound and most are resistant to penetration. The most common constructions are graded as shown in table 3.3.

Table 3.3. Roofing: grades of resistance to attack	
Grade 1	Reinforced concrete (including hollow pots) metal decking
Grade 2	Tiles or slates on close-boarded timber
Grade 3	Corrugated metal sheet on steel trusses
Grade 4	Asbestos cement sheet on rafters (unlined)
	Tiles or slates on rafters

The weak spots in roofs are of course the various openings.

3.5.2   Any doors leading on to a roof must be treated as external doors (see section 3.3) and constructed accordingly, in the awareness that they will probably be concealed from view. The entrances to lift motor rooms and tank rooms are typical examples which are often forgotten.

3.5.3   Duct terminations, louvres and fan housings should be carefully examined to establish whether they are removable, and if so whether access to the building could be possible. They are usually too small to allow this, but any opening over 250 mm square should be regarded as suspect.

3.5.4   Clerestory glazing does not provide easy access to the building interior because the windows are usually some distance above floor level; this is balanced by certain external advantages for the intruder:

The criminal works from a flat base
He is likely to be concealed from view from the ground
Opening vents are unlikely to be fitted with security fastenings
Glazing systems (eg patent glazing) are often easy to dismantle
Monitors and northlights present similar problems and are even more difficult to protect. Some countermeasures which may be considered are:

Restrict access to roof openings of this type
Consider roof lighting at night
Use good remote control openers (*not* cords)
Use clutch head screws for glazing fixings

3.5.5   Isolated rooflights in flat roofs are the most obvious openings and those most used by the criminal. The location should be taken into account and accessibility will vary according to roof pitch, access, height and degree of concealment. The most vulnerable are probably those in the centre of a flat roof where the criminal may force entry while being invisible from the ground. It should also be noted that access to roofs can easily change following alterations to the building or to adjoining property.

Ventilation openings may be required for smoke extraction and may also be automatically controlled. The system should be inspected to ensure the opening is secure when shut. Lights in roofs which are beside a higher building will often be required to be fire resistant; in effect this means that they cannot open and must be glazed with wired glass, both of which factors increase security.

A substantially constructed and fixed non-opening rooflight will provide adequate protection against vandals and opportunists. The detailing of the kerbs should be examined to ensure that the construction and fixings are to the same standard as the roof and light: it is sometimes found that the rooflight, though sound in itself, is inadequately fixed to a thin timber kerb which in turn is nailed to the roof structure, enabling the whole assembly to be levered off.

Fixings should either be inaccessible from the outside or made resistant to removal by the use of clutch head screws, rivets or drive screws.

The glazing material is relevant: it is necessary to protect occupants below and so some form of reinforced glazing will be used as a matter of safety, particularly when there are taller buildings nearby and there is danger from articles falling from windows or from icicles. Highly impact-resistant plastics such as polycarbonate and cab will also give some protection against a forceful attack, but there may be a conflict with fire requirements. The glazing should not be transparent: it should be translucent or obscured so that the intruder cannot study his target, assess any further barriers or detect whether he will be observed.

If opening lights are essential for other reasons, secure fastenings must be fitted, such as the conduit type of remote control gear or at least a rod operated screw-jack.

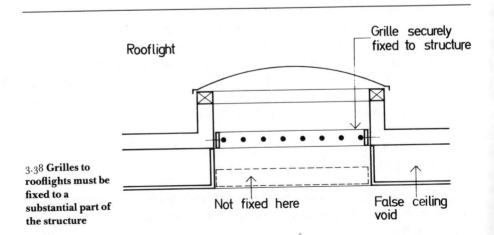

3.38 Grilles to rooflights must be fixed to a substantial part of the structure

Rooflight

Grille securely fixed to structure

Not fixed here

False ceiling void

The cam types of over-centre fastener are not recommended: they can be tripped from the outside and their operation is less secure if the fit of the opening section deteriorates because of trapped dirt or leaves.

If high security is required and rooflights cannot be omitted, the opening must be blocked by bars or grilles fitted below the kerb, fig 3.38. This must also be done if there is any doubt about the construction of the rooflight or its fixing. Some manufacturers offer grilles as standard fittings on their rooflights; this is a good principle to adopt and it also demonstrates that security has been actively considered. The fittings and kerb are critical, however, and must be examined to ensure that they are strong enough to resist force. Alternatively, the grilles can be fitted at the bottom of the shaft, hinged and padlocked for ease of maintenance. The fixings must be sound and must *not* rely on the false ceiling framing alone. The construction of the grille should be similar to that for windows set out in section 3.4.

Internal areas such as cashier's offices are liable to attack while occupied, and any rooflights should be fitted with anti-bandit glazing to BS 5544: 1978 Glass block pavement lights in concrete frames are also acceptable.

3.6 Floors

3.6.1 Floors are not common as means of access for the intruder, as there will almost inevitably be easier routes to the inside. Even so, their construction should be considered as there is some risk of penetration into secure areas either from underground or from a floor below, which may be in a separate tenancy. There is also a risk of interference with services running inside the floor structure, such as communications or alarm wiring. If the floor construction is continuous, the intruder will require time, concealment, and tools and will be unable to avoid making a noise.

Suspended timber floors are usually limited to older domestic premises but they are obviously weaker than solid concrete construction and the void below assists access from the outside. Services in such floors are also more accessible.

Floors below very high risk areas like strongrooms must be given special treatment and are covered in chapter 10.

Checklist 3

The building envelope

Walls

      Define likelihood of vandalism
      Consider physical strength/construction
      Check protection from vehicle approach
      Blast resistance (if any)
      Building Regulations

Entrances and exits

      Keep number to minimum
      Designate final exit
      Locate for security
      Establish locking routine
      Reconcile escape with security disciplines
      Consider attack resistance of doors and threat energy
      Open security doors outwards
      Avoid double leaf doors
      Protect doors from vehicle approach
      Check doorframe fixings
      No panelled or hollow cored doors
      Steel sheet for medium risks upwards
      Avoid low-level glazing
      Care with ironmongery specification
      Fix bolts properly
      Avoid rim locks
      Provide deadlocking facility
      Consider multiple locking
      Close shackled padlocks
      Define likelihood of vandalism

Windows

Check location (ground floor or easy access?)
Any dimension over 125 mm?
Consider bars or grilles
Opening mode
Glass type
Pane size: ideally 500 cm² maximum
Risk of explosion and glass injuries
Shutter protection

Roofs

Examine access
Examine openings and rooflights

Floors

Is penetration possible?
Can services be interfered with?

4 Inside the building

4.1   General

4.1.1   Earlier chapters have set out the principles of security with regard to the main physical barriers: the site boundary and the building envelope. Though these are certainly the main lines of defence, the problems of security do not end with them and further measures are required within the building, which become of particular importance if the outer shell is breached and during the hours of normal occupation.

Theft of goods must be prevented and occupants protected against attack and these risks arise from the presence of:

Intruders (i.e. unauthorised visitors)
Authorised visitors (delivery men, contractors, customers)
Dishonest occupants

Whatever physical measures are taken, control of these risks depends heavily upon human management, so the degree of control will vary from time to time according to the attitudes and capabilities of the different people involved. In addition, because such procedures are essentially contingency plans, the routines and disciplines to be followed will decay in the absence of attack and gradually become ineffective. This environment is ideal for the opportunist criminal and it is not surprising that he is the main type of culprit. Most intrusions occur once decay has taken place; detection and control of this decay will be easier if a formal security plan is followed.

4.1.2   The security problems inside the building vary according to the time of day and the state of occupancy of the premises; whereas the protection of a building full of people relies heavily on management, the same building when empty is best protected by physical barriers and detection systems. The security plan should set out a deliberate routine for changing over from one régime to the other.

4.1.3   Multiple tenancies, common in housing and offices, complicate the definition of interior and perimeter; the security established can also be confused in a like manner. It is assumed here that the boundaries of the *tenancy* are regarded as the building envelope and dealt with in accordance with chapter 3, and in this chapter only those areas within the tenancy are treated as the interior. This often leaves communal areas—toilets, lifts stairs and stores—outside any formal control, and if this is so then they must be examined with an attitude similar to that set out in chapter 2 for the grounds and site.

The individual tenant must strive not to become an obvious weak component in the whole building, otherwise he will be under even greater threat from the intruder who has penetrated the outer shell and is about to pick his target.

4.1.4 There is also a matter of principle to be decided before raising the level of the physical barriers within the building, since intruders breaking *through* a building can easily cause damage which is more expensive than the likely loss of property. This is an extremely difficult matter to rule upon and no hard and fast guidance can be given. The principal factors to be taken into account are:

> The value of the property at risk (i.e. the value to the criminal and the loss to the owner: see chapter 1)
> The attitude of the intruder

The latter is an unknown factor but it is probable there will be some malicious damage done in addition to that done to any barriers broken in the course of the crime. This is more likely to occur with amateur criminals and is not fully understood. The risk decreases as the crime becomes more planned and deliberate.

The police will usually advise that internal doors should not be locked in domestic premises, because they are expected to be hollow-cored lightweight construction and easily smashed. In non-domestic premises many of the doors will be fire-resisting (i.e. solid) and otherwise more substantial, so that when locked they provide a reasonable barrier. Unfortunately this does not help matters, as the amount of malicious damage which occurs in private houses is likely to be much higher than in commercial premises (except in cases of arson). It is interesting to note that this conflicts with the general conclusions on vandalism in chapter 8, which are that private space which is tended is less likely to be vandalised than areas seen to be in diffuse or public ownership. The published studies on vandalism do not draw attention to this, but it remains unexplained and could usefully be given more consideration.

Damage to furniture and equipment can be especially costly, and it is foolish to lock a cupboard to protect items of comparatively minor value such as drinks or stamps while a building is unoccupied. This principle is well known in shops, and tills are quite sensibly left empty with open drawers at night.

4.1.5 A further matter of principle to be considered is that of prosecution, and whatever policy is decided upon must be included in the management of the security plan. It used to be the case that failure to report a crime to the police was an offence in itself (misprision of felony) but it is no longer so, subject to the provisions of the Criminal Law Act 1967, that there must be no gain when dealing with the detected offender. It may be thought wrong to forgo the prosecution of an offender—and indeed the moral issue may take precedence—but in many cases there will be greater harm done to security by drawing publicity to a target than is gained by public punishment of an offender. It is not generally known that some police forces maintain arrangements for the local press to examine their records and reports and so any information given to the police cannot be expected to remain confidential.

4.2   Planning

4.2.1 Where specific target risks are present, such as cashiers' offices, strongrooms or data storage, these should be surrounded by concentric zones of progressively rising grades of security, and the outer zones of accommodation should themselves be protected to a higher degree than normal because of the presence of the special target area. The reason for this is first that the intruder will encounter increasing resistance as he approaches the target, and second, the deliberate arrangement of these zones encourages an overall consciousness of security throughout the building.

4.2.2 This principle must not be followed to the extent that wages offices are located deep within a secure zone so that many people have to enter the zone to collect their pay, as this would affect the security of the area unnecessarily. Neither should the wages office be so close to the building entrance that criminals have quick and easy access. Though these principles may seem to conflict, they are not in practice too difficult to achieve if some skill is applied to the planning, figs 4.1, 4.2, 4.3.

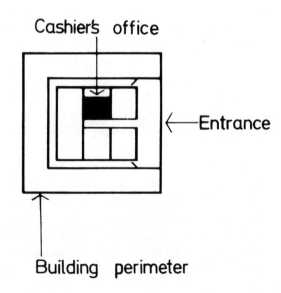

Cashiers office

Entrance

4.1 **Visitors penetrate freely into the centre of the building, surrounded by secure areas. Unnecessary risk**

Building perimeter

4.2 Cash is at risk from casual intruders as it is too close to the public area

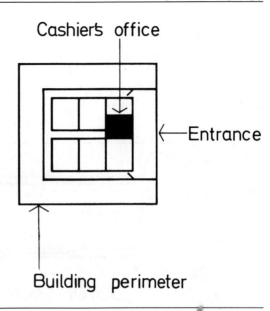

Cashier's office

Entrance

Building perimeter

4.3 A better solution: a lobby approach for visitors, easily secured for whatever periods are necessary

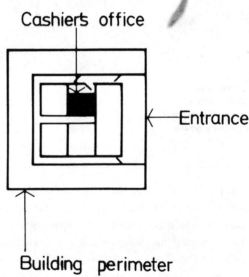

Cashier's office

Entrance

Building perimeter

4.2.3. Access to internal high security areas is often gained by duress (i.e. personal threat). Apart from providing personal alarms (see chapter 5) there are other precautions which can be taken.

 Ensure that there are always at least two people working in secure areas

 Allow access one at a time, not in pairs or groups

 Include a duress code in any access control system: see chapter 7

 Establish a routine to operate in such circumstances

With regard to the latter, it should be remembered that personal threats, like fire, will be dealt with in an atmosphere of crisis—which will not be the right time to be planning what to do next—there must be a drill and staff must be aware of it, so that it can be carried out efficiently.

Cash offices are best approached through a lobby or lock with some form of interlock between the doors.

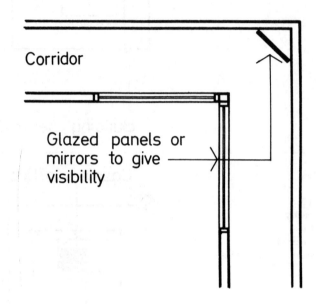

Corridor

Glazed panels or mirrors to give visibility

4.4 **Internal movement of valuables: protect against ambush**

4.2.4 Visibility must be maintained through circulation areas where valuables are present in the building. There should be extensive use of glazed panels and mirrors should be placed at the appropriate points in corridors, to prevent attacks from criminals in hiding, figs 4.4, 4.5. Indeed, when there is a major movement of cash or valuables a special routine should operate: all circulation spaces should be policed to ensure they are clear, and visitors to the building must be excluded. The route designated for the cash should be able to be isolatd from normal circulation during this period.

4.2.5 Proper facilities should be provided for the delivery and despatch of goods and the first principle is that the two functions must be physically separated. There should be enough room to unpack and check deliveries, and one load must be passed through to storage and the area cleared before another load is accepted, fig 4.6

Delivery bays for cash and valuables should wherever possible operate on an air

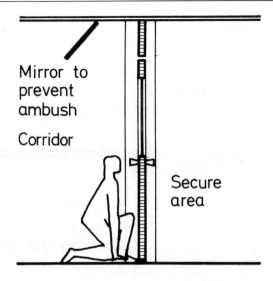

4.5 Secure areas: protect points of exit

Mirror to prevent ambush

Corridor

Secure area

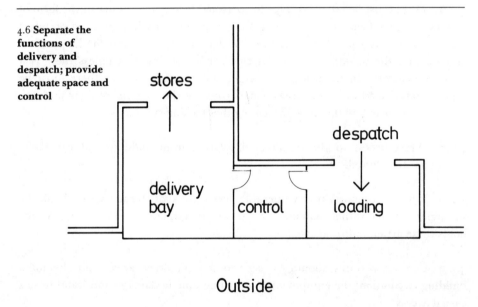

4.6 Separate the functions of delivery and despatch; provide adequate space and control

stores

delivery bay

control

despatch

loading

Outside

lock principle: that is, vehicles and delivery personnel must be admitted to an area which can be secured against outside attack before the vehicle is opened, fig 4.7. Many thefts take place at the vulnerable time when security vehicles are open for the transfer of their contents, but unfortunately space necessary for such an arrangement is not often available.

The inner barrier of the air lock must also be secure to the rest of the building to guard against the risk of a bogus security vehicle entering for the purpose of attacking the valuables kept on the premises.

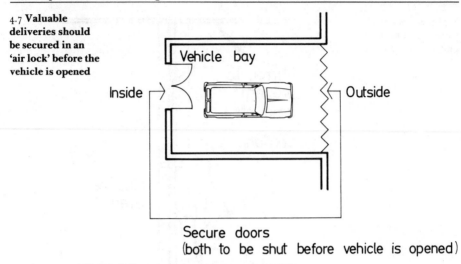

4.7 **Valuable deliveries should be secured in an 'air lock' before the vehicle is opened**

4.2.6 There must be secure storage for personal belongings, either in the form of lockers (with padlocks) or lockable desks. It is particularly important in premises where pilferage is a problem to ensure that handbags, cases and the like are not brought into the workplace, and this rule cannot be enforced unless there is a secure depository. In premises with larger staff changing rooms there must be supervision of access to these areas. Coats (but not the contents of their pockets) can be safeguarded by the use of patent clothes locking systems.

4.2.7 Direct access to the building circulation from underground car parks should not be allowed.

4.2.8 Where a proportion of vulnerable goods are kept storage areas should be subdivided so that rather than one large secure area, there is an inner 'cage' which holds those articles most at risk.

4.2.9 Computer suites should be separated from other areas and the main building circulation: the equipment is too vulnerable to damage and fraud to risk casual access.

4.2.10 There are other real forms of loss suffered by employers through the misuse of office facilities. Postal franking machines have their own seals and locks but their use should be restricted to a post room, controlled by management routines and the issue of keys firmly regulated. Substantial costs can be incurred by the use of telephones for private calls; many types of exchange and switchboard can be arranged so that external dialled calls are either barred, limited to local calls or specific extensions. The flexibility in this respect is growing with the availability of microprocessor-controlled switchboards. Alternatively, dial locks can be fitted.

Photocopying machines are commonly misused and, surprisingly, they are not usually fitted with locks. If abuse is a problem, they should be kept in a locked room or restricted to the use of designated operators. Since both these principles rely on management routines and are extremely inconvenient for bona-fide users, any attempt to enforce them usually falls rapidly into decay. Considering the amount of electronic technology that is included in modern photocopying machines it would seem a simple matter for both job number and personal codes to be keyed in along with the number of copies; this would provide both authorisation and accounting at the same time. Particular care must be taken over confidential documents and the copying of these must obviously be most carefully controlled. Special paper is available for original typing which will dazzle some copiers and prevent reproduction, but it is not foolproof. Paper shredders should be used to destroy confidential documents.

4.2.11 Internal vandalism can occur, particularly in large industrial premises where machinery may be stopped or maliciously damaged for a variety of reasons. The routing of circulation corridors around production areas at high level where they can act as observation galleries can help to prevent this, as well as contributing in a more general way to management and supervision.

4.3   Public buildings

4.3.1 Those premises which are open to public use without hindrance cannot rely on either access control systems or physical barriers for their security during occupied hours, but must establish a combination of management and surveillance. Museums, art galleries and libraries are examples. A simple precaution is the requirement to deposit bags and packages at the entrance and a secure supervised space must be provided for this. All the public spaces should be under supervision to prevent damage and the contents should also be connected to an alarm system: see chapter 6.

The division between public and private space must be clearly defined, both to the visitor and to the staff, and in a multi-occupancy building this division should be regarded as the boundary of a tenancy and protected accordingly. This is a most important principle and will apply in other sorts of open buildings including theatres, public offices, hotels, shops and hospitals. Both access control systems (chapter 7) and intruder detection systems (chapter 6) must take the division into account.

4.3.2 Retail losses are high and continuous: the most generally quoted estimate sets the figures at approximately 2% of turnover in the UK, but there are other estimates ranging from 5 to 9%. There is some consistency over the direction of the losses, which are usually said to consist of:

10% errors and wastage

30% customer theft

60% staff theft

Losses are higher in larger shops. This is no doubt a result of scale, together with the differences in incentive between owners of small shops and managers of larger ones.

Customer theft is euphemistically known as shoplifting and it is unfortunate that it. is sometimes seen as mischievous rather than criminal, as evidenced by a reluctance to use the more accurate term for the crime.

The great majority of shoplifters operate in a very simple manner: they walk into shops, pick up goods and walk out with them in pockets, bags or in the hand. Few use special clothing or containers, though long coats or coats draped over the arm should immediately arouse suspicion. Shoplifters frequently work in pairs, when one will distract a shop assistant with an innocent enquiry while the other steals the goods. It is clear that the most attractive environment for the shoplifter is a poorly observed area with goods on open display and no checkout till near the exit. Many department stores correspond closely with this description, but most are fully aware of the risks involved and apply design and management principles in an attempt to reduce the losses. The main defences are threefold:

Observation

Verification

Protection

Observation of the sales area will deter theft. Display shelving should be kept down to a height of 1.2—1.5 m and tills should be slightly raised and sited for maximum observation of the sales area. Convex mirrors are effective and can be installed to cover hidden areas of the display; they must be kept clean and repositioned as necessary when the display is rearranged. Observation booths raised from the retail floor are said to be better but are more expensive to set up and run. Closed circuit television (see chapter 9) is also a working deterrent and can be coupled with video recording to provide evidence of the theft. Dummy cameras are advertised but are not recommended: security should be intentional and not part of a bluff. In any case, dummy cameras will do little to deter staff theft. If alertness and attention to the customer is encouraged among staff, this will be a most effective defence, as well as improving sales and customer relations. One major retail chain in the USA reduced its losses from 2.2% to 1.4% in a year by giving employees 50% of the savings, but it was not known what proportion was a reduction of customer theft and how much was staff pilferage. Warning notices and the presence of detectives are effective in larger shops.

Verification of sales makes a plausible defence by the thief more difficult and the object is to make clear which goods carried by a shopper have been paid for. This is a management matter; the main routines are to ensure that all goods carry a substantial price tag with the shop name included, and to wrap each purchase and include a dated sales ticket inside the wrapper.

Goods can be wired individually to an alarm system or can be fitted with persistent tags which can only be removed at the till and will be detected electronically if they are taken past detectors at the shop entrance. This system is a deterrent but is not foolproof as the tags can be masked.

Protection of goods by physical means obviously depends on the nature of the articles themselves, and though some may be enclosed in locked showcases or chained to a shelf, this is not practical with many others.

Most of the above precautions are quite consistent with good customer relations, and unlike many security measures will not detract from sales. Indeed, there is a sales advantage to be gained when a shop displays a confident secure attitude, because some customers are reluctant to shop where theft is commonplace in case they are themselves accused; at the very least an uneasy shopper is not likely to be an eager customer.

Apart from the simple theft of goods there are other losses inflicted by the customer. Credit card and cheque frauds are especially difficult to avoid, and one of the major credit card companies in the UK sets the figures for its own cards at 1200 cases per year, including many multiple purchases. Violent attacks on staff are increasing, particularly in shops with all-female staff, and these are usually variations of till snatching. The first defence is to reduce the target value by installing counter-caches into which the cashier can regularly transfer money so that till contents are low, or for the management to establish collection rounds for the same purpose, though the latter introduce a new target for attack. Personal alarms can also be fitted to the till area (see chapter 5) and the tills themselves should not be in isolation near the entrance. Modern electronic cash registers can be activated by a pressure mat, so that they are more secure when unattended.

In self-service and larger shops where theft may be more frequent there should be a room located near the entrance and designated for search and interview. It will be used by shop security staff and by the police when they are called.

Staff pilferage is the largest proportion of the losses and is both more difficult to control and more distressing to experience; the morale of employees can be seriously affected by accusations, suspicion and the guilt of colleagues. Though the problem is fairly widespread there is no doubt that major losses can be caused by a small proportion of staff. The following methods are common.

Theft of goods

Theft of cash

Under-ringing on the till and keeping the difference

Mis-accounting for returned goods

Altering duplicate copies of bills

Undercharging an accomplice for goods

Dishonest arrangements with delivery drivers

Short-changing customers

Introducing false invoices for goods

Extra items on the customer's bill

There may also be theft from other employees. Access to receiving bays and stockrooms should be restricted, and these therefore should not be used as through routes for staff access. Secure areas within stockrooms will enable valuable or vulnerable goods to be separated and more easily controlled. Handbags and cases should be banned from the shop floor but this can only be reasonably enforced if there is a properly secure staff locker room where they can be left in safety. The allowance of generous staff discounts is also seen as an effective disincentive to theft. Other precautions to be taken are:

> Always take up references for new staff
> Establish a strict routine for handling cash
> Apply rigid rules for till operation
> Carry out routine random till checks

4.3.3 In hotels and restaurants there are similar problems with staff pilferage, especially of food, because it is more difficult to account precisely for the amounts used. There are additional opportunities for dishonest arrangements with delivery drivers, so that food of a lesser quality is accepted or a lesser quantity is delivered, the difference in cost being shared.

There are more complex risks in hotels however, and the pattern of crime varies with the class of hotel and the area: broadly, the higher class hotels must concentrate their defences against their staff, whereas lower class hotels encounter different risks, for example from prostitutes and from the guests themselves.

All staff contracts must include a right of search and there must be a master-key system for staff lockers.

There are traditional continuing losses: linen is stolen by staff and guests at an alarming rate, and the security of bar stocks is always a problem. The physical security of and access to wine stores must be clearly established; in practice it nearly always is, because the alternative is immediate losses which are quickly detected.

The planning principles in a hotel, which involve the separation of public and service areas, do not ease the task of creating a simple circulation pattern. This is important in the control of the service areas and the reduction of pilferage: there must be clear logical flows of goods and services so that there is no blurring of function between one area and another, and staff have no need to enter or pass through areas outside their own responsibility.

The planning of motels often places the bedrooms in a separate unsupervised and unstaffed block with direct access from the car park. It must be expected that losses here will be high.

General theft from rooms is in the souvenir class—towels, ashtrays etc—but larger items such as televisions are also vulnerable. Some hotels are efficient enough to order a fast room check to be made while the bill is being made up, so that the guest is surprised to see his souvenirs appearing on the bill. There are some novel approaches: one chain applies notices reading 'this picture has been stolen' behind the prints which hang on the bedroom walls.

Guests' property is also stolen from rooms by staff, intruders and other guests. The room doors must be secured without the need to deadlock them, and continuous balconies with opening windows should not be constructed. A staff location system that signifies which rooms are occupied by chambermaids is a deterrent. A hotel must also expect false allegations of loss from guests who are attempting to defraud the hotel out of compensation. Safety deposit boxes for guests' valuables are to be encouraged, together with strict procedures for their use: 'please watch me put your property into this box'.

The reception area should obviously be sited to give control and supervision over the main hotel entrance, but it should also have a view of the main waiting area to discourage its use by itinerants. The reception desk is also the place where room keys are issued and returned, and there are several weak practices which reduce security: first of all, the key board should not be on view so that anyone approaching the desk can tell whether a room is empty; secondly, there should be a counter slot and box for returned keys and they must never be left on the counter; and finally, keys should not be issued by reception staff on demand, without some proof of identity.

The control of room keys is most important and most thieves are caught with keys in their possession. For this reason in the USA it is now law that an innkeeper may not let a room unless he is aware of the location of all the keys to that room and this legislation is leading to the adoption of a number of electronic keyless access control systems ideally suited to hotels; these systems are described more fully in chapter 7.

If keyed systems are used, however, all is not lost and several simple precautions will significantly reduce the risks:

> There must be a lost-key register and an established procedure to be followed
>
> Room keys must *not* be marked with the hotel name, address and room number
>
> Locks with removable cores allow easy substitution and regular rotation, especially if a number of spare cores are kept
>
> Master keys must be guarded and not used unless absolutely necessary

Abuse of rooms is a possibility: it can be either for criminal purposes or as a form of fraud. All rooms must be inspected at least once each day, whether in use or not.

A proper luggage room is necessary where guests' luggage can be left after they have checked out. It must be controlled, so that the contents are protected against theft and so that any suspicious cases are detected.

4.4 Visitors

4.4.1 Non-public premises will have more control over the access to the building, but they will always need to admit visitors in one form or another.

The walk-in petty thief is well known in large commercial premises where he may prowl through the building unchallenged, seeking the odd empty office or unattended handbag. There is a good living to be made from sundry cash and calculators, together with subsequent cheque and credit card abuse. Smaller organisations often consider themselves immune from such theft, but this is by no means true.

It has become accepted as common practice that visitors are checked at the point of entry and an escort is sent to accompany them to their destination. This is all well and good as security practice, but there are always gaps in the system, such as allowing a visitor to leave the building unescorted, presumably on the assumption that he has been vouched for by his dealings with an occupant. This is bad practice and gives rise to other weaknesses:

> There will always be unescorted strangers in the building, and so challenge
> is unlikely
> No one leaving is checked by security staff
> The overall need to escort strangers is called into disrepute

It is, in any case, common courtesy to greet guests at the door and to see them out.

Some visitors such as workmen carrying out maintenance are more regular and require some freedom of access. They must carry some form of personal authority, which must be inspected: the simplest form is a combined pass and identity card. This should be displayed permanently and be colour-coded for date.

It is good security to know who is in the building at any time, and it is essential following detection of any crime. The simplest way of providing such a roll-call is by signing in and out; if this system is adopted then *all* occupants and visitors must go through the routine. Some decay may be expected.

Some of the better card-access systems (chapter 7) will give a roll call at a central point, based on which cards have passed which locks. This is intended for use in an emergency where a building must be evacuated. This works well in isolated and highly disciplined circumstances where the need is fully understood, such as aboard oil rigs, where the occupancy of each compartment is checked; in the more relaxed atmosphere of a normal building there will be a proportion of abuse.

4.5 Security office and staff

4.5.1 If the premises are patrolled or if there is a security officer appointed, then separate office accommodation must be provided. The office need not be near the entrance or even close to other administrative offices, and in fact there are advantages in completely separating the functions.

Internal patrols are effective, and may be required to record their progress by clocking in at various points on their round. The supervision and administration of patrols is a professional matter and should not be left to the general management of the business.

The security staff may be permanently established employees or members of a specialised security firm. In the first case, all the security personnel will be under direct control and will be thoroughly familiar with the premises, but there is a risk of decay as informal relationships naturally develop with other permanent staff. On the other hand, uniformed strangers can cause resentment.

If a security company is employed, which may be more economical, especially if part-time cover is required, then the company must be selected with care as there are many plausible cowboys in the business. The British Security Industry Code of Practice should be followed and references obtained.

An example will serve to illustrate the dangers: a London teaching hospital was about to be commissioned—this period is a well-known time for widespread theft, as new and old supplies and equipment are delivered to an unoccupied building by a multitude of people. The hospital wisely employed a security company to monitor the whole process, but did not enquire thoroughly enough into their capabilities. At the end of the commissioning period, the permanent hospital security staff took over and within the first two weeks it was necessary to arrest and charge five of the contract security officers: over £5000 worth of property was recovered as a result. Whoever the security staff are, they should be responsible for:

> Lock and unlock procedures
> Routine and random patrols
> Escorting cash
> Providing pay-point protection
> Testing alarm systems
> Protecting employees' belongings

4.6 Cleaners

4.6.1 The access allowed to cleaners during unoccupied hours presents a difficult problem. Indeed, the principle is so full of security risks that it is often completely ignored, with the result that cleaners have free unsupervised access at night to areas which are strictly policed during the day. Wherever possible, high security areas should be cleaned during the hours of occupation, and the cleaners treated like any other visitors. The following general principles apply:

> Do *not* issue cleaners with a master key
> If keys are issued to contract cleaners, change locks when the contract expires
> Make telephones, photocopiers, inoperable
> Carry out random checks during hours when cleaners work
> *Plan* cleaners' access to sensitive areas (i.e. lock rooms normally, remove contents for cleaning)

Some security companies offer the services of their own screened staff to carry out cleaning, thus offering an alternative approach to the problem.

4.7   Fixtures, fittings and equipment

4.7.1   The routine confidentiality associated with pay and personal records can be maintained by the ordinary locks provided on filing cabinets and cupboards. Locks on furniture must be used sensibly however, bearing in mind that few are capable of resisting any real or determined force and that the cost of the incidental damage can easily exceed the value of the contents lost.

The protection of highly confidential material is best achieved by the restriction of sensitive information, on the military principle, to those who need to know. The physical protection of the paperwork is achieved by safes and specially designed filing cabinets: see chapter 10. Paper shredders effectively destroy confidential documents and notes after use.

4.7.2   Vending machines are commonly damaged for one of three reasons:
Theft of the cash inside
Theft of the stock
Frustration
Theft can be controlled by careful siting of the machines, and it is obvious that those with valuable contents on display, such as cigarette machines, are the most vulnerable. Where cash is the attraction, as with telephone coin boxes, the machine should be designed so that it is obvious that the coins fall into a separate substantial receptacle and cannot be obtained simply by breaking into a thin-skinned casing. The prevention of damage by frustrated users is easier to achieve and the management should ensure that:
The machine is of a reliable type
It is kept stocked
It accepts a variety of coins
Reference to chapter 8 will show that if a machine is left in a damaged condition, there is an incitement to vandalism in the area surrounding.

4.7.3   Inventories of equipment are essential, but many organisations do not maintain them, and in the event of fire or burglary are unable to list the number of items missing, far less give details of serial numbers: ask a company how many typewriters are owned and the odds are that they will have to send someone to count them! Losses are often undiscovered until stocktaking takes place; management systems should allow random spot checks of vulnerable items so that losses can be identified before the thief has covered his tracks.

4.8   Internal doors

4.8.1   Many of the factors influencing the design and construction of internal doors are identical with those for external doors: see chapter 3. There is an additional level of vulnerability, however, in that once the intruder has penetrated the outer shell he is relatively free to take his time and to expend more effort on forcing entry through the more concealed internal barriers. The damage caused can be considerable and it is recommended that an internal door only be locked specifically to protect the contents of a particular room. The police usually advise that in domestic premises, internal doors should not be fitted with locks at all.

4.8.2 As in previous chapters, the question of locking is dealt with in the context of providing a physical barrier and not with regulating admission, which is covered in chapter 7.

The reason for locking a door should be clear. Some doors are locked as a matter of convenience, such as the cleaner's room, where other occupants of the building must be deterred from depositing rubbish inside or borrowing cleaning equipment for odd spillages. These doors are unlikely to be forced and the quality of the lock is of little importance. Stationery stores, photocopying and post rooms are targets for the opportunist petty thief, for the contents themselves or their unauthorised use; they will require a little more physical security but only minimal force will be anticipated.

In many buildings the majority of doors are open much of the time, so it is not surprising that a survey of an older building will reveal that although most of the doors are fitted with locks, no one knows what has happened to the keys! In the days before cost planning, little thought was given to the possibility of reducing ironmongery costs by omitting unnecessary locks.

Where locks are fitted to provide security against risks on the level of the walk-in thief, they should have a minimum of three levers. There is also some merit in bolts, in which case, there is nothing on the outside of the door to be attacked, though bolts can only be used in rooms with several doors. During occupied hours it is unlikely that an unattended room will be deadlocked, as such a deliberate action is too inconvenient for the users, so night latches are more suitable because they are automatically locked on each closing. There are night latches available with a special hold-back mechanism (snib) which can only be operated by a separate key, so that unauthorised occupants cannot de-activate the latch and the possibility of decay is reduced.

It is common practice to hide spare keys. Unfortunately, the criminal mind seems to be far better at finding them than the occupant is at hiding them. There must be an agreed procedure for lost keys, and whereas in the lower levels of security it will not usually be necessary to replace the lock, there are certainly circumstances in which it would be essential to do so; these would include loss in suspicious circumstances and loss during a burglary or where it is believed that the key is held by a previous occupant or employee. The casual duplication of keys must be positively discouraged. The management of keys is important and a register of keys and keyholders should exist and be kept up to date.

Where higher security is required, then the locks should follow the principles set out for external doors and comply with BS 3621: 1980, but in occupied areas with heavy traffic it will be necessary to fit a good mortice night latch with an anti-thrust mechanism *in addition* to the deadlock, so that protection is maintained during working hours. Key-in-knob sets are not suitable for high security doors. If protection of the occupants is necessary, as is the case of cash offices, there is much to recommend fitting bolts to the door, as they are unpickable and simply operated from the inside without a key.

Average physical security is obtained by the use of mortice night latches with antithrust bolts or 5 lever locks. Cylinder locks may also be used.

4.8.3 The construction of the door must also be considered. Sliding doors are not very satisfactory as they are difficult to lock, and if little thought is given to the possibility of forced entry they can often be lifted off their tracks, or at least far enough for a hook bolt to become disengaged.

Simple hollow core flush doors give minimal security but even so are better than panelled or part-glazed doors, in which the inserts can be broken to give access to a night latch or a lock with the key left in.

If more physical resistance is required, then a more substantial door should be used and, as a rule of thumb, any door and frame with a fire rating will be adequate for the average building risk. Frame fixings will require attention but there will be little difficulty in providing an adequate fixing. Glazed panels should be avoided if possible, but if they are required for fire safety reasons the glass must be located well away from any night latching device. Loose pin hinges should not be used.

Higher protection is available through the use of steel or steel-reinforced doors and frames. It may be possible to incorporate bullet resistance (see 3.3.10) through a sheet of steel within the door construction. Hinge bolts should be fitted. Door glazing is not compatible with this standard of construction, but fish-eye viewers are recommended and the occupants of areas containing valuables should be instructed and encouraged to use them.

4.8.4 Signs on doors have a limited effect and it is pointless to suppose that 'keep out' or 'private' will deter the deliberate criminal, but these signs do have some value in that the opportunist has a less plausible excuse for entry. Such signs also give occupants a reason to challenge strangers, though in practice they very rarely do so.

4.8.5 Turnstiles are useful in regulating access and have been described previously.

4.8.6 The provision of very high security doors for a building entails specialist design and construction which is considered in chapter 10.

4.9   Partitions, floors and ceilings

4.9.1 Just as the design of the security of the building envelope must not be restricted to doors and windows, so the internal fabric must be designed to an overall standard appropriate to the physical strength required.

If the interior of the building is properly constructed, partitions, floors and ceilings will normally be imperforate and will deter vandals and opportunist criminals from attempting access. Even the most deliberate criminal is more likely to attack the doors of a room than the walls or floors. This is partly because he cannot see inside the construction and will not be certain of the design or the time that it will take to penetrate; but it is also because there is a strong pressure of habit to enter through entrances. Nevertheless, when the attack on the door fails, the intruder will seek alternatives.

4.9.2 Some of the weakest partitions in general use are those found in modern offices: the movable demountable types have obvious flaws, but some of the more permanent system partitions include screwed or clip-on sections which can easily be removed to allow whole infill panels to be lifted out quickly and quietly. To be fair, these are not sold with any claim to security; but on the other hand, neither is any attention drawn to the weaknesses. Stud and plasterboard partitions also offer little physical resistance to attack.

Stockrooms should be subdivided so that valuable goods are separated into a secure area. The partition need not be highly resistant to force and, as observation of the area is an advantage, some form of steel mesh division is ideal. The mesh should go from floor to ceiling and be fixed to a timber or steel frame. The same type of division can be used to secure cars in communal garages.

Where the separation required is more temporary, as in hotel bars, rolling grilles can be fitted into removable vertical guides. These are made to a decorative pattern and are a good deal stronger than they look; failure usually occurs at the counter fittings, which can be reinforced with padlocks.

Apart from the specialist walls round strongrooms and vaults (chapter 10), normal high security can be achieved by the use of ordinary half-brick or 100 mm block partitions, plastered on both sides. If required, resistance can be increased by including expanded metal in the bedding joints or, better still, vertical steel dowel bars in the brick or block perforations. These extra precautions would be appropriate in, say, stores for drugs, poisons, guns and ammunition, where the specific risk of attack is higher, but a strongroom is not justified. These areas are often referred to as secure rooms and, as may be imagined, there is some degree of overlap with strongrooms proper. In order to achieve appropriate security, the purpose of the room must be formally stated and clearly understood by designer and user.

It should also be remembered that all four walls should be considered and not just the three which abut the party wall: though there are seldom problems in this respect, there is no control over access to the other side of a party wall, and the security risk is therefore higher.

4.9.3 Openings other than doors are weak points and cannot be forgotten about: vents, grilles and hatches must be examined, since any opening more than 250 mm square is a possible access route.

Glazing is provided in partitions for various reasons, including the need to observe the outside from a secure area. Panels near a door are subject to the same restrictions as those in the door itself. Obscured glazing is a deterrent as the criminal is unsure of the activity on the other side and is also prevented from making any reconnaissance.

The construction of glazed screens is particularly important where there is a risk of deliberate violent attack, as in banks, building societies and other counter or cash handling areas. In these cases ordinary glass should never be used and the screens should be designed in consultation with the building management, who will be aware of the specific threats which are likely and may indeed have their own standards of construction. It must be appreciated that improper so-called security glazing is not only likely to be ineffective, but may even increase the danger to occupants during an attack. The main object is in fact personal protection, with the deterrence of the criminal second. The attacks may be made by:

> Tools (hammers, bars, pickaxes)
> Missiles (bricks)
> Small arms
> Shotguns
> Rifles
> Flame
> Chemicals

Danger to the occupants arises from:

> The criminals themselves
> Projectiles
> Fragmenting glass

The protection is divided into two main classes: *mechanical* and *firearm* resistance.

Mechanical attacks are resisted by the installation of *anti-bandit* glazing as set out in BS 5544: 1978; the glass is tested by having a 2.5 kg steel ball dropped on it from various heights, fig 4.8.

Any use of the term safety glass should be forbidden as, in this context, it is a particularly dangerous misnomer, referring usually to ordinary toughened glass which provides safety in the event of accidental breakage but no protection against attack. Anti-bandit glazing may be made from laminated glass or plastics.

Firearm attacks are resisted by *security glazing* to BS 5051 Part 1: 1973, Part 2: 1979: As may be expected, the forces involved are greater than manual attacks but they also vary much more and the BS is graded accordingly for levels of attack

4.8 Anti-bandit glazing for protection against mechanical attack

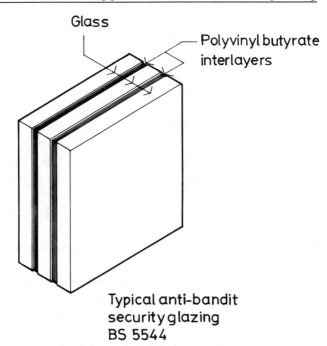

Glass

Polyvinyl butyrate interlayers

Typical anti-bandit security glazing BS 5544

4.9 Security glazing for protection against attack by firearms

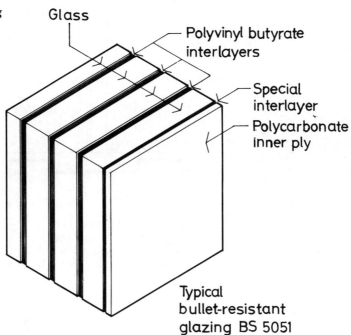

Glass

Polyvinyl butyrate interlayers

Special interlayer

Polycarbonate inner ply

Typical bullet-resistant glazing BS 5051

from smaller handguns to high velocity military rifles: categories go to G3, fig 4.9. The glazing must resist three shots from short range in a limited area and is usually constructed from glass laminated with layers of polyvinyl butyrate. Grade G3 may have ten layers and be over 75 mm thick. In addition, there is a separate section of the BS (category S) dealing especially with shotgun attacks for situations where these are thought to be more likely. It is important to note that the two sections are not interchangeable: category G panels are not necessarily shotgun resistant and those in category S do not automatically give any bullet resistance.

It is fundamental to bullet-resistant glazing that no splinters of glass should be ejected from the rear face, and an alternative approach to the design is the duplex screen, in which a primary panel resists the projectile and a second, separate panel acts as a shield against splinters. BS 5051 'suggests' that bullet resistant glazing will be highly resistant to mechanical attacks, but it must be emphasized that the reverse does not hold true: anti-bandit glazing to BS 5544: 1978 *must not* be used as a defence against firearm attack.

If any form of security glazing is used over a counter, the protection should extend not only to the lower section of counter but also to any external windows, rooflights, partitions, and doors which surround the target area.

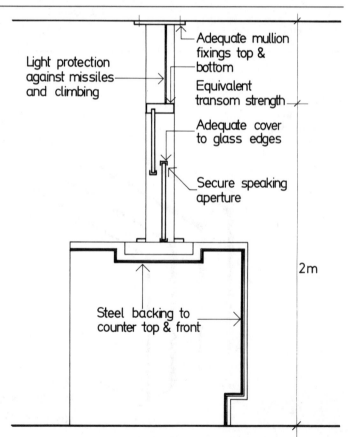

Light protection against missiles and climbing

Adequate mullion fixings top & bottom

Equivalent transom strength

Adequate cover to glass edges

Secure speaking aperture

Steel backing to counter top & front

2m

4.10 **Counters and fronts should be carefully detailed to protect staff and deter attacks**

The installation of security glazing generally is covered by BS 5357: 1976; there is much detail, but the main points are listed below and shown in fig 4.10:

Glass must have adequate edge cover of at least 10 mm of 3 mm thick mild steel

Plastics must have an increased edge cover of 25 mm

Mullions should be adequately fixed top and bottom

Transoms should have equivalent strength

The screen should extend to 2 m above floor level and the gap above should include protection to prevent climbing, vaulting, or throwing objects over

Counter fronts should be backed by 6 mm sheet steel increased to 8.5 mm armour steel if category G3 (BS 5051) is to be resisted

Counter tops over 25 mm thick should have 3 mm mild steel sheet fixed to the underside (increased for thinner tops)

Shielding should extend below transaction trays

Speaking and transaction apertures should not allow a firearm to be aimed through the screen.

Flame and chemical attacks are not so common but are effective against some plastics. As they are more time-consuming processes they are limited to periods when the building is unoccupied and the criminal will be allowed more time to penetrate. A standard for bullet-resistant opaque sheet materials is to be published to complement BS 5051 and will allow whole assemblies to be constructed.

Self-contained cashier kiosks are manufactured for isolated use either inside or outside the building and they offer varying degrees of protection.

4.9.4 The penetration of floors is only likely in high risk areas; the floors tend to be substantial building elements and offer considerable physical resistance. There is some risk of penetration from within the building into a secure area and there is a risk of tampering with services, communications, or alarm wiring. The level of this risk must be estimated but it is obviously greater where there is an underfloor void, as with suspended ground floor construction or the raised floors used in computer rooms. In the latter case, access is by definition easy; so firstly, passage from neighbouring areas below the floor must be obstructed and secondly such floors offer a good 'priest-hole' in which an intruder can conceal himself during working hours to emerge later when the building is empty. It is sensible to restrict access to the computer room and to provide detection systems to cover such an eventuality: see chapter 6. A further risk is the planting of explosives by terrorists.

4.9.5 Suspended ceilings are much more common and there are similar risks: passage between one secure area and another should not be possible and the criminal should not be able to hide in the void or to conceal stolen goods there for subsequent collection. This latter risk is worth special attention in shops, schools and building sites where considerable caches may have been built up over a period of time. The motives are sometimes obscure and theft may be difficult to prove, as the goods have not been removed from the premises. The physical barrier provided by a false ceiling is often flimsy.

There may also be the following motives for illicit access to ceiling voids:

Interference with alarms and communications

Tapping into electrical services to provide power for tools

Observation of high security areas and their procedures

Trapdoors into ceiling voids and attics should be bolted from below. Pitched roof construction usually gives better space for the intruder than flat roofs, and the ceiling itself is likely to be well enough supported to allow free movement. A 600 mm void can be enough to allow access however, and although false ceilings may appear insubstantial they are usually capable of supporting the weight of a man. The simple lay-in systems give quick and easy access and should not be used: systems should be preferred which take more time to penetrate, such as metal clipped tiles, or those with a non-demountable grid.

4.10   Lighting

4.10.1 In the protection of premises against the major risk of burglary by night, the question of internal lighting will arise; once again there are two basic approaches: first, there should be no lights whatever allowed inside the building after hours so that any seen from outside will create immediate suspicion. Alternatively, planned levels of lighting are left on, to aid surveillance from the outside and leave the criminal in doubt as to the occupancy of the building.

The first method is likely to fail in practice, as it is difficult to ensure that all lights are switched off every night, and in any case someone may be working late quite legitimately. The second principle is more reliable and its introduction of uncertainty should not be underestimated. This system is also quite appropriate for domestic premises. The main exception to the use is the building site, which should abide firmly by the first method of no lighting.

The majority of buildings require some provision for means of escape in case of fire, and the routes designated require emergency lighting independent of the main power supply. This is accomplished either by centralised battery packs, emergency generators, or self-contained light fittings containing batteries on constant recharge. Whichever system is installed it is sensible to consider security in the planning, and extend the system if necessary to cover additonal sensitive areas which are at risk. For their purpose the self-contained fitting is the best.

Safes should be visible from outside their secure area for observation by police or patrols, and should be illuminated at night by more than one fitting, so that darkness is cause for suspicion and is not put down to simple equipment failure.

Security lighting outside the building is a different matter and is covered in chapter 2.

4.11   Lifts

4.11.1 The criminal can use lifts for several purposes: he can obtain access to areas without being seen; he can carry away heavy spoils; and he can ambush personnel carrying cash. Lifts should be immobilised when the building is empty and during the times of major cash transfer.

Although lifts should not slip through the net of the security plan, it is not unknown for inconsistencies to arise: a typical oversight is the goods lift which opens onto a loading bay and to each level of storage, with the lift controls secured only by a simple cylinder key switch, as compared with the substantial protection on the adjacent entrance door.

4.12   Commissioning

4.12.1 Irrespective of the overall building security proposed, the period during which a new building is first occupied is one of special risk because:

>   Goods are in transit
>   Protection is divided between owners, suppliers and carriers
>   Local risks are not fully apparent
>   Management is heavily occupied on other tasks
>   Personnel are likely to be depleted
>   The premises are strange
>   Security routines, even if developed, are unlikely to be fully operational

One of the problems which can occur has already been mentioned in section 4.5 above, but clearly there are others. It is sensible for any organisation unfamiliar with the process of commissioning a building to employ the specialist advice of a reputable security company to oversee the whole process; the larger and more complex the organisation the greater the benefits, and the money is likely to be well spent.

4.13   Search

4.13.1 Searches for explosives and similar threats are dealt with in chapter 5. There are businesses however which suffer greatly from pilferage, especially of small items, and which can only control the amount of loss by personal searches. These are always distasteful and can, understandably, create significant difficulties in industrial relations. There are three cardinal rules:

>   *All* occupants and visitors are liable to search and no one must be exempt in
>   principle or practice
>   Contracts of employment must include the right of search of both person
>   and spaces such as lockers and desks
>   Searches must be random, routine, thorough and discreet

There must also be an invariable and well-publicised procedure when illicit material is discovered.

4.14 Industrial espionage

4.14.1 This is essentially the theft of information and is not a crime in the UK, unless the Official Secrets Act is involved or unless some other criminal activity, such as burglary, is coincidental. It is difficult to detect, more difficult to prove and often impossible to recover from the loss.

At the simplest level, information can be carried away by an employee and in the case of a simple tender figure for example, may not even require any documentation. There are management remedies in the restriction of access to sensitive information and the control of the documents themselves, but it is difficult to be confident about their efficacy.

Eavesdropping is another matter: the bugging beloved of popular novels. Though it is by no means as common, as easy, or as reliable as fiction suggests, electronic eavesdropping does take place and like the rest of electronic technology is becoming cheaper and more readily available. Indeed, concern has been expressed recently about the advent of small cheap bugs in the form of self-contained VHF microtransmitters. These have been advertised in the general press and transmit a voice signal to domestic radio recivers several hundred metres away. The main classes of eavesdropping device are:

Self-contained radio transmitters

Microphones wired to remote transmitters

Tape recorders planted for collection

Telephone attachments (local or remote)

The detection of these devices is a specialist matter and, if their use is suspected, then expert advice should be sought from a security company.

Equipment is also available for scrambling telephone conversations to prevent eavesdropping; its use may be illegal in the UK and its efficacy is unknown, so specialist advice must be obtained.

Checklist 4

Inside the building

Multiple tenancies

  Define perimeter
  Strive for comparability

Risk areas

  Locate cash offices etc within
   protective surroundings

Zoning

  Design concentric zones

Visibility

  Avoid ambush traps, especially
   on cash routes

Goods

  Separate despatch/delivery
  Provide checking area
  Provide staff changing rooms and secure personal
   storage

Facilities

  Secure machines/photocopiers/telephones

Retail losses

  Establish observation
  Operate verification of sales
  Protect goods

Install counter caches
Include search room
Establish routines for staff

Hotels

Simplify planning
Good room locks
Staff location systems for chambermaids
Safety deposit box routines
Reception area sited for supervision
Control of room keys
Consider electronic access control
Include proper luggage room

Visitors

Escort visitors in and out
Establish authority for entry
Consider electronic roll-call

Security staff

Locate office/base
Establish patrols
Decide on contract/employed staff
Follow BSIC code of practice
Obtain references

Cleaners

Do not issue master keys
Change locks when cleaners change
Plan access

Fittings

Do not rely on ordinary furniture locks
Site vending machines carefully and maintain stocks
Maintain inventories

Internal doors

Decide locking policy
Minimum 3 lever locks,
    5 lever for average security
Control key issue

Avoid sliding doors
Avoid panelled/glazed doors
Fit fish-eye viewers to risk areas
Turnstiles for secure areas

Partitions, floors

Avoid demountable partitions/stud and plasterboard
for secure areas
Subdivide stockrooms
Solid (100 mm block or brick) for moderate security
Avoid glazing, especially near doors
Fit *Anti-bandit glazing* to resist mechanical attack BS
5544: 1978
Fit *Security glazing* to resist firearm attack (BS 50TX:
Part 2: 1973 and Part 2: 1979
Install security glazing in accordance with BS 5357:
1976
Guard against concealment in computer floors

Ceilings

Check access possibilities area to area
Check vulnerability of services
Bolt trapdoors from below

Internal lighting

Leave planned lights on at night
Illuminate safes (visible from outside)
Use multiple fittings

Lifts

Immobilise in empty building

Commissioning

Take specialist advice

Search

Establish routine and plan
Publicise policies

5 Terrorism and personal safety

5.1 General

5.1.1 Twenty years ago in the UK there was little cause for an individual to believe he might be at some risk either from violent criminal attack or from terrorism. In the nineteen-eighties the probability of either event is high enough to justify its inclusion in formal security plans.

5.1.2 The organisation and planning of security against terrorist attack is quite different from that for normal crime prevention. The major objective of the plan will be personal safety, the protection of property will be secondary and the apprehension of the terrorists themselves will not be of immediate concern to the parties involved. Terrorist attack is a catastrophic event and will be dealt with in an atmosphere of crisis: therefore a security plan will only be successful if contingency procedures operate immediately and automatically without the need for personal management decisions.

5.1.3 The designation of a building as a potential terrorist target is an obvious first step towards protective measures; but it is not always a straightforward matter. In the UK, government buildings are deliberately protected but except in Northern Ireland few others are; though this may seem logical at first, there is a world-wide trend for terrorists to direct their attacks at corporate targets, so that multi-national companies are probably more vulnerable. Political aims, and therefore targets, change from time to time, and the situation should be kept under review.

When the frequency of terrorist attacks rises to the point where military resistance is required, as in Northern Ireland, the question of target definition ceases to be relevant because attacks become random and overall protection is required.

5.1.4 It may be thought that the risk is unpredictable and unmanageable but this is not so, and the attraction of the target will be affected by:

The nature of the occupancy or business

The approach to the premises

The possible damage related to the effort needed

Escape routes

The likely degree of local disruption

There is also the question of the terrorist's perception of the target's vulnerability and the consistency of any defensive measures. If the latter are not maintained at a constant level, the attackers, like opportunist criminals, are likely to wait for complacency.

The risk should be viewed constructively: compare the probability of terrorist attack with that of earthquake; then compare the insurance cover.

5.1.5 It must also be remembered that the purpose of terrorism is to create fear: that is what the word means. There is no doubt that this fear can be quite widespread, and one example is the death list of business men published by the IRA, which unsettled the business community in Northern Ireland for some time. The freedom from fear must therefore be seen as the prime objective of anti-terrorist activity, but it should be said that this is rarely achieved, not least because fear is a subjective emotion and once created is not easily removed by reassurance.

5.1.6 Figures for terrorist activities are not easy to compile, partly because of political attitudes and problems of definition: one man's terrorist is another's resistance fighter. An analysis of *international* attacks reveals a trend, however. These are cases in which the culprits have crossed borders and the figures *exclude* Northern Ireland: in 1978 there were 1511 attacks, compared with 293 in 1970. In Europe in 1978 there were 674 attacks including IRA activity. Typically, 50 per cent of the attacks were bombings.

On an international assessment it is clear that some 80 per cent of attacks are 'successful'—though once again there is a problem of definition and it has been assumed that 'success' need not be complete, eg a kidnapping is regarded as successful if the victim is abducted, irrespective of subsequent ransom or release.

5.1.7 There are three main forms of attack:

Personal attack: Threat, kidnap, hostage or murder of individuals or groups.

Direct assault: Buildings are attacked from the outside with offensive weapons (usually military). Defensive measures are limited to the means of construction of the perimeter and external walls.

Indirect assault: A delayed action explosive is left, either inside or near to the building. There may or may not be a warning of the time of the explosion, and if there is, then the warning itself may be inaccurate or intentionally deceptive.

5.1.8 Buildings may include protection against criminal attack by explosives or firearms, but it should be noted that terrorist action using those means will not be limited to unoccupied hours, and that firearms are likely to be used in any area, and not just where valuables are located. The effects of blast and firearms have been dealt with in chapters 3 and 4 for specific areas. It is unlikely that a building in daily civilian use could be designed to resist an attack by modern military weapons.

Many of the bombs planted in buildings are, in the official jargon, improvised ordnance devices (IODs) and are made from stolen explosives. It is important that the storage of explosives on building sites and elsewhere should be carefully controlled. There is also a proposal that batches of explosives should be labelled with chemical or radioactive 'taggants' which would persist after an explosion and enable the source of the material to be traced.

Where the risk is high, protection against snipers should be included, and fortunately this requires nothing more substantial than a visual screen.

5.1.9 The importance of restricting vehicle access was mentioned in chapter 2, and it should be repeated that the use of a vehicle is essential to large-scale terrorist activity and the restriction of vehicle access is a vital principle.

5.1.10 Taking into account all the factors outlined above, the defensive measures established against terrorist attack should contribute towards one of four basic aims.

> Make the attacker find an alternative, softer target
> Cause the attacker to take time and be exposed
> Minimise injury
> Minimise damage

5.1.11 Of course, terrorism is not the only threat to personal safety—in fact it is one of the least likely—but the nature of the threat makes defence and reassurance most difficult.

5.2   Alerts and warnings

5.2.1   The threat of explosion may be discovered in three ways:
> A bomb is found and identified
> A bomb is suspected
> A warning is received

A telephonist or other suitable person must have a checklist to operate in these circumstances, which should be developed in consultation with the police, bearing in mind that those people notified of the emergency will be those who will control any search and evacuation necessary, and will not automatically relate to the normal management hierarchy.

5.3   Searches and evacuation

5.3.1   In the event of an unspecified bomb threat it will be necessary to search the premises, and this can be done with minimum disruption and maximum efficiency only if a search plan has been developed as a contingency. The search should be carried out by a minimum number of people. In general, though the police will be present and can advise, they will *not* carry out the searches themselves, on the principle that they are most unlikely to know the building as well as the occupants and so their search would not be as efficient. Where the risk is high, searches should be carried out regularly, to prevent the gradual accumulation of caches of explosives or weapons.

5.3.2 Vehicle searches may also be carried out as a matter of policy on entry and should also follow an established plan. In chapter 2 mention was made of the need to provide adequate space for proper examination of the vehicles.

5.3.3 Explosives in vehicles, deliveries, mail and on the person may be detected in a number of ways, none of which is entirely reliable:

Personal search: cannot be thorough for practical reasons and may well harm trade in many businesses. A simple frisking to the standard practised at airports is a deterrent but is unlikely to prevent bombs being brought into the premises in pieces. There are however certain classic components of IODs such as clothes pegs, which are used in timing devices and should arouse suspicion.

Metal detectors: are useful as it is difficult to make a bomb without the use of metals; they are not very discriminating though, and there are many legitimate metallic objects which will be detected and will require further examination.

X rays can be seen in use at airports. They are expensive and require some skill in use; as this operation is boring there is a high possibility of decay in efficiency. Cylindrical objects, tubes and wires are regarded as suspicious. There is some risk to films and microprocessors even with low dosage machines.

Vapour detectors are highly discriminating and detect the distinctive gases emitted by chemical explosives (but not firearms). Different models work on different principles and therefore sense different vapours; none are able to guarantee the detection of *all* available explosives but, in the context of IODs this may be thought unnecessary.

Dogs can be trained to detect the smell of explosives and are effective. They are expensive to train and keep, requiring a skilled handler and for practical reasons may not be acceptable in many situations or where there are members of the general public entering.

5.3.4 Evacuation may be necessary and must also be carried out to an established plan. This will be similar to a fire evacuation plan with two major differences:

Occupants must take with them their bags, cases and packages

Occupants must *not* be allowed to disperse from the external assembly area, as they may be required to identify property thought to be suspicious.

5.4   Kidnap and hostage

5.4.1 In some countries these threats are more likely to arise from the general criminal community than from terrorist action, but in the UK there is no current criminal trend in this direction.

5.4.2 The victim of a kidnapping is likely to be a corporate executive or a member of his family, in the hope that the ransom can combine substantial sums of money with some political concession by the corporation and maximum publicity. Companies with interest abroad in areas of political conflict should regard themselves as potential targets.

The victim must be active in his own protection and should realise that the preparation for the kidnap is usually carried out very carefully. Attacks are likely to be made while he is in transit, especially during routine journeys. The first principle to be followed is therefore to avoid regular patterns of activity, either by the target or his family. In addition, the vulnerable person should be instructed in the need to watch out for any signs of surveillance being carried out on him. The risk is increased during any regular trips abroad, especially to those countries which have a record of kidnapping.

5.4.3 It is predicted that this crime will become more common in the future. The establishment of ransom insurance, by both companies and by individuals, is a known growth industry in the USA.

5.5   Control

5.5.1 In an emergency, be it terrorism, fire or anything else, there will be a need for clear communication and control; much of the communications will be outside the normal pattern and with strange bodies such as the fire brigade and police. In an organisation of any size, the management is likely to be compartmented in a way which does not assist this type of communication, and an incident control room should be considered. This is part of the standard brief in some government buildings and a simple room of 7–10 m^2 is sufficient, with connections to the main switchboard and an independent telephone line. The room should be sited on a main circulation route at ground level and be close to, but not part of the main entrance area. It need not be on an outside wall and there are advantages in a wholly internal location, so long as suitable provision is made for emergency lighting. The room should contain documented contingency plans and communication checklists for use in emergency. These must be set out in such a way that they can be used by strangers.

In most organisations, particularly commercial offices, there will be pressure on the use of space, and such a room is likely to become at best a storeroom and at worst may be used as another working office. If this cannot be resisted then the room must be abandoned for incident control: there is no point in pretending to keep a facility—it is like having empty fire extinguishers.

5.6 Violent crime

5.6.1 Although terrorism presents the most extreme deliberate threat to personal safety and any one incident will threaten numbers of people, it is not the most likely occurrence and it is clear that other violent crime is more frequent.

5.6.2 There is evidence that the use of violence in the course of criminal activity is increasing, and this has come as no surprise either to the police or the security industry. As mentioned in chapter 1, there is also a tendency in circumstances of high security for the attack to be transferred from goods to those people who have access to them. It is therefore clear that the higher the level of protection provided, the greater the need (and responsibility) actively to consider the safety of the people involved.

In 1982 there were 109 000 cases of violence against the person in England and Wales, and 2 700 serious injuries from firearms. Social characteristics and the framework of the law both change over a period of time, and the figures will reflect these changes. In this context it is interesting to examine the situation in the USA where:

> Murder is one of the major causes of death
> The average age of killers is 21
> 25 per cent of killers are women
> Only 2 per cent are criminally insane

It must be pointed out, however, that whereas in 1980 there were 621 murders in England and Wales, there were over 50 000 in the USA.

5.6.3 The greatest danger is obviously where cash is involved and the risk is greatly increased where the cash is in transit, either outside or within the premises. Many of the problems are those of management policy. It should no longer be acceptable to despatch staff casually along the street to the bank night safe with the day's takings. Night safes are not recommended and are gradually falling into disrepute: better to arrange random deposits during banking hours or to contract with a security company for cash collections as necessary. If night safes are used or cash is being transferred otherwise, it must be carried by an adult male with at least one companion, instructed in and prepared for the risk. This applies to both pedestrian and vehicle movements. The escort should walk immediately behind the man carrying the cash and should also carry an alarm of some kind (even if only a whistle). Both should walk facing the oncoming traffic.

5.7   Duress

5.7.1   If an employee is charged with the protection of cash or valuables he should be told what is expected of him in the event of threats or menaces: this is only fair, so that he does not put his safety at risk unnecessarily.

5.7.2   Some access control systems include a duress code so that a person who is menaced may include an innocent signal (such as extra digit) and gain access while also making an unperceived signal for assistance.

5.8   Personal alarms

5.8.1   Alarm systems designed to give warning of personal attack may be portable or static.

5.8.2   The static types are the most common and are suitable for use in banks or post offices and in housing areas. They can be part of a general intruder detection system (see chapter 6), and are in fact covered by part of the BS for intruder alarm systems BS 4737: Parts 1 and 2: 1977–79 as deliberately operated devices. The operating mechanisms may be latching—the alarm stays on until the switch is reset by a key—or non-latching, as with a simple push button. The latching type is intended to ease operation and maintain the alarm signal under duress, whilst introducing a disincentive to casual or mischevious use: it is detectable on the same principle as a railway communication cord.

In either case it is important that the alarm should be operable without perceptible body movement, so that the personal threat is not increased. Foot switches are useful for people working at counters; an alternative is a continuous sensitive strip will allow contact to be made anywhere along its length, thus minimising hand movement.

In houses the greatest risk occurs when the occupant is answering the door, or during the night. The alarm switch should be located by the front door frame at shoulder height: the hand can naturally rest there and it is out of the normal reach of children. An additional switch can be beside the bed.

5.8.3   The portable type of alarm is not covered by the BS but there is a need to give some protection to those who are carrying cash, are vulnerable to kidnap or on security patrol and who do not have the benefit of any physical barriers. The simplest system is entirely self-contained and is designed to give an instant alarm at the point of attack, to summon help and to confuse, frighten or deter the attacker. Devices available include whistles and sirens powered by compressed gas and intense repeating flashing lights, working on the same principles as a camera flashgun. Gas and chemical deterrent aerosol sprays are also available illicitly but are not considered safe in the UK; their use against an innocent person would be regarded as assault.

There are variations on this principle which can be fitted to cases used for cash transit; these are usually operated by a wrist chain. A dye can be released on the money inside, making it difficult to dispose of and marking anyone who handles it, or coloured smoke can be released. This is particularly effective in preventing escape by car as it rapidly fills the car to the point where driving is impossible.

Mobile alarms connected to a central system are necessary in some instances, but they introduce technical difficulties which are difficult to overcome. The reception of the radio signal cannot be guaranteed as it is subject to the same areas of masking and transmission weakness as voice signals. A simple radio signal is also vulnerable to external interference and as they operate on the fail safe principle, there is a high probability of false alarms. These problems are partially overcome by reducing the operating range to about 300 m, and by modulating or encoding the signal so that it is unique. An 8-bit data stream is least likely to be duplicated. VHF radio is essential.

The actuating device can be in the pocket or disguised as a watch, but some delay should be included to prevent accidental operation; it is suggested that the switch has to be held for 750 milliseconds.

5.8.4 A decision must be made about the sounding device. In circumstances of personal threat a sudden loud alarm may increase the danger, so a silent confidential signal is preferable. The argument for this principle is strenghtened when there is also a degree of physical protection present, as behind bank counters, and where it may be assumed that help can be summoned from wherever on the premises the alarm does sound. In sub-post-offices, for example, all the people on the premises may be subject to the same threat and a silent alarm would not be appropriate.

The BS allows the alarms to be 'normal' (i.e. loud) or 'quiet' as with intruder alarm systems, or silent.

5.9   Fire

5.9.1 There are major hazards to personal safety arising from fires in buildings. In the UK the legislation and standards governing the design, construction and use of buildings with regard to fire safety is of a high standard. It is continually being reviewed and developed, and the information available is comprehensive. It would not be possible to cover the subject in a book about security and neither is it necessary to do so, but the basic principles may usefully be aired:

5.9.2 The dangers caused by fires are not always appreciated; they fall into five categories which are given in order of severity.

Smoke can rapidly spread through a building, travelling along corridors, false ceiling voids, ventilation systems, ducts and cableways. First, visibility is impaired to the extent that escape routes cannot be found, then breathing becomes difficult and asphyxiation can occur through lack of oxygen. Finally, the smoke temperature may be so high that lungs are damaged or breathing is impossible. It should also be noted that the smoke damage to buildings and their contents is likely to be extensive in itself.

Toxic gases are generated by a number of burning substances, particularly plastics. The gases vary according to the amount of oxygen available for combustion and the ambient temperature. They can be lethal or incapacitating long before other dangers arise, and as they do not necessarily have the same visual characteristics as smoke, they can develop without so much alarm and suspicion. Current studies are concentrating on the problem, which has become more important in recent years as the use of plastics in furniture has increased

Radiation of heat from surfaces exposed to the fire can cause secondary ignition, but it can also prevent the use of escape routes. The protection against this can have a particular effect on the observation of one area from another, in that the amount of glazing in the division is severely restricted. There is a nomogram in BS CP 153: Part 4: 1972 which allows the area of glass to be calculated, considering the need to walk past the panel and the time taken before the point of unbearable pain is reached.

Structural collapse can cause injury and block escape routes. It occurs when timber structure burns away, steel softens, masonry cracks and fixings melt.

Flame is the most obvious and least severe of the hazards: by the time there is direct danger from flame it is likely that people will have succumbed to one of the other effects of the fire.

5.9.3 Precautions are established according to the degree and combination of the two categories of peril.

High *fire* risk arising from flammable substances, unattended areas or hazardous processes

High *life* risk arising from the presence of people who are specially vulnerable, such as those sleeping, the sick and elderly, or concentrated numbers unfamiliar with the premises.

There may also be quite specific consideration of the risk to property including stores, equipment and data.

5.9.4 The detection of a fire may be by:

Observation

Heat detectors

Smoke detectors

Combustion detectors

The automatic detectors can be incorporated in the more comprehensive types of building alarm systems along with intruder detection: see chapter 9.

5.9.5 Following detection, there must be a policy for signalling alarms and for deciding whether to evacuate the building and in what order. This must be predetermined and should be included in the security plan. There is a single overriding principle in planning for fire safety:

People must be able to move away from the danger to a place of safety.

This may seem obvious but there are many buildings—mostly older ones—in which it does not apply, and where an occupant can leave his warm comfortable office or hotel room on hearing the alarm to emerge into a smoke-filled corridor with no guarantee that, whichever way he goes, he will not encounter greater danger.

A place of safety is ideally the open air, but not necessarily so. The time needed to escape to the open air from a large building can be unacceptable, and indeed in hospitals and the like there may be equal danger in moving the occupants down stairways. It is a well-tried principle that buildings may be divided into compartments surrounded by an envelope of specified fire resistance, so that in any fire the neighbouring compartment (which is ideally on the same floor) provides a place of safety; there must of course be alternative means of escape from each compartment.

5.9.6 Fire fighting other than immediate first aid is a skilful business, and if it cannot be done without any risk to personal safety it should be left to the fire brigade. If there is a delay in calling the brigade, the firemen themselves may be put at greater risk, so they should be called automatically, even if a fire appears at first to be minor. Fire fighting appliances include:

Blankets for smothering flames
Extinguishers *of the correct type*
Hosereels
Automatic sprinklers
Automatic gas saturation

The provision of buckets of sand or water is deprecated because they are likely to get taken away for other purposes, and in any case are unlikely to be kept full. Automatic sprinkler systems are excellent for unattended areas, and in most cases where a fire has begun a single sprinkler head has been sufficient to control it. The cost of installation can be offset in part by a specific reduction of insurance premiums. Water damage can be extensive however, and it is important that a facility is established for a connected alarm and easy subsequent manual cut-off.

Checklist 5

Terrorism and personal safety

Terrorist attack

> Define likelihood
> Establish planned response and drill
> Establish review periods
> Include blast protection
> Consider visual screen for snipers
> Restrict vehicle access and approach

Bomb alerts

> Establish checklist
> Establish search and evacuation procedures
> Check incoming vehicles

Kidnap or hostage-taking

> Establish risk and define targets
> Brief target personnel
> Avoid regular patterns of movement
> Consider ransom insurance

Control

> Designate incident room
> Establish documented procedures

Violent crime

> Protect cash-carrying staff

Duress

    Brief staff for response
    Include codes in access control systems

Alarms

    Install in risk situations
    Consider sounding or silent alarms

Fire

    Consider fire risk or life risk
    Escape security
    Appliances and training

6 Intruder detection

6.1 The purpose

6.1.1 Strength is the main principle of good security, but it is a variable property and difficult to measure; it can be overcome at any time by greater strength, so it must be accepted that any physical barriers set up around the property can be breached.

If this breach occurs undetected, then no more security exists and the property is lost. Bearing in mind that the current clear-up rate for burglary in the UK is approximately only 30%, it is clear that some remedy must be found and the most obvious solution is the detection of the intrusion as early as possible, so that action can be taken to prevent or reduce the loss as it occurs.

6.1.2 An intruder detection system can have the following characteristics:

It warns that an intrusion has occured. This warning need not be made known to the intruder

It may allow the intruder to penetrate to a degree, becoming a trapping device

Activation can scare an intruder away before he has completed his entry; many opportunists and casual criminals are not prepared to expose themselves to attention or to risk

Visible evidence of the installation can deter attempts to gain entry: the criminal will seek an easier target elsewhere

The value of the last point should not be underestimated: only 3% of Britain's homes have any security system installed. Beware of the dummy alarm boxes which are sold, however, as experienced criminals are rarely fooled by them and manufacturers who find their logo used on empty bell casings fixed to walls are understandably annoyed.

Conversely, it is sometimes held that the obvious presence of an alarm system advertises the fact that the premises contain articles of value, and increase the attraction to the criminal. Notwithstanding this theory, a detection system cannot ever *reduce* the overall level of security, if only because the opportunist is always deterred and he is more common than the hunter.

6.1.3 The concepts and detailed design of intruder detection systems are in a state of rapid and radical change. Some see this as the single transition of the industry from low to high technology but the more far-sighted security companies have realised that this state of change is likely to continue into the future and are planning accordingly. An examination of the three main factors shows why this is so:

> Intruder detection systems are concerned with the processing of information. The silicon microprocessor has revolutionised the technical capabilities of even the simplest systems, and it is clear that once linked to this line of development alarm systems will change as it changes

> Changing systems add another dimension to security, in that the criminal has to keep pace with developments, and is more frequently confused or presented with uncertainty

> The security industry is one of the fastest growing in the world. A survey in five EEC countries estimates their fire security products markets at £2 billion, and in the face of such growth and commercial competition no company will be able to remain static in its products or services

6.1.4 The policy of both the local police authority and the insurance company involved must be taken into account when specifying alarm systems. There is sometimes a conflict between the two, in that the police want to catch criminals and the insurance company is satisfied if there is no loss.

The police are likely to have strong views about the type of system installed, and their opinions are not necessarily consistent from one area to another: it is not easy to demonstrate results from crime prevention, so the resources allocated to this branch tend to be limited. However, because their detection rate is so low, any system which will cut down the number of break-ins is bound to be welcomed by the police, especially if the installation is reliable.

Insurance companies exert a great influence on the type of system installed, and are frequently the prime movers. Managements often ask their insurance company to recommend a system and oversee the appointment of an alarm company. Unfortunately, insurance companies are not always as constructive as they might be: the attitude is too often 'If you don't install system x we will not maintain cover' rather than 'If you install system x your premium will be £A, but if you install system z your premium will be £B.'

6.1.5 Though the technology available is impressive it has not always been so, and neither has the security industry been able in the past to control its overall standards and quality. The result is an overwhelming reputation for false alarms and this affects the attitude of the general public as well as the main parties involved: customers, criminals and police.

Major efforts are now being made to remove the problem and there is evidence that significant advances are being made. The problem is discussed in more detail in section 6.5 following, and in selection chart 6.1. All parties (except the criminal) accept that an improvement in the general standard of intruder alarm systems is essential.

6.1.6 It must be accepted that a system has a useful design life. This is not only because of wear and tear on the components, but also because of the concepts of the original protection. Just as the industry as a whole changes, so must an individual installation be kept under review so that it does not become vulnerable because of:

> Wear
> Advances in equipment for attack
> Becoming an easier target than updated premises nearby

6.2   The level of protection

6.2.1 As with the other aspects of security, the level of protection provided by an intruder detection system must be assessed carefully, so that resources are used economically and too much is not expected of the system itself. The risk varies between premises, but it may also vary within them; different areas of the building are likely to require different types of protection.

The target can be, say, a petrol station at one end of the scale and a nuclear power station at the other. A survey is carried out on existing buildings (if a security company does this it is usually free) and account is taken of the location, history, type of attack likely and insurance company before recommending a level of protection.

A major consequence of burglaries is the damage caused, either in the process of entry or as a deliberate act. Indeed, in many cases, the damage exceeds the loss of property and deliberate fouling and destruction is common, especially in domestic premises. The likely degree of this damage must be estimated and included in the value of the property to be protected when assessing the intruder detection system needed.

6.3   System configuration

6.3.1 Any intruder alarm system is made up of three separate components:
The sensor
The control unit
The alarm signal
The components are linked by a communications medium (usually wiring) which also should be regarded as a part of the whole system. The components are discussed in detail later, but it be stressed that their compatibility is critical to the acceptability of the system as a whole, so they should all be supplied by a single reliable source.

6.3.2 Simplicity helps and can affect which level of security is practicable: simple physical protection will allow easy electrical protection.

6.3.3 The intruder detection system may be *on* or *off* (somewhat confusingly known as closed or open) but in its inactive open mode, it is only the signal which is interrupted, while the other components remain active. This is because some sensors require time to settle down into a stable condition after being switched on, and so are left permanently under power. It is probable that in the future this principle will change, as there is some concern being expressed about the possible long-term health hazards arising from continual exposure to low energy microwaves and ultrasonic emissions. There is no evidence to support this theory at present.

6.4 The geometry of protection

6.4.1 Intruders can be detected:
When they cross a line (linear protection)
When they enter a space (volumetric protection)
When they contact an object (point protection)
Figure 6.1 shows the places in which these principles may best be applied, from the perimeter inwards.

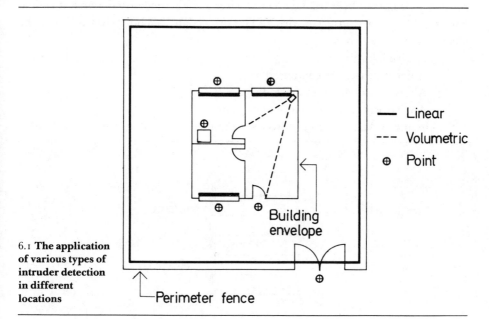

6.1 **The application of various types of intruder detection in different locations**

6.4.2 Perimeter protection can only be established in conjunction with a good physical barrier, especially if the site is unmanned. Protection of the external area will depend on the nature of the risk and the need to raise the alarm as soon as possible following an intrusion. There are some common risks: vehicle tyres for example, which are habitually stored in the open air.

6.4.3 Often, the correct solution will be a combination of linear and volumetric detection systems.

6.5   Sensors

6.5.1 Considerable ingenuity has been applied to the design of the sensing mechanisms for intruder detection systems, and it has to be said that much of the unreliability which such systems are credited with stems from their innovative technology. The problems in fact are numerous, and there is no single device which is suitable for every location. The British Standard (BS 4737 *Intruder alarm systems in buildings*) covers a number of different sensors but is not exhaustive. The various types currently available, together with their advantages and limitations are set out below and summarised in selection chart 6.1. Many are falling into disuse as volumetric protection becomes more reliable.

6.5.2 *Continuous wiring*. Wires are stretched across an opening and form a double pole circuit. The wires must be at a maximum of 100 mm spacing, and fixed every 600 mm, fig 6.2. Alternatively, they can be run in tubes or grooved rods. Extra protection is offered by a second layer of wires at right angles to the first; it is then known as mesh or transverse wiring. The protection is mainly electrical and the alarm is generated when:

> A wire is cut
> Adjacent wires are connected *or*
> Alternate wires are connected
> Any wire is displaced more than 50 mm

If the circuitry is known it can be overcome quite easily. It does not look very nice.

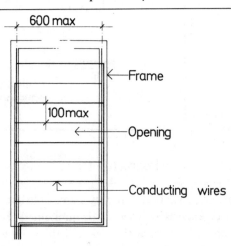

6.2 **Continous wiring**

6.5.3 *Foil on glass.* Thin conductive tapes of lead or aluminium foil are applied to the inside face of the glass, and form a single or double pole circuit, fig 6.3. The strips are normally run around the edge of the pane between 50 mm and 100 mm from the edge. They must be carefully applied so that there is no blistering or loosening, and they must not be taken across cracks or over the junction of butt jointed glass. The alarm is generated when:

      The glass under the foil is broken

      The foil is cut

      Adjacent strips are connected (double pole circuit only)

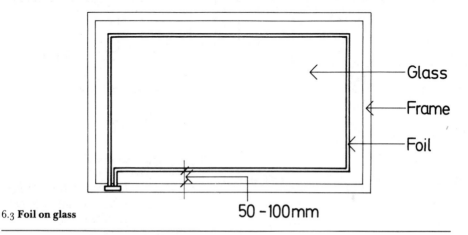

6.3 **Foil on glass**

The appearance is quite acceptable if carefully applied, but there are problems with window cleaning. A hole can often be cut in ordinary glass away from the foil and to counter this the strips can be arranged to give greater cover. This is more obtrusive though, and is not necessary for toughened glass which cannot be cut in the same way. This system like continuous wiring is labour-intensive, and is being replaced by other methods.

6.5.4 *Protective switches.* These are the most traditional and well-tried devices for intruder detection. They are simple mechanical or magnetic electrical switches which are located so that they operate when another part moves, fig 6.4 a, b. The moving part can be a door, window or a set of fine wires stretched taut across an opening. This latter is one of the most reliable and most difficult to overcome of all devices; the wires should not be more than 100 mm apart and the switch arranged to operate when the wires are cut or stretched. The switches take a variety of forms and can be open or closed circuit; i.e. can either make or break the circuit to alarm. It must not be possible to tell by inspection which way the switch is wired.

    Simple mechanical contacts operate in a similar way to the courtesy light switch on a car door and they are largely obsolete because they suffer from the same problems—they get dirty and stick—and in addition the door can warp. There is

**6.4 Protective
switches: an
arrangement
linked to wires
a Mechanical
protective switch
b Magnetic
protective switch**

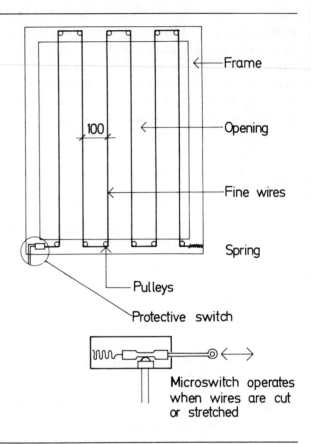

Frame

100   Opening

Fine wires

Spring

Pulleys

Protective switch

Microswitch operates
when wires are cut
or stretched

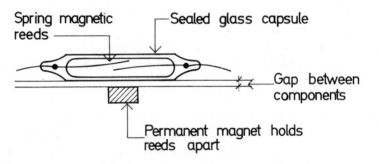

Spring magnetic
reeds

Sealed glass capsule

Gap between
components

Permanent magnet holds
reeds apart

no protection of the glazed area of the door or window, which must be covered by a taut wire system or by knock-out rods that span between spring loaded microswitches. The rod system can be overcome and is not in general use.

Magnetic reed switches are easier to seal hermetically and are not so prone to accumulating dirt. A flexible strip is held away from a contact by a magnetic insert in the door or window. The simpler types can be overcome by the application of another magnet and they also suffer a gradual deterioration of the magnetic property if the door is continually banging.

Protective switches generate an alarm when:

The wiring is tampered with in the wrong way

The moving part allows an opening gap over 100 mm

They can be defeated if the method of wiring is known and, in many cases, they can be cut around, leaving the critical part of the door in position whilst the rest is opened.

6.5.5 *Rigid printed circuit wiring.* Boards are prefabricated with double pole wiring printed irremovably onto the surface. The printed side is always inwards and though they can be used for walls and doors the system is not popular and is little used except, occasionally, for safes. The circuits are vulnerable to mechanical damage and faults are difficult to trace and repair. The alarm is generated when:

Any conductor is cut

Adjacent or alternate conductors are connected

Any conductor is displaced more than 50 mm

6.5.6 *Pressure mats.* These devices are akin to protective switches in that a simple electrical contact must be made or broken. The mats contain layers of foil or strips which make contact when pressed together by a person standing on them. They are intended for use in strategic places within the building where an intruder might be expected, such as door mats, under windows, stair treads and in front of showcases and safes. As they are easily avoided they have no value at all unless they are well hidden and as they are usually placed beneath a carpet they can become visible after a time as the carpet wears differently over the edge. Small animals can activate them if they are too sensitive. The alarm is generated when:

A force greater than 100 N is applied over a 60 mm circle

6.5.7 *Vacuum glass.* Two sheets of glass are made up into a sealed double glazed unit and a partial vacuum is created between them. One of the sheets can be laminated for extra physical protection and the thermal and acoustic properties are excellent. The units are best in small panes as larger sizes require unsightly distance-pieces to keep the glass apart and to prevent the vacuum fluctuating when the glass drums. The system is highly expensive however, and as other methods of protection show significant savings it is rarely used. Gradual leakage into the vacuum can occur. The alarm is generated when:

The glass is broken

Vacuum is lost

6.5.8 *Beam interruption detectors.* Sometimes known as fences, these are true linear detectors in that a beam of radiation passes in a straight line from a transmitter to a receiver. The radiation may be light, infra-red or radiowaves, and each has different characteristics.

Light beams are not useful outside as they cease to operate in fog. Their main drawback however is the ease with which they can be masked, either by an additional light source impinging on the photoelectric cell receiver, or simply by an intensely high ambient light level. It is possible that the use of laser equipment could overcome this in special circumstances. A light beam is always obtrusive.

Radiowave (microwave) beams are used for linear protection externally and the signal can be modulated with the receiver matched accordingly so that masking is prevented. The beams have a typical range of about 200 m and are usually set up in vertical interconnected pairs so that the movement of grass, birds and animals does not generate alarms, fig 6.5. There is a loss of sensitivity in the rain and some risk, with older models, of mutual interference between neighbouring transmitters. The system is only useful on flat terrain and though it is not as obvious as an optical system, an experienced criminal will be able to spot the posts and may well be able to avoid the beam.

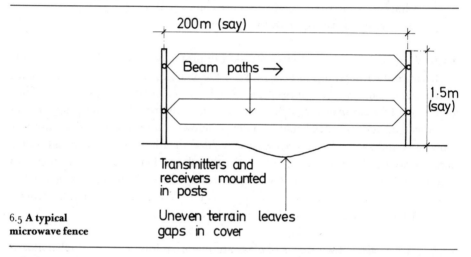

6.5 A typical microwave fence

Infra-red beams can also be modulated though they are badly affected by fog and rain and are always obtrusive. They are not commonly used. The alarm is generated when:

> The beam is interrupted for more than 40 ms
> The power supply falls
> The casing is tampered with

6.5.9 *Radiowave doppler detectors.* Commonly known as microwave detectors, these devices are volumetric and are designed to transmit and receive radiowaves of a fixed frequency (approximately 10.7 GHz). If the waves are reflected from a *moving* object such as a person, the returning signal changes in frequency and this is detected by the sensor, fig 6.6

The devices are extremely sensitive and their area of coverage extends round corners; this can be a problem in itself and movement of parts of the structure (such as doors swinging) or wave penetration through glass can create false alarms. Penetration of lightweight block walls is also possible, so the area of coverage must be carefully considered. Blind spots and shadow areas are possible behind metallic objects, which can allow security weaknesses to arise in warehouses where, for example, piles of refrigerators are stocked. The sensors themselves can be focussed to some extent by fitting cones (horns) to the head. Coverage should not be extended casually by installing more units because it can be expected that, on average, there will be one false alarm per year per unit. The area of highest risk must be designated and a survey is essential to determine this. When used outside, some 1–2 false alarms per week can be expected, so they should not be used on an unmanned site.

Interference with the signal can be caused by fluorescent lights, but in practice, this is rarely a problem. Older units were subject to mutual interference; this has now been overcome with current models, though it is unwise to site units in line. The microwaves themselves can cause a nuisance and, even though very low energies are involved, there is some possibility of a health hazard from long term exposure. Because of the problems of coverage and false alarms, the BS lays down a seven-day test period for the system to settle down during which no false alarms must be given, before it can be connected to a police notification device. An alarm is generated when:

A 40–50 kg person moves 2 m at average speed

Power supply falls

The sensor is tampered with internally

The usual means of defeating the system is by placing metal foil over the sensor while the system is open. A few devices are able to detect this and there are also check-receivers made which monitor the presence of the microwave signal: these however increase the risk of system failure and false alarm, and are not proving popular.

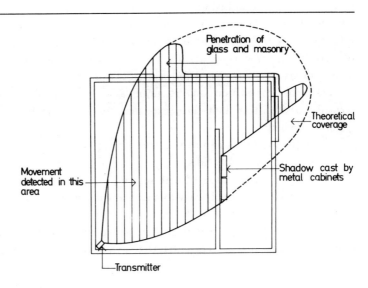

6.6 Microwave detection: the pattern of coverage

6.5.10 *Ultrasonic movement detectors.* A doppler shift in the frequency of ultrasonic reflections from a moving object is detected in the same way as a microwave sensor and a similar volume is covered, fig 6.7. The other operational characteristics are quite different. The signal generated is higher than 22 KHz and as penetration of surfaces is almost nil, the siting is less critical. There is no mutual interference between units, as the crystals which determine the precise frequency are carefully controlled and matched between transmitting head and receiver.

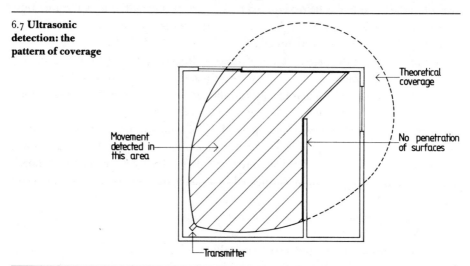

6.7 **Ultrasonic detection: the pattern of coverage**

Theoretical coverage

Movement detected in this area

No penetration of surfaces

Transmitter

There are two main drawbacks to the use of these detectors: firstly, moving objects such as curtains are easily detected (unless these are foil lined a microwave sensor will probably not respond) and secondly, the devices are sensitive to differing air densities. This means that they are not suitable for use in buildings in which there are draughts, or where a warm air or space heating system operates. The total area covered increases where the enclosing surfaces are relatively reflective and high ambient noise levels reduce their effectiveness. In general, ultrasonic sensors cover a greater area for a given cost than microwave sensors. The systems must be tested for seven days in the same way as for microwave sensors before connection to police notification systems. There are possible health hazards arising from long-term exposure to ultrasonic radiation. An alarm is generated when:

A 40–50 kg person moves 2 m at average speed

The power supply falls

The sensor is tampered with internally

These devices are relatively easy to mask, as their penetrating power is so low, and masking can be achieved in the open mode by placing cling-film over the head. Check receivers are not feasible, as there are so many random sources of ultrasonic frequencies generated. It is essential that a walk-test be carried out as the system is closed.

6.5.11 *Passive infra-red detectors*. These devices radiate no energy themselves but are sensitive to a change in the infra-red radiation within a space. A heat sensor within the unit is set at the focal point of a multi-faceted mirror and, as the geometry of the mirror is known, the pattern of coverage is entirely predictable, fig 6.8. Penetration of surfaces is nil.

Single-element types respond to changes within a finger pattern so that radial movements can be detected. False alarms can arise through extraneous heat sources such as central heating systems cutting in and changing sunlight patterns on walls and floors. To overcome these problems, the more advanced units contain dual sensing elements arranged as positive and negative, so that static hotspots are ignored. The typical range of a unit is 12–15 m, though passage in front of the detector within 2–3 m is usually possible without generating an alarm.

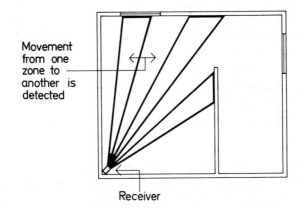

Movement from one zone to another is detected

Receiver

6.8 Passive infra-red detection: the pattern of coverage

The sensors themselves deteriorate with time, as they incorporate a thin gelatine screen at the front which becomes dirty and cannot be cleaned, thus attenuating the signal. For this reason, these detectors are not popular and are not highly regarded. Their main use is in areas where neither microwave nor ultrasonic devices can be used, such as draughty environments with moving objects. They should not be used in high ambient temperatures (over 27°C) although the BS indicates their use up to 40°C. An alarm is generated when:

A 40–50 kg person moves 2 m at average speed

The power supply falls

The sensor is tampered with internally

Passive infra-red sensors are easy to mask, simply by covering them while the system is open. In addition, it is possible that an intruder could wear clothing which would not radiate to the extent that an alarm was given.

6.5.12 *Volumetric capacitive detectors*. Capacitance is an electrical property associated with an insulator such as air. It can be measured for any space and, as the introduction of a new object into the space will change the capacitance, the measuring device can be made to trigger an alarm signal. These sensors are passive and there is no emission of any radiation. They are rarely used and their performance is uncertain. Sudden changes in humidity, static electricity build-up and ionization of the air caused by electrical equipment can all give rise to capacitance changes. As with the other volumetric systems above, a seven-day test period is required before connection to a police notification device. An alarm is generated when:

> A 40–50 kg person moves 2 m at average speed
> The power falls
> The sensor is tampered with internally

6.5.13 *Capacitive proximity detectors.* These operate in a similar way to the volumetric detectors described above except that they are intended to protect single objects, such as safes, and so their range and sensitivity is adjusted accordingly. An alarm is generated when:

> An object is touched by a person *or*
> An object is approached closely by a person
> The power supply falls
> The sensor is tampered with internally

6.5.14 *Vibration detectors.* A range of devices is available to detect the vibrations which are characteristic of a physical attack. The common requirement of all the types is that they must distinguish between natural environmental vibrations and those which occur during an attempted intrusion.

The simplest device is the trembler, usually consisting of a leaf spring attached to a weight and a contact. Some can be overcome by the application of an immobilising magnet, others by the injection of setting chemicals or foam. They have largely fallen into disuse.

Inertia switches and accelerometers of various designs respond to sudden movements and are often clamped onto safes and filing cabinets. Their sensitivity is such that a fairly stable environment is required. The more sophisticated seismic detectors have a memory capacity so that vibrations can be analysed over a period of time; they are particularly suitable for vaults.

Piezo-electric crystals generate an electrical current when subjected to pressure such as may be applied by a vibrating diaphragm. They are particularly sensitive to the frequency of the vibration and so are ideally suited to application to areas of glass where they can be designed to respond only to those frequencies typical of breaking glass. They can be overcome by melting the glass and they can be detached. An alarm condition is generated when:

> Vibration characteristic of an attack occurs

The power supply falls

Any casing is tampered with

6.5.15 *Acoustic detectors.* A passive microphone receives sound and an electronic device analyses the input with the intention of detecting the sounds characteristic of a physical attack on a solid structure. The BS is specific in that these devices are intended for use in strongrooms and vaults. They are not suitable where there is a high ambient noise level, as the trigger level of their operation must be at least 15dB above this level. It is possible that they could be defeated by a micro-processor-controlled 'anti-noise' generator to nullify the perceived sound pattern of an attack. Access to the sensor would be necessary. An alarm is generated when:

A sound in excess of the trigger level continues for more than 5 s in any 30 s

A sound in excess of 120 dBA continues for more than 100 ms

The power supply falls

The mechanism is tampered with

There are two further variants of acoustic detectors.

The geophone is designed for burial outside, preferably under a bed of shale, and is intended to detect the characteristic sounds of footfalls: the shale makes them noisier. Each detector has a range of about 6 m, but they can be bridged and they are made ineffective by any substantial layer of snow.

The vandal alarm is specially designed for unoccupied school premises. It registers noises on an accumulative basis, each new input raising the stored signal level until a pre-set threshold is reached and an alarm generated. On the principle that vandals take their time and usually make a lot of noise, the system is highly effective, as a single unit can cover a large area.

6.5.16 *Fibreoptic detectors.* A continuous fibreoptic cable is run around an area. Light is introduced at one end and received at the other, any variation being cause for alarm. The cable can be woven into a fence or used as part of a special barbed tape. It cannot be cut without detection or short-circuited, but as it is only a single wire it is usually not difficult to avoid it altogether. It is also expensive and difficult to repair when damaged, but it is useful where other systems cannot be used, such as under water, on uneven ground or where flammable gases are present. An alarm is generated when:

The light signal is interrupted

6.5.17 *Passive optical detectors.* In areas which are naturally dark, a simple photoelectric cell can generate an alarm if light intrudes through an open door, lights switched on or torches. As the room must be completely internal, these sensors are usually only used in vaults and strongrooms, often combined with acoustic detectors. An alarm is generated when:

Light in excess of the trigger level falls on the unit

The power supply falls

The units are easily masked, simply by covering the receiving aperture.

6.5.18 *Differential air pressure detectors.* The pressure within a closed area is kept artificially higher or lower than normal by a fan in one of the walls, and the differential between inside and outside is monitored. Any open door will reduce the difference and a signal can be generated. The system used to be installed in strongrooms but is not generally used in new installations. An alarm is generated when:

> The pressure differential falls
> The power fails
> The fan fails

6.5.19 *Liquid pressure sensors.* Twin plastic tubes are filled with antifreeze and buried 600 mm apart in the ground. Sensors on the end of each tube register any differential between them and so the passage of vehicles or pedestrians can be detected. An equalising valve is included between the tubes to allow a slow bleed over a period of, say 30 s to compensate for static pressures such as parked vehicles. The system is extremely sensitive and does not require flat terrain. It is difficult to detect and repair leaks however, and the system is not often used in commercial installations. An alarm is generated when:

> The difference in pressure between the two pipes exceeds a trigger level
> The power fails
> A pipe is cut

6.5.20 *Magnetic sensors.* Cable is buried below a road surface to form an induction loop and vehicles moving overhead are detected in the same way as they are at traffic lights and car park barriers. Pedestrians and bicycles will not be detected. An alternative use often suggested is the installation of these loops below parked vehicles in loading bays so that their removal would be detected. This is not recommended, since if the presence of the loop is known it can be held activated by the presence of other pieces of metal like dustbin lids placed on the ground. In the normal mode, an alarm is generated when:

> A metallic mass is in proximity.

6.5.21 The detection of intruders by observation by patrols or other surveillance is covered in chapter 9.

6.6   Selecting detection systems

6.6.1   It is impossible to give firm guidance on the use of a particular device in a general location as there are many areas in which potential uses overlap; there are also situations in which no system will be wholly effective. Nevertheless there are some principles which must be followed when selecting equipment.

Selection chart 6.1. Sensors

Type	Advantages	Disadvantages	Use
Continuous wiring	Simple Obvious presence	Vulnerable Unattractive	Windows
Foil on glass	Simple Reliable Acceptable appearance Obvious presence	Application difficult Cleaning problems	Windows (especially toughened glass)
Protective switches	Traditional Proven Most types are reliable Inconspicuous Simple	Some types vulnerable	Moving parts Doors/windows
Rigid printed circuit wiring		Can be damaged	Safes Obsolescent
Pressure mats	Simple	Vulnerable	Stairs Under windows
Vacuum glass	Good thermal and acoustic properties	Deteriorate Expensive	Rare
Light beams	Simple	Vulnerable Obvious line Fog	Lines
Radiowave beams	Not vulnerable to masking	Rain Interference Flat terrain only Obvious line	200 m max line
Infra-red beams	Not vulnerable to masking if modulated	Fog Rain Obvious line	Rare
Radio wave doppler	Sensitive Covers 'round corners' and penetrates solids	Sensitive Masked by metallic objects False alarms Some vulnerability	Volumetric Movement detection Internal use best
Ultrasonic	No penetration on surfaces High area/cost ratio	No penetration of surfaces Confused by moving curtains etc. Confused by air densities Affected by high ambient noise False alarms Vulnerable to masking	Volumetric movement detection Internal use Not with warm air heating
Passive infra-red	No radiation No penetration of surfaces Predictable coverage	No penetration of surfaces False alarms Deteriorate	Volumetric Movement detection Internal 12–15 m range Unpopular

Selection chart 6.1. Sensors

Type	Advantages	Disadvantages	Use
		Vulnerable Affected by high ambient temperatures	
Volumetric capacitive	No radiation	Unreliable False alarms	Volumetric
Capacitive proximity	No radiation	Limited use	Objects
Vibration	Simple	Vulnerable Stable environment required	Obsolescent Fences
Acoustic	No radiation	Not effective in noisy locations	Strong rooms Vaults
Fibreoptic	Simple	Avoidable Expensive to repair	Fences Under water Uneven ground
Passive optical	Simple	Vulnerable	Dark areas Vaults
Differential air pressure			Obsolescent Vaults
Liquid pressure	Works on any terrain	Expensive to maintain	Linear external
Magnetic	Reliable	Only vehicles detected Unreliable	Small external areas

6.6.2   To begin with, the whole system must be designed and installed by a single organisation, so that the components are matched for performance, sensitivity and reliability.

6.6.3   A decision must be taken as to whether there is to be an intruder detection system for the external area of the site. This will depend on the need and the practicability; the latter is determined by:

      The nature of the perimeter barrier

      The climate (winds or other phenomena lead to false alarms)

      The activities of the neighbours

If a system is needed then it must be decided whether the fence itself is the base for the detectors and though this might seem the most logical place, it should be avoided if possible. Fences are difficult and expensive to maintain, and if detectors are fixed to them this maintenance must always be carried out; the sensors used have to be very sensitive and require high maintenance themselves: and lastly, the outside of the fence is likely to be exposed to too much interference from passers-by, neighbours and scratching animals. Detectors, then, may only be fitted to the fence in high maintenance, high security areas such as nuclear power stations. Suitable devices are:

Beam interruption detectors (on top of walls)

Vibration detectors

Fibreoptic detectors

The external area is a more practical place to install detectors, particularly if a sterile area can be declared immediately inside the perimeter fence, fig 6.9. This zone should be wide enough to prevent bridging or jumping (say 4 m) and ideally should itself be separated by a second fence. Suitable devices are:

Beam interruption detectors (level terrain)

Radiowave doppler detectors (manned sites only)

Vibration detectors (seismic)

Acoustic detectors (geophones)

Liquid pressure sensors

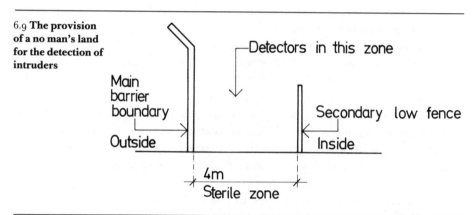

6.9 **The provision of a no man's land for the detection of intruders**

6.6.4 Simple, stable physical devices are not the best for external use because of the unstable environment and the loss of performance as they gradually deteriorate.

6.6.5 The building envelope is the most common line of detection, followed by the use of volumetric devices in the interior spaces. The most reliable systems are those which are physically stable; that is to say, no change of state is involved between the watch and alarm modes, and there is no measure required of a changing environment. These are followed by those devices with moving parts such as protective switches and lastly—as far as reliability is concerned—by the movement detectors which need to monitor environmental changes typical of human movement.

6.6.6 For the building envelope, suitable devices are:

Continuous wiring (windows, doors, rooflights)

Foil on glass (windows, glazed doors)

Protective switches (windows, doors, rooflights)

Rigid printed circuit wiring (doors)

Vacuum glass (windows)
Vibration detectors (windows, doors, walls, rooflights)
Acoustic detectors (walls)

6.6.7   For the interior of the building, suitable devices are:
Protective switches (internal doors)
Rigid printed circuit wiring (internal doors)
Pressure mats (floors)
Beam interruption detectors (doors, corridors)
Radiowave doppler detectors (spaces)
Ultrasonic detectors (spaces)
Passive infra-red detectors (spaces, corridors)
Volumetric capacitance detectors (spaces)
Acoustic detectors (spaces)
Passive optical detectors (dark spaces)
Differential air pressure detectors (small closed spaces)

6.6.8   In many buildings there are particular items requiring protection, either during occupied hours, as in museums and art galleries, or against special risks at night, such as safes or confidential filing cabinets. In addition, the hardware of the intruder detection systems themselves requires special protection against tampering. Suitable devices for the protection of individual items are:
Foil on glass (showcases)
Protective switches (showcases, cabinets, pictures)
Rigid printed circuit wiring (cabinets, safes)
Pressure mats (in front of showcases, safes)
Vacuum glass (showcases)
Capacitive proximity (pictures, sculpture, safes)
Vibration detectors (safes, cabinets, showcases)

6.6.9   The protection of empty buildings and those which are partially complete is a field which has not received much attention to date, although there are many examples of vandalism and arson of empty premises. Temporary protection can be provided by vibration detectors fixed to the floor and it will probably be necessary to connect to a telephone calling system.

6.7   Wiring and power supply

6.7.1   There are several ways in which the wiring of an intruder detection system can be arranged to add to the uncertainty of the criminal and to make his task more difficult. On the other hand, it is clear that the wiring has a degree of vulnerability because it is relatively unprotected by tamper-proof casings. It is probable that wiring will remain as the connection medium for alarm systems:

optical fibres are expensive and there are considerable problems when they break; radios need batteries, must be checked more frequently and are subject to interference; and signals passed through other building wiring such as mains reduce the integrity of the security system.

6.7.2   Many of the detailed technical requirements for wiring are set out in BS 4737: Part 2: Section 2.1: 1977 and there are additional principles followed by individual alarm companies as part of their own policy. It is important that the method of wiring is not obvious and that records should not be available. The wires themselves must not be marked or colour-coded and they should be concealed as far as possible.

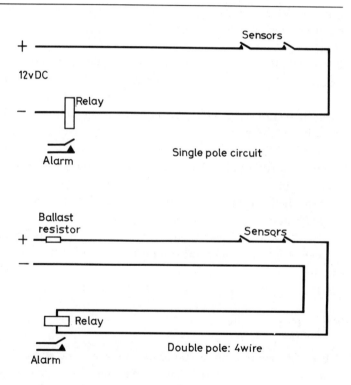

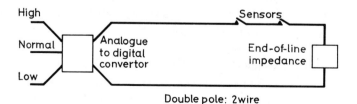

6.10 **Single and double pole circuitry. Double pole wiring must be used on detector circuits**

6.7.3 Wiring should be run in conduit, in a roof space, in trunking or an inaccessible void. There is no doubt that conduit systems are more secure and it should be possible to have these installed with draw wires during construction, without compromising the secrecy of the system.

6.7.4 The circuit configuration varies. A simple single conductor arrangement can be made ineffective by short-circuiting and so, on detection circuits, a double pole circuit must be used. The diagrams show how an alarm is generated when short circuiting is attempted, fig 6.10.

6.7.5 The other simple variation on the detection circuit is the choice of an open or closed configuration; i.e. whether the sensor is required to make the circuit to generate an alarm, or to break it. It must not be possible for the intruder to discover which by inspection.

6.7.6 It must not be possible to put the alarm system out of action by disconnecting the mains power supply, so some form of self-contained power suppy is essential. Rechargeable batteries can be included with the equipment or inside a separate secure casing. They are on permanent charge, and should the mains fail, must be able to maintain normal operation for eight hours. A separate system is required within the casing of the external audible alarm and must sound for 30 minutes. Alternatively, the system can be powered solely by batteries with no mains connection, in which case the minimum operational times are 75% of the battery shelf life in normal operation plus 4 hours in an alarm condition; the batteries in the external audible device must run it for 2 hours.

There is a move away from standby battery systems because it is felt that the change of power supply and complication reduces the overall reliability; because the rechargeable batteries are likely to receive little maintenance; and because modern systems require very little power to run.

6.8   Control units

6.8.1 The control unit is responsible for accepting and processing the input from detection devices, actuating signalling equipment accordingly, and for opening, closing and testing the intruder alarm system. Its complexity is directly dependent on the nature and extent of the system as a whole. Single simple domestic systems are fitted with a matching control unit, but there is a rise in complexity with larger systems because of the zoning necessary, the different detection circuits incorporated, and the probable inclusion of other systems such as fire detection.

The main property of the microprocessor in intruder detection systems is its ability to sample more input data. This means that with modern equipment:

More and varied sensors can be connected to a single control

Greater analysis of sensed signals can be carried out, enabling false alarms to be identified and avoided more easily

A variety of responses can be selected within the system

6.8.2 The control equipment must be inside the building and should not be visible from outside. It must be housed in a substantial casing made from 1.2 mm mild steel or its equivalent and it must be fitted with an anti-tamper device: i.e. it must be locked, and if opened the alarm must sound immediately.

6.8.3 Each zone or detector circuit must have its own display on the control unit so that it is obvious whereabouts in the premises an alarm has been raised. The system must be able to show this whether it is in the open or closed condition as, clearly, both intrusions and false alarms are of interest during occupied hours as well as at night.

6.8.4 The equipment should not respond to short anomalies in the detection circuits, as these are characteristic of some sensors. It will signal an alarm raised by a detection circuit which lasts more than 800 ms.

6.8.5 As the control units must be within the building, there must also be a legitimate way of entry without tripping the alarm allowed. A route must be designated from the outside to the control unit for entry, and for exit. It is obvious that there are potential weaknesses in security here and the facility must be arranged most carefully:

>A time control can be included so that the system opens and closes automatically at certain times. There are few premises where this can work successfully.

>A delay is arranged, so that there is enough time to proceed from the entry door to the control unit. This can include a control over the designated route so that the delay suppresses only those signals generated by detectors on that route.

>A shunt lock is fitted to the entry door. It contains a microswitch so that, when the key is turned, the alarm system is muted.

>A shunt switch has a similar function but need not be connected to the door and is normally outside the protected area

A shunt system increases the danger of personal attack and briefly—at opening and closing time—removes the protection of the intruder detection system. This is because the keyholder will be in front of an open door with the alarm system inoperative: see also section 6.13 below. Shunt switches can be arranged to operate on partial systems, routes or zones.

6.8.6 The system must not be able to be closed if an alarm condition exists, and the normal closing procedure should not itself generate an alarm.

6.8.7 No documentation regarding the control unit must be kept on the premises except for opening and closing routines, which should be permanently kept adjacent to the unit.

6.9 Signalling

6.9.1 Intruder detection systems are often classified according to their signalling method. As the signal is the end product it is rightly seen as crucial, and alarm companies pay great attention to both the hardware and the operation of signalling systems. There are three main categories:

> Audible alarms
> Remote telephonic
> Private wire

6.9.2 Audible alarm systems are the simplest and are fitted in about 35% of the new installations each year. As they are the cheapest type, there is a concentration of use in housing and small shops. A sounder (usually a bell) is fitted inside a casing outside the premises, and must be located where it is not likely to be damaged or interfered with. Any visible connections must also be protected in conduit. It is activated by an alarm generated at the control unit, or by tampering with the casing, or by disconnection, and it is self-powered, capable of running for 30 minutes (rechargeable batteries) or 2 hours (replaceable batteries). Further response arises from either the public or the police noticing the alarm. In fact under pollution control legislation, the bell is not allowed to ring for an extended period as the keyholder may not be available and a nuisance is caused. The Department of the Environment's code requires bells to be stopped within 20 minutes and this is enforced by the local Environmental Health Officer. The better quality units have a variable time unit on the bell. An additional unit can be fitted inside the premises.

6.9.3 Remote telephonic devices are intended to notify either the police or an alarm company by automatic dialling through the normal public telephone network, and these account for about 50% of the new installations each year. They may be used with or without an audible device and, if a bell is used it may incorporate a delaying mechanism up to 15 minutes in order to give the police a chance to arrive. The delay is variable and should be set in consultation with the police and the insurance company. The bell should be constructed as set out above but should not sound in the case of personal attack.

The weakness of this type of system is that it relies on the telephone line and exchange equipment, both of which are outside the control of the building owner or alarm company. The telephone line must be reserved for outgoing calls only during the time that the alarm system is closed or should be ex-directory. The telephone wires should be underground and the system itself must monitor the connection; if any fault is detected, the bell delay is cut out and an alarm will sound within 30 seconds if one is signalled.

The automatic dialling equipment should not be visible from outside the premises. The mechanism can work by disc, tape or electronic dialling and either dials 999 and asks for the police, or dials the number of the alarm company. In the first case, only one try is permitted and if the 999 call fails it cannot be repeated so the system reverts to an audible signal only. If an alarm company is called, the equipment can attempt the connection repeatedly, usually up to five times.

Even so, there can be misunderstandings and faults with recorded voice communications, so modern systems which dial alarm companies are digital communications, where there is some mutual interrogation and verification between the equipment at either end, and where the message itself is shorter, more reliable and better understood.

6.9.4   In high security premises, a private wire system would always be used, and about 10% of new installations use this method of signalling. Once again, it can be used with or without an audible alarm in the same way as the telephone system, but it does not rely on the ordinary public telephone lines. The private wire supplied by British Telecom leads either to the local police station or to the alarm company. However, it is gradually becoming a national policy that the police do not want this type of alarm in their stations, and it is expected that this option will cease to be available.

The advantages of a private wire are substantial: it is always open, never engaged; it can be monitored continuously; and it can accept opening and closing signals. However, such private wires are becoming more expensive, especially over long distances, and the economic catchment area around alarm company central stations is becoming smaller.

6.10   Networks

6.10.1 In order to maintain the areas covered by alarm companies with private wire systems, and to make such cover economic, adjacent subscribers may share multiplex signals without any loss of security. Some alarm companies have installed local 'collectors' to extend this facility so that there is only one long distance line from each locality. It is anticipated that this type of system will expand.

6.10.2 There are also several proposals for local area networks to be set up to carry digital information and it is possible that alarm companies will make some use of these, though once again, a part of the signalling path would be out of control.

Selection Chart 6.2. Alarm signalling

Signal	Advantages	Disadvantages	Use
Sounder	Common Simple Obvious Cheap Self contained	Nuisance Some vulnerability	General
Remote Telephonic (Auto-dial)	Relatively cheap	Relies on Telecom equipment Single 999 call only allowed Some vulnerability	General
Private wire	Most secure Always available	Expensive	Higher security
Networks	Secure Digital information Cheaper than private wire	Shared connections	Higher security

6.11   Response

6.11.1 The intruder is detected, the alarm system is activated—so what is to happen next? The time between the alarm being raised and the arrival of the police or security patrol is important and to a certain extent uncontrollable. Some criminals will race a detection system, knowing that particularly on domestic premises they will have a few minutes to steal a substantial amount of goods before the police arrive. Nevertheless, better an intruder who is pressed for time than one who can work at his leisure.

6.11.2 Police response time is governed by the location, police workload, patrol patterns and the likely cause of the alarm; if the premises have a record of false alarms then the police may suspend emergency response and merely visit the premises in the normal course of a patrol. It is the police who must be involved in the apprehension of any criminals, however, and so it is they who are expected to attend alarm calls.

6.11.3 There is a possibility that in future it will be the alarm company who send uniformed patrols to respond to alarm calls in advance of the police being called, but this is a matter of some political debate within the security industry.

6.12   Control rooms

6.12.1 Automatic dialling systems and private wires which call alarm companies are received in special control rooms. As the room is itself part of the alarm system it must be physically secure to a high standard, and ideally will be linked to control rooms in other areas so that a continous level of monitoring is possible. A number of procedures must be followed quite rigidly in order to preserve the integrity of the many alarm installations which terminate in the room.

6.12.1 As a matter of policy, all subscriber keyholders are given a card and personal number so that they can be identified before discussing their installations on the telephone, whether in an emergency or not.

6.12.3 If an intruder alarm is registered, the control room staff will notify the police and they in turn will notify the registered keyholder, who is expected to attend the premises and notify the alarm company of the cause of the alarm. Notification of the police by the control room is often complicated by geography and the different areas of coverage of control rooms, police authorities and telephone exchanges. Some police forces are reluctant to accept notification from outside their area, even if the premises concerned are within. In addition, the security companies are heavily discouraged from using the 999 system and if they do so, there will be complaints against them.

6.12.4 The direct line may become faulty, in which case the alarm company will attempt to contact a keyholder direct unless they believe the system to be closed, in which case the police will be called. The police will be called immediately in any case where a fault develops in a system fitted with a personal attack facility.

6.13 False alarms

6.13.1 The frequency of false alarms in intruder detection systems has been a considerable problem over the years everywhere that the systems are fitted. The usual figure which is quoted is that 95% of alarms raised are false; and though this is a massive proportion it must be said that many of these false alarms are in fact evidence of a potential intruder having been scared away. A balance must be struck between the risk of false alarms and the different risk of under-providing security. The security industry is conscious of the problem and over the last few years has made great efforts towards reducing false alarms. It is also noticeable that since the publication of BS 4166: 1979 and BS 4737: 1977–79 the incidence has reduced and there is certainly less deliberate or careless ringing of the bells. More diagnostic procedures can be included in modern microprocessor based systems and this too helps to eliminate faults.

6.13.2 There are several typical causes of false alarms; in order of frequency:
Misuse by subscriber
Equipment failure (including poor specification)
Environmental faults
Telephone line faults

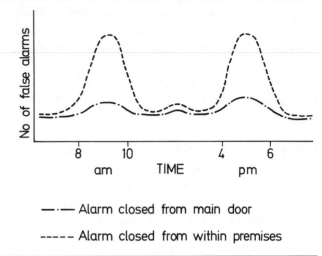

6.11 **Opening and closing disciplines can have a dramatic effect on the incidence of false alarms**

—·— Alarm closed from main door

----- Alarm closed from within premises

Many of the subscriber faults occur as bad management of opening and closing routines; examples can be heard in any high street each morning and evening when shops open and close. Such bells are, not surprisingly, ignored by passers-by and police alike, though there are many cases of intrusions taking place at these times and for this reason. Equipment failure can arise from age, damage, poor quality, a wrong specification or the wrong calibration. The hair-trigger principle on which many alarms work does not help. Some detectors are sensitive to environmental factors such as heat, vibration, noise, and dirt, which may not have been apparent at the time of installation. Faults monitored in telephone connections will in some circumstances give an alarm condition.

6.13.3 The police vary from force to force in their attitude to false alarms: all are concerned and some simply withdraw their response to premises with a poor record, while others adopt a more constructive attitude to diagnosing the reasons. This enables them to build up a useful bank of experience and they are able to give real advice on the installation and use of new systems. To give an example, one force exerts strong pressure on alarm companies with regard to lock-up shop premises and insists that the alarm system is opened and closed from the main entrance door. Although this caused some resistance because of the immediate security weakness (see section 6.8 above) there has been a dramatic drop in false alarms, as can be seen from the diagram, and it is felt that, in the broader sense, security has been improved, fig 6.11.

6.13.4 Should the problem continue to the extent that Government action is necessary to bring about an acceptable level, as has happened in other countries, then some reconsideration of alarm philosophy will be needed. The first principle under review will probably be the fail safe operation whereby any fault in a system automatically generates an alarm.

6.13.5 Much of the false ringing occurs as a result of poor re-setting procedures following a previous activation of the system. If an alarm sounds and there is no obvious cause, it should not simply be reset and left to repeat the fault; some positive diagnosis must be made of the reason. Some systems have a single response and must be reset manually after an alarm, while others reset automatically after a predetermined period, even if there has been no attendance. In the former case, there is clearly a security weakness, for criminals can deliberately trigger an alarm and then enter the premises later, knowing that they have in effect disabled the alarm.

6.13.6 Alarm fittings and wiring can get accidentally damaged just like any other part of the building or its services. The installation must be regarded with care, and water and heat sources must be kept away; any faults are more likely to cause false alarms than to make the system inoperative.

Changes in the building layout or alterations to its structure should be taken into account and the alarm company asked to examine them. On no account should building maintenance staff be allowed to modify alarm wiring. Regular maintenance checks by the alarm company will also help to detect any illicit tampering or masking.

6.13.7 The British Security Industry Association has produced a code of practice concerned with the management of false alarms on the basis that positive action is required by the alarm companies with respect to their own installations. The first step is to nominate an individual within the alarm company to have a responsibility for dealing with false alarms. This enables a higher level of skill and experience to be available, especially for recurrent problems, and brings the whole matter into the formal management of the company so that the appropriate resources can be allocated and faults are not left in the normal reactive maintenance responsibility of field engineers. The code sets out a sequence of action for false alarms which is designed to bring more resources to bear progressively on the more recurrent problems.

6.14 Regulatory bodies

6.14.1 The BSIA, mentioned above, is a trade association and though not concerned solely with intruder alarm installations, it is expected to contribute in general terms to the philosophy of their design.

6.14.2 The British Standards Institution publishes a comprehensive standard (BS 4737: Parts 1 and 2: 1977–1979) and much of the contents have been discussed in sections above. BS 4166: 1979 covers private wire connections.

6.14.3 The National Supervisory Council for Intruder Alarms also publishes

Codes of Practice and maintains a list of approved installers. It tests equipment—particularly power supplies—and it inspects installations and issues certificates. It also enforces compliance with the BS amongst its members.

6.15   Installation

6.15.1 The procedures followed during installation and commissioning of intruder detection systems are most important for their subsequent operation. The object is that the whole system should not only provide the protection which has been designed, but that also the user should understand it and be capable of operating it satisfactorily.

6.15.2 First of all, the installation must be tested. The detection circuits, power supplies and signalling equipment must all work correctly and be electrically sound. Proper records are prepared including any modifications found necessary. Secondly, for systems with remote signalling where beam interruption, vibration or volumetric detectors are used, there must be a seven-day settling down period free of false alarms before the signalling equipment is connected.

6.15.3 Lastly, the installation must be handed over to the subscriber. This is a formal procedure and should be carried out by a qualified alarm company representative (who should not have been involved in the installation). The subscriber must be trained in the operation of the system, particularly with the routines for opening and closing it, and the action that he is to take for both normal and emergency service. The NSCIA Certificate of Status and Competence should be issued, together with full and clear written instructions for operation. The local police must then be informed that the installation is in operation.

6.16   Maintenance

6.16.1 The British Standard (BS 4737: Section 2.2: 1977) includes specific provisions for maintenance and records relating to intruder alarm systems. There are two separate sections dealing respectively with those systems which only have audible signalling and those which have a remote signalling connection; the latter sets out more stringent requirements, because the systems tend to be more complicated and because the police demand higher reliability if they are to be called out automatically.

6.16.2 The BS is intended to form the basis for the contract between the subscriber and the alarm company. Such a contract is necessary and is normally signed over a five-year period; it is subject to the code of practice published by the NSCIA. The alarm company will usually be split into divisions covering:
    Sales

    Installation
    Service
Servicing personnel require specialist training, particularly for detecting faults on complex installations or those which include computerised equipment.

6.16.3 Routine maintenance must be carried out at six-monthly intervals (twelve-monthly for audible signalling installations). The company representative must be able to identify himself and the police must be informed that the system is under test during these visits. Clearly they should be carried out in the shortest practicable time and they will include tests on:

    Installation location and siting against recorded details
    Operation of detectors
    Flexible connections
    Power supplies
    Control equipment
    Automatic dialling and direct line equipment
    Audible alarms
    Operation

6.16.4 The alarm company must also keep records of the installation, which should include a log of all alarm calls, visits, alterations and maintenance. The record must of course be kept in a safe place with limited access, and for additional security, the name and location of the subscriber should be coded.

6.16.5 Maintenance is not restricted to the installation itself. The user has a responsibility for those parts of the building under his control which affect the operation of the alarm. Doors and windows can be damaged, for example, either causing an alarm condition to register or in the opposite case, making a detector inoperable. Small animals and birds allowed in can activate movement detectors and the operation of these can also be made more or less sensitive by the stacking level and physical stability of stock.

6.16.6 It is essential to keep the police informed as to the status of an intruder alarm system, its maintenance and any alterations. It is also important that they should be informed when a system is removed.

6.17 Cost

6.17.1 Protection costs money and protection in depth can cost a great deal of money. The value of goods to be protected must be considered and it should be realised that comprehensive protection is likely to entail substantial expense, but that no intruder alarm system will be completely reliable or proof against attack.

6.17.2 Guidance on cost is difficult to give in general terms because of the difference in design between one building and another. To give some idea of the sums involved:

> In domestic premises, a simple bell device with 5–8 simple detectors, say £300
>
> In a single high street shop unit, a standard commercial installation, say £1000

More complex systems will obviously cost more and this will depend on a number of other factors. There is a proportional rise with the number of electronic detectors, for example, and connections to alarm company central stations are bound to be more expensive, though some savings may be possible by multiplexing or connecting into local connectors.

6.17.3 There are several budget systems on the market aimed at domestic and small commercial premises. They usually consist of isolated electronic movement detectors with minimal control equipment. These devices tend to lack reliability, and it should be noted that their failure is likely to give false alarms rather than allow intrusions.

6.17.4 As there are usually no rebates on insurance premiums following the installation of intruder alarms, there is no direct saving to be set against the cost. It has been suggested however that this cost should itself be regarded as a single premium insurance.

6.18   Integrated systems

6.18.1 The interior alarm may be part of an integrated computer-controlled security system which will control and record:

Intruder alarms
Fire alarms
Plant failure alarms
Environmental sensors
Access control
Roll call of occupants
External lighting
Patrols
Personal attack
Theft of tagged goods
Tampering

6.18.2 Development of such systems is in its early stages but is seen by the industry as the way ahead. Details are set out in chapter 9.

Checklist 6
Intruder detection

Systems

> Check with police and insurance company
> Define design life
> Check for wear and changes in resistance or new
> modes of attack
> Define risk level of protection required
> Estimate consequences of failure

Geometry

> Decide on linear, volumetric or point protection

Sensors

> Specify type for location
> Ensure compatibility within whole system

Wiring and power supply

> Comply with BS 4737 Part 2
> Do not mark or code wiring
> Route with care
> Select open or closed circuit
> Use double-pole wiring
> Provide standby power

Control units

> Locate discreetly inside building
> Designate access route and procedure
> Keep documentation remote

Signalling

Select audible or silent or telephonic
Protect sounder
Private wire system for highest security
Avoid auto-dialling for high security

False alarms

Avoid poor or cheapest equipment
Establish proper opening and closing routines
Apply correct maintenance to equipment
Investigate causes of false alarms and rectify:
    nominate individual
Protect alarm installation and wiring from damage
Alarm company only to carry out all modifications

Installation

Ensure proper testing procedure
Carry out handover checks
Carry out handover training and provide instructions

Maintenance

Keep records
Keep maintenance contract

7 Access control

7.1 The principle

7.1.1 The term access control is often used in the security industry to refer only to the more sophisticated electronic systems. This is misleading, however, and it must be established in a much broader sense that the principle encompasses the whole discipline of allowing access to authorised personnel and denying it to others by whatever means are appropriate.

7.1.2 It is assumed in this chapter that the physical barriers have been established and that they are reliable: that is to say, for example, that all doors once locked are as effective as the walls and roof. For this reason, the *strength* of doors and the constructional *strength* of locking mechanisms has been set out in chapters 3 and 4 so that the authorised use of these doors by unlocking them could be considered separately here. This is an important distinction and bears repetition: the strongest door can be opened by a keyholder, whereas the most secure locking mechanism is useless when applied to a flimsy door.

A further distinction to be drawn is that between access control and *secure* access control. The former may be introduced within a building for any number of managerial reasons and will be quite satisfactory for routine operation. If a system is to be crime-resistant however, a much higher level of planning and operation will be necessary. It is important that the user should be under no illusions as to the value of his system: there often exists a false idea of security which arises through ignorance.

7.1.3 In a secure system, access for people is not always necessary, and much thought should be given to alternative means of communication. In fact, most of the practical problems experienced in access control systems arise directly from human characteristics which cause the system to decay in its operation and to become distrusted. The management of a system is therefore crucial and must include both maintenance of the hardware and response to infractions. This response must be local to be effective.

7.1.4 A secure access control system should stand in its own right and should not need to be supported in its normal operation by intruder detection systems. There is, however, an advantage in appointing a single organisation to install all aspects of the security system so that an overall level of protection is attained.

7.2   Planning

7.2.1   Access control is not limited to the final exit/first entrance door. The way in which a building is occupied may well require a number of access points, both on the perimeter and within, and different methods may be necessary at each. For example, a hotel will need to control the movement of:

> Residents
> Visitors to residents
> Restaurant and bar customers
> Staff
> Goods deliveries
> Maintenance personnel
> Vehicles to the car park

Details of systems for hotels are given later.

7.2.2   There is no doubt that the design of systems for special or complex buildings is difficult, and the planning of these, however carefully done, should incorporate a review phase so that any shortcomings found in use can be remedied.

7.2.3   The need for a system of access control is not only generated by the wish to prevent theft. It can also eliminate the need for dangerous searches in the event of terrorist attack or fire. In addition, there are premises in which only limited numbers of people are present at night, and their personal safety and their perception of it is more assured if access to their area is properly controlled. This is particularly relevant to office premises where computers are run all night, attended by a skeleton staff, and the contrast in them is most apparent: by day both the premises and the streets around are likely to be bustling with activity, whereas at night the building is empty and the business area deserted.

7.2.4.   If an access control system is to be introduced to existing premises, whether in the form of additional locks or electronics, then organisational changes will almost certainly be necessary. Occupants must be familiarised with the reasoning behind the installation as well as its operation, and there may well be problems of political acceptability. The hardware is the least important part of the planning.

In fact, the system itself should be kept as simple as possible. If queues develop at points of access, it may be assumed that failure is likely, because the pressures for abuse will not be resistable for long. For this reason, application of a system to the 'front' door alone should normally be resisted, especially at peak times; adverse weather will make the pressure exerted by queues even worse. In addition, it will be difficult to deal with visitors. Of course, this is not always practical and is particularly difficult in housing schemes, which are discussed in section 7.7.

7.2.5 Although the object of access control is to regulate the entry of people, nearly all the systems available ignore the people themselves and respond to tokens carried by them, such as keys, electronic cards, or combinations of numbers. There are inherent security weaknesses here, as clearly these tokens may be carried by unauthorised persons or may be physically duplicated. In the case of memorised codes, even though there is a more personal attachment, this is outweighed by the fact that illicit possession is undetectable.

Personal verification has always presented problems. The most obvious method is by facial recognition by security staff, compared against a photograph. This is not entirely satisfactory as there is always a reduction in the efficiency of recognition over a period of time and a gradual decay arising from familiarity; if such a method is used, rotating contact staff will maintain a higher level of security. It is also the most expensive method: 24-hour coverage of a point all year round with one man on duty will cost about £30,000 per year.

Other methods of personal recognition are in various stages of development:

Signature recognition by an optical scan linked to a computer is quite reliable but time-consuming (often requiring more than one signature) and inappropriate for mass use. There is an error rate of about 5% (which means in effect that 5% of authorised personnel are refused admission)

Voice recognition again involving computer analysis of a sample against stored data is promising, though the error rate remains stubbornly around 1%

Thumbprints operate in a similar way to signatures and the error rate is similar. There are practical difficulties in producing samples for examination

Though it is likely that the increased computing power becoming available will make these and other personal recognition methods feasible in practice in the reasonably near future, none are suitable for general use at present.

7.2.6 Visitors require special authority for access. They should always be treated as visitors and should not be incorporated into the routine system: no keys or coded cards should be issued to them. Visitors should be seen by appointment and escorted both in and out: see chapter 4. Some form of identification disc or pass, colour coded for date, will also be appropriate where strangers are otherwise unlikely to be challenged.

7.2.7 Another traditional weakness in operation is the access allowed to cleaners, which has already been mentioned in chapter 4.

7.3   Locking

7.3.1   The decision to fit locks to doors should not be taken too lightly. A policy frequently adopted during planning that 'all doors shall be lockable' is an easy way out, but if it is followed there will be problems:

   The reason for locking a particular door becomes blurred

   Key inventory and control is unnecessarily complicated

   The money available for locks is thinly spread and the quality of each is
      reduced accordingly

   Money is wasted on superfluous locks

In any case, it is usually a simple matter to fit additional locks to doors, whereas money cannot be recovered from those fitted unnecessarily.

   In access control terms, locks do not always need to be highly secure or resistant to attack, and the example quoted in chapter 4 of the cleaner's cupboard and stationery store illustrate the point.

7.4   Locks

7.4.1   The history of locks is fascinating and has received much attention. Ever since man has built shelter, he has felt the need to secure it. The first locks were probably constructions of cord or rope tied in various complex ways so that they operated as a kind of intruder detection system as well as a securing device. Simple wooden latches followed and in Egyptian times timber beams were used across doors, held in place by falling pins: the pins were raised by pegs on a separate piece of wood used as a key and the principle is identical to that used in pin-tumbler locks today.

   The craft of lock-making continued to develop through the ages and it is clear that locks of astonishing ingenuity were constructed in early times. Unfortunately, it is often the keys which survive rather than the locks themselves and some are in forms so strange that it is impossible to deduce the mechanism of the lock which they operated. In Germany, the Lock and Hardware Museum at Velbert near Wuppertal houses an international collection of some 10000 items.

   In mediaeval times, most locks operated on the principle of *wards*, with both locks and complex keys being made individually by hand. In the eighteenth century society became more acquisitive and the industrial revolution made available new metals and new technology, encouraging a general atmosphere of invention. These factors fostered both the need and the ability to design new locking mechanisms, and the first lasting new development was the *lever lock*, arising from Robert Baron's patent double acting tumbler of 1778. The *Bramah* lock was patented in 1784 and is still in use today as a high security mechanism; it combines the Egyptian sliding principle with the rotary action seen in some Roman and many mediaeval locks.

   In the nineteenth century competition between manufactures was fierce and in

7.1 **General lock types and their terminology**

A Lever mortice lock (upright)
B Horizontal lever mortice lock
C Cylinder mortice lock
D Cylinder mortice deadlock
E Cylinder rim nightlatch
F Cylinder rim drawback lock

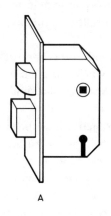

A

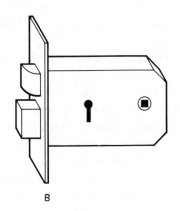

B

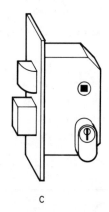

C

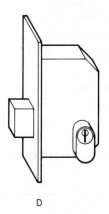

D

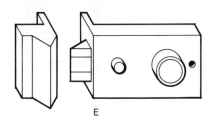

E

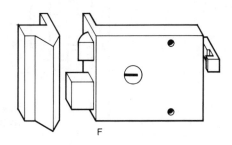

F

the spirit of the age many outrageous claims were made. These led to a spate of public lockpicking contests and challenges, in which various 'impregnable' locks were offered, with prizes in the event of their being overcome. A famous name then (as now) was Chubb who offered their six-lever lock and were dismayed to find it opened in half an hour by a veteran American lockpicker called Hobbs. The same man set to work on a Bramah lock and though he opened it eventually, it took 44 hours and entailed making a special key, forcing him to declare it virtually unpickable. By this time lever mechanisms were beginning to incorporate detector levers to reveal picking attempts, detainers, false notching, steel rollers in the bolt and monitor levers.

The invention of the pin-tumbler lock by Yale introduced another mechanism which is still in common use today. It combined a mechanism which was good in principle, enabling many key differs, with the acknowledged advantage of a small keyhole which restricted access to the interior workings of the lock.

Modern developments have not been so radical and, in the main, have been restricted to the introduction of new materials and much more accurate machining. Much ingenuity has been applied to the design of locks (and much to defeating them!) and there is no doubt that lockmakers retain a sense of history and pride in their craft today. However, there are, and have been throughout the centuries only two mechanical principles by which the security of key-operated locks is achieved. One is by means of fixed obstructions to prevent wrong keys from entering or turning in the lock. The other method, which is much superior, employs one or more movable restraints which must be arranged in pre-selected positions by a key before the bolt is allowed to move.

7.4.2   The configuration of a lock is a matter of specification and usually depends on the location and use. The case, bolts and surface operation are the main variants and fig 7.1 shows the range generally available together with the appropriate terminology. The following paragraphs set out the mechanisms currently in use and their relevance to key security.

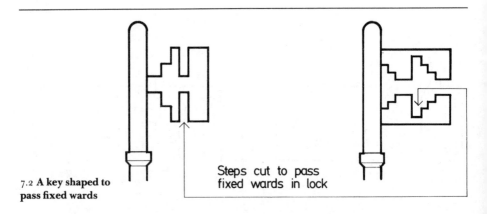

Steps cut to pass
fixed wards in lock

7.2 **A key shaped to pass fixed wards**

7.4.3 *Warded locks* are the cheapest kind and, as might be expected, the least secure. Wards are fixed obstructions behind the keyhole and the key must be shaped to pass over them before it can turn the mechanism, fig 7.2. Although the wards can be complex, a key can be cut away to miss them completely, and this is the origin of the term skeleton key. In fact this is the only type of lock in which a skeleton key is effective. Nowadays very few locks of this kind are made, but the principle is still used to provide more differs on lever locks (qv) than would be available by using levers alone.

On a similar principle, the shape of the keyhole can be altered to restrict entry of wrong keys, fig 7.3. This is more applicable to pin tumbler locks (qv) but occasionally bullets are fixed to the bit of the key to correspond with slots in the keyhole. Differs are limited. A further variant in the size of the key itself, and differences may be introduced in the diameter of the key shank and keyhole. Once again, differs are extremely limited.

Warded locks will not be appropriate in any situation where a degree of security is required.

7.3 The keyhole shape can vary to provide limited differs

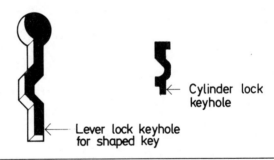

Cylinder lock keyhole

Lever lock keyhole for shaped key

7.4.4 *Lever locks* contain a mechanism in which a lever is raised by the key so that a peg attached to the bolt may move through a gating which is machined into it. The form of the gating varies and the height of the notch on the bit of the key must match, as fig 7.4 shows.

The number of key differs can obviously be increased if a number of levers are placed side by side, and though statements are often made as to the security of a particular number of levers, the matter is not that simple. Firstly, most locks are operated from both sides, so the key must be symmetrical; secondly, one of the notches must operate the bolt stump directly, so the lever at the other extreme must be the same height for the same reasons of reversibility.

In a four lever lock with a five step key, one step operates the bolt and the opposing step is thus determined; of the remaining three steps, two must be symmetrical, and so the same height, and one remains; there are thus only two differing levers and if each has three heights available the differs are 3^2 which is 9. However, keys with all steps the same look like blanks and are unacceptable, so the practical number of differs available with a four lever lock is only 4. In practice this is raised to 48 by including twelve differing wards but it can be seen that key security is still minimal. Close manufacturing tolerances can raise the number of heights available on each step though this is usually only worthwhile if more levers are also included.

If a fifth lever is introduced the differs are improved considerably: three of the levers can vary and if, in addition, seven different heights are available for each step, a maximum of 7^3 differs are possible (343) which is reduced in practice to 250.

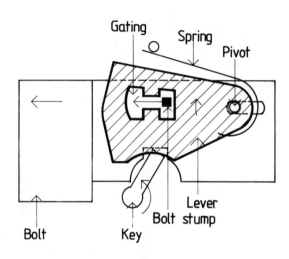

7.4 The mechanism of the common lever lock

If the key steps are released from the need to throw the bolt by including an additional mechanism, then on the same basis as above, 7^4 differs are possible (2401) which, again, is reduced in practice to 1000. This figure meets the requirement of BS 3621: 1980.

Seven to ten lever locks are also available but in some cases the inclusion of extra levers is a substitute for the finer machining necessary in order to have extra lifts available on each one. The important factor is the number of key differs available before warding.

7.4.5 *Detainer locks* (Butters system) operate in a similar manner to lever locks except that a system of movable notched detainers is used instead of levers, fig 7.5. The notching in the ends of the detainers is engaged by a mechanical linkage and the greater flexibility offered by this system allows nine steps in the height of each lift of the detainer. In addition, there is a bolt-throwing mechanism and so, in a lock with 5 detainers—the most common—the maximum key differing is 9^5 (59049), which is reduced to a practical number of 25000. The practicability of overcoming the lock by trial of keys is eliminated as this number of keys weighs about one tonne! As warding is not used, skeletonising of the keys is useless.

The diagram shows an extra notch cut in the detainer; this notch is used where a master keyed system is needed: see section 7.5. Ordinary lever locks usually rely on warding for mastering facilities, so their flexibility and security are severely limited compared with the detainer mechanism.

Security locks manufactured in this way—such as the Chubb range—include various refinements in the mechanism, like false notching on the detainers, to prevent picking and may be regarded as unbeatable for most practical purposes.

Several other devices have been used in the past to increase the level of security, but most have been discontinued as unnecessary in the light of the high resistance obtained by modern standards of manufacture. One such device was the detector lever: an additional lever included in the lock for the express purpose of detecting trial of keys or attempts at picking: a false key or instrument would lift the lever into a special position so that when the correct key was inserted it would not operate until given a sharp reverse turn.

Where lever or detainer locks can be single sided (as in safes and strongrooms) the key differs available are greatly increased.

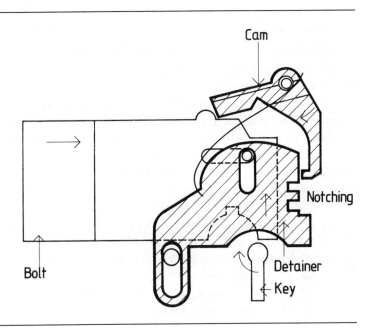

7.5 A Butters system or detainer lock

7.4.6 *Pin tumbler locks* are a form of cylinder lock invented by Yale in the nineteenth century. For many years they were expensive and so were not widely used. The original threaded cylinder was costly to manufacture, but modern through-cylinders are much more competitive. The principles of operation are simple and are illustrated in fig 7.6. The security of the locked cylinder is provided by the spring-loaded pin tumblers in sets of four, five or six which prevent the plug from rotating to operate the bolt. When the correct key is inserted the pins are lifted to a predetermined height and the split in each coincides with the joint between plug and cylinder barrel so that rotation is possible and the bolt can be thrown.

7.6 **The principles of pin-tumbler locks**

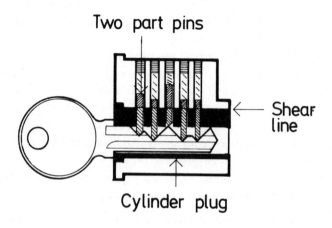

Two part pins

← Shear line

Cylinder plug

Keys of different sections are made and, with the variations in pin length, this enables the differs to be regarded as practically infinite with the better-made locks. Hundreds of thousands are available even on the simpler types.

It is in the nature of the mechanism that two-sided operation is only possible if the cylinder assembly is duplicated, though this in itself allows some flexibility in the configuration, as locks can be fitted with different operation on each side. The most common variants are: key one side and thumbturn on the other (used for escape doors) and key one side and the other side blank. Pin tumbler locks have many advantages, for example:

Practically infinite key differs
Ease of standard key replacement
Good key security when master keyed
High flexibility in master key systems
Keys are easily carried
All types of lock configuration can be suited together
Cylinders can be easily replaced

In security terms, however, they are physically vulnerable. Instead of the lock mechanism being securely contained in a steel case inside the door, as with lever locks, it is outside the case and exposed on the face of the door. Indeed, with the majority of cylinders the length is fixed by the number of pins and this means that the cylinder will often project from the face of the door, increasing its vulnerability still further.

The projection enables the whole cylinder to be gripped by a pipe-wrench and turned bodily or twisted off. Ordinary cylinder plugs can also be drilled out or punched through, shearing the pins. To counter this, some variants have tapered shrouds around the projecting cylinder and the plug and pins are hardened. Picking is also possible by the use of mechanical devices such as lock guns, which are carefully controlled by locksmiths and somewhat nervously regarded by police.

7.4.7 *Disc tumbler looks* are much more resistant to picking. They operate in a similar way to pin tumblers in that the key lines up shaped discs into a position where the cylinder is permitted to rotate. As the discs can be adjacent however, more can be included in the same space and it is common to see 10-disc cylinders offered as security locks. The cylinders are still vulnerable to physical attack, though some ranges—such as Ingersoll—include many features designed to reduce this as far as possible.

7.4.8 Though cylinder locks generally cannot provide the same strength as lever mortice locks, they are ideal for access control applications where flexibility may well be more important than resistance to physical attack.

There are several unorthodox cylinder locks which have been developed in an attempt to increase key security as well as the resistance to picking. The unorthodox itself adds to the general security of the mechanism. Examples are:

Magnetic locks
Kaba system
Zeiss Ikon system

7.4.9 *Magnetic locks* work on the pin tumbler principle except that instead of the pins being lifted by raised points on the key they are magnetised and can be repelled by like poles on magnetic inserts in the key. These inserts can be north or south poles or blanks. The keys are smooth and convenient to carry and high key security is claimed, though there are equal claims that the locks are easily defeated. Lock-guns cannot be used.

7.4.10 *The Kaba system* also operates on the pin tumbler principle but it includes four rows of pins on different axes, fig 7.7. The pins bear onto depressions specially machined in the key and differs are practically infinite. Mastering facilities are extensive and lock-guns cannot be used.

7.4.11 *Zeiss Ikon locks* are pin tumblers engineered to fine tolerances and some models include wings on the key similar to the bullets found on some lever keys. There is also an alarm facility incorporated in the mechanism to detect attacks, tampering, attempts at picking or trial of keys.

With all three of these unconventional systems it is difficult to obtain casual copies of the keys, as blanks are not commonly available: see 7.5.3.

7.7 Multiple axis pin-tumbler locks

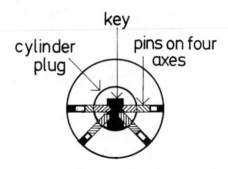

7.4.12 *The Bramah lock* also has an unconventional mechanism: slots in a small compact key correspond with a rotating barrel and discs which allows the bolt to be thrown. Its main use in the past has been for cabinet and despatch case locks and although this type of mechanism is available in the form of mortice deadlocks, the range is limited and it is not suitable for any extensive access control system.

7.4.13 *Combination, change-key* and *time locks* are more suited to strongrooms and are described in chapter 10.

7.4.14 Modern security locks are highly resistant to picking and, in any case, force is the more likely form of attack. Picking is not impossible however, and there are even publications (like the *Locksmith's Ledger* in the USA) which set out the correct methods to use.

Selection chart 7.1. Lock selection

Type	Advantage	Disadvantage	Use
Warded	Cheap	Minimal security	Limited
Lever	Cheap to medium (varies with number of levers) Reliable	Pickable Limited mastering	General (security varies from low to medium with number of levers)
Detainer	More secure More mastering capability	Relatively expensive	Security locks Master key systems
Pin tumbler **Disc tumbler**	Cheap to medium Extensive mastering Small key High security types available All types of locks	Vulnerable mechanism Some pickable	General Master key systems

7.5   Keying

7.5.1 Good key security and physical security go hand-in-hand. Keys should be respected for what they are—a means of opening a door—and kept in a secure place with formal control. They should not be lent or left where they can be taken or copied, nor should they be left in locks where they can be shaken out from the other side.

7.5.2 Key boxes hold a number of keys in such a way that those missing are immediately obvious. It is also easy to keep a register if keys are stored in this way. The boxes are themselves lockable (though not very secure) and the keys inside should therefore be identified by colour and number alone and the index to location removed when the box is locked.

In fact, keys should never be labelled specifically with their location in case they are lost, when misuse will be easy. The most common example of bad practice in this respect is the hotel room key which has both hotel name and room number on it, inviting the finder to use it in the most obvious way.

7.5.3 Key copying presents security problems and should be discouraged. For some building types many keys may be cut for the main entrance door over a period of time, so that control over them is gradually lost (hostels and nurses's homes are typical examples). Keys may also be copied deliberately for illicit reasons and there are many places like heel bars where copies of common keys are made quickly and easily.

There are companies whose only business is the manufacture of key blanks for copying to fit various locks. They operate world-wide and aim to be comprehensive in their range. In any case, a key is only a shaped piece of metal and it is impossible to prevent copying by a determined craftsman. There are however ways of minimising the problem:

Change locks: This can be done periodically as a routine or whenever the number of keys in circulation becomes too high. If the lock is of a type where the change can be made simply be exchanging the cylinder, the process is cheap and easy. Spare cylinders can be kept to increase the differs.

Use locks with unusual keys. There is an inevitable time lag between the introduction of a key profile and the availability of copy key blanks. Even when they are produced they will only be held in limited locations. There is limited stock generally of:

>   Master key blanks
>   Seven pin cylinder blanks
>   Magnetic keys
>   10-disc tumbler blanks
>   Exotic profiles (Kaba, Bramah, Zeiss)

7.5.4 Keys are often hidden with the astonishing belief that the criminal mind is not clever enough to find them. This is futile; the criminal is likely to have had more experience searching for keys than the occupant has had of hiding them.

7.5.5 It is likely that the control of access throughout the premises will not be a simple matter of go and no-go areas, but that various people will need access to different areas. This may be necessary in a most complicated and overlapping way, so some form of *master keying* or *suiting* of locks will be required. Master keying and suiting are often poorly understood. They are facilities intended to increase convenience in the use of locks and flexibility to access control; *not* to increase security. In fact, the overall level of security in a locking system is lowered by the introduction of master keying, simply because there are more keys in circulation for any one lock, and because the number of key differs available is reduced. All the keys are vulnerable to loss, theft or abuse, and the greater the complexity of the master keying system, the greater is the theoretical reduction in security. Of course, there are many buildings where the advantages of convenience in use far outweigh the drawbacks and, provided the system is carefully thought out, the reduction in security can be minimised. The main principles to be followed are:

> Do not include high security areas under a mastered suite: they must be kept quite separate
>
> Do not include entrance doors in the system. These should have individual locks which can be changed whenever necessary, so that the security of the building envelope is not compromised
>
> Do not ask too much of the locking system. Though the facilities may be available, highly complex mastering has the effect of using up many of the key differs. Four and five lever locks can be mastered but systems of any size must be designed around a minimum seven lever, detainer or cylinder locking range
>
> Take special care over the authorisation of use of master and grandmaster keys. They are frequently issued for reasons of status rather than need

In fact there may be no need to provide a grandmaster key at all: who really needs (or should be allowed!) access to every door in the building so frequently that a single key is the only practical answer? If the grandmaster key is lost, the whole system is compromised: depending on the circumstances of the loss, all the locks may have to be changed, which can be a very expensive exercise.

7.5.6 Each lock in a suite can be opened by at least two different keys: the lock's own key and the master key. The system can become more complex by the addition of sub-suites involving grandmaster keying and common locking. The possibilities are extensive and are best considered diagrammatically, fig 7.8.

The simple master key shown opens locks one to nine, each of which has its own differing key.

Two or more master key suites can be linked by a grandmaster key.

Common locking can be introduced as shown, in fig 7.8, where lock C1 is passed by the grandmaster, both submasters A and B, the keys to locks A4 and B1 and its own key. The security of such a common lock will be very low.

Further complexity is illustrated by the addition of two more options: three locks are shown (C1, C2, C3) which are controlled only by the grandmaster and their own keys, fig 7.9. Secondly, an overlapping submaster suite A/B has been

7.8 A simple master key system: Key A opens locks A1–A5; Key B locks B1–B4; the grandmaster key opens all 9 locks

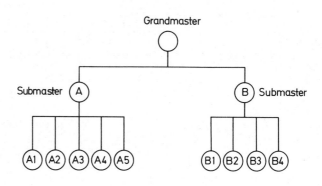

7.9 Common locking: the system operates as in 7.8 above, but common lock C 1 is opened by the keys to A4, B1 as well as the two submaster keys A and B and the grandmaster key

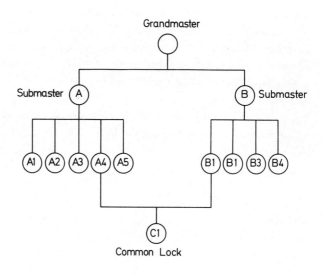

introduced to control locks A4, A5, B1 and B2 only, fig 7.10. This is known as cross-suiting and is useful where access is required by one keyholder to specific rooms in different buildings.

Using these facilities, a total system may be built up and a comprehensive scheme for a hotel is illustrated in fig 7.11. More security will be available on simpler systems with limited areas of suiting. The complex arrangement will only be possible with high quality locks (almost certainly cylinder locks) which have been designed by the manufacturer with master keying in mind.

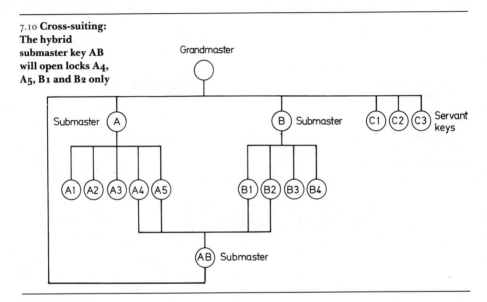

7.10 **Cross-suiting: The hybrid submaster key AB will open locks A4, A5, B1 and B2 only**

7.5.7 Manufacturers adopt two different approaches to the structure of master keyed suites. On the one hand is *lock control*, in which a lock is made to open to a number of different keys; and on the other is *key control* where a particular key is designated to open specified locks. The difference may be difficult to appreciate at first, but the latter system relates more to the needs of security in that it is designed around a keyholder and his authority for access. The extent of cross-suiting available on lock control systems is limited.

7.5.8 Mastering and other operational access controls needed in hotels is often achieved by the use of locking knobsets. The physical security offered by these is negligible, as the whole of the locking mechanism is inside the projecting knob and can be knocked off.

7.5.9 Emergency master keys are also useful in hotels and give access to the bedrooms alone. They will operate even if the guest has set his lock for privacy and will also lock out the guest's key. They are used when a guest has collapsed, for example, but they should normally be kept in a sealed pouch in the safe.

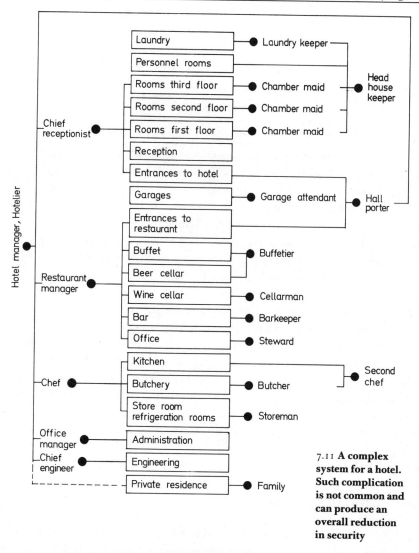

7.11 **A complex system for a hotel. Such complication is not common and can produce an overall reduction in security**

7.5.10 Where building security is to be high and there is concern over the possible loss of key integrity during the building process, *construction keying* may be considered. During the course of construction, all the appropriate locks are fitted to their respective doors but all the keys—including master and grandmaster keys—are issued separately to the building owner. The builder is given a special construction master key which will operate all the locks fitted. On completion or handover of any section, the building owner operates the locks with his own master key and this action renders the construction master key useless from that time onwards. The facility is only available on cylinder locks and the precise mechanism varies and is confidential between manufacturers. The general principle is that the first use of the correct master key disengages the special construction pin and deposits it permanently in a side gallery in the cylinder. There is some loss of facility on differs and mastering, as a potential line of pins is no longer usable. The feature is not standard, is not offered by all manufacturers and entails an extra cost on each lock.

7.6   Electronic systems

7.6.1   As a means of access control, electronic card access systems are becoming more commonly applied. They are cheaper and more effective than manned supervision of access, with the proviso that it is only the cards which are recognised and not the bearers. The most successful use of these installations is where electronics and manpower are combined. The automatic system is not seen as a complete replacement for manned security but rather as an enhancement, so that personnel are released for the beat and the other more constructive duties. Remote card readers can be backed up by CCTV cameras.

7.6.2   All systems operate on the principle that a unique card will cause a door to be electronically unlocked, and it is this unlocking which can reveal weaknesses in the operation. It is most important that the hardware fitted to the door—both the lock and the electrically released striking plate—is adequate for its purpose. It should be at least as resistant to attack as an ordinary mechanical lock in the same situation, and this is *not* easy to achieve on an external door which opens outwards, as the electrical striking plate is exposed. In addition, the wiring to the door release must be secure and tamper-proof if secure access control is to be provided.

7.6.3   A hierarchy which uses cards is much easier to establish than one with locks and keys. Moreover it can be revised whenever necessary in the future, without capital expenditure on new locks.

7.6.4   Many facilities other than access control can be included in the electronics of the system, and are set out later in this section. Where security is important, it will be found that these extra facilities sometimes tend to negate the original aim of the installation, confuse its purpose and cause an overall loss of security. The function of the system should be automatic, requiring no continuous management and therefore, as with many other aspects of security planning, it should be kept as simple as possible.

7.6.5   High security installations should be operated in conjunction with turnstiles.

7.6.6   As with master keys, the issue of access cards is regarded as something of a status symbol in many organisations. If there is to be a proper control arranged on the basis of need, this must be discouraged, and it should never be obvious from the appearance of the card (colour or coding) that the bearer has access to one area or another. This is also good security planning in the case of card loss. Many of the more capable systems record which cards are used in which doors, and it is possible to review this use so that cards which are not used for certain areas can be withdrawn or reprogrammed accordingly.

7.6.7 The cards themselves may take several forms. Punched cards are sometimes used for car parks and dry cleaning collections but they are easily reproducible and therefore insecure. Magnetically coded cards are the most common. They can be prefabricated or in some cases coded by the user as necessary. If the user has programming equipment it must be most securely kept—preferably off the premises in a safe—and the various instructions and register kept separately. The cards can be had with or without personal codes. There is in theory an extra level of control if personal codes are used, but there are difficulties in practice because people become lax and codes are either forgotten or written on the cards themselves 'for convenience'. In addition, the process of entry takes longer if a code is to be entered and any subsequent frustration or queuing will threaten the operation of the scheme.

Magnetic cards are difficult to copy but it is still quite possible to do so. They are also prone to corruption, especially in industrial environments where many magnetic influences may be present, and much ingenuity has been put into the development of alternatives. One of the most successful is the Securimaster system operated by Group 4 and Securitas International Products. Each card is laminated with a series of discs concealed below the surface. The arrangment and composition of the discs is not reproducible and it is scanned by a radio frequency device in each reader.

7.6.8 Other devices which may be useful in particular circumstances are proximity readers and radio releases.

The proximity reader uses a magnetic card which, instead of being pushed into a slot, needs only to be held within a critical distance of the reading head. The head itself may therefore be covered or even concealed and it is particularly useful where vandal resistance is needed.

Radio release of locks (the Mastiff system) uses an individual transmitter which is carried by each person and which emits a modulated signal for acceptance by the receiver at each door. Indeed, a door is not necessary, as the signal can be used merely to suppress an alarm device. The system is convenient, since no deliberate action is required by the user, but security is not complete because the devices must be transferred for recharging, and though they die quite quickly, lost units can be used for some time.

7.6.9 For the same reasons that keys should not be identified by locating labels, access cards should neither bear the address of the premises nor the name of the carrier. If identification is essential, a photograph may be permanently affixed, but this could be dangerous in situations in which hostages might be taken.

7.6.10 There is a clear procedure for establishing a card-based access control system.

First, the broad specification of the installation must be set out:

How many reading units and points of access?

How many personnel are involved?

What categories do they fall into?

A range of codes is then selected and reserved for the system from the differs available. The cards must be unique and the range which is set against a particular installation must take account of any growth predicted. The cards are then made according to the planned hierarchy of access. They are given a serial number but no other label.

It is important that at no stage of planning or manufacture can records of the installation come together with the numerical coded information on the cards: the two should be separated by both time and place. Personal codes are generated in a random way and are issued directly to the card bearers for them to memorise.

7.6.11 Cards can be lost, bearers can leave or their status can change, so readers must be programmable to reject certain cards when necessary. Eventually, to save wastage of the total number of cards assigned to any one installation, a second set of personal codes is issued, so that all cards previously voided are available for re-issue.

7.6.12 Several other features can be included as part of the system:

Anti-passback units are designed to prevent a bearer entering the premises and then handing the card out to an unauthorised person: the reader will reject a card on entry if it has not previously exited through the systems.

Time-barring only allows access for certain cards at specified times, such as the hours when supervision of an area is available.

Duress can be revealed by a card carrier by entering a special extra digit on the personal code, whereupon a silent alarm signal is transmitted. It is a difficult facility in practice, as it is easily activated by mistake or abused. In any case, the response to the alarm is also unreliable because of the uncertainty as to the registration of the signal and the location of the person under duress.

Rollcalls are possible on the more sophisticated systems and the more basic may have a tally-roll. The principle is that for both security reasons and evacuation control it is desirable to know who in the building at any time. With extra readers it is also possible to know the whereabouts of the cards which have entered, as the system will record which readers have been passed. Staff discipline makes operation of such a system extremely difficult and the rate of decay is high. There are exceptional circumstances—such as nuclear reactor halls and offshore oil rigs—where the catastrophic nature of a possible emergency and the life risk involved in rescue attempts justify such a feature. In such cases staff discipline is more likely to be maintained. Marshalling points must also be designated, for personal checking.

Time records can be kept, as the hardware can note a card entry, identity and time used. The records should be transferred to a medium such as punched tape for later analysis.

Last card memory helps to detect malfunctions and abuse, and can be useful following an incident. An individual reader stores the number of the last card which operated it, which can be retrieved by a special procedure.

Unlock time can be limited so that passage of more than one person is inhibited and loitering in lobbies is detected.

Abuse can be detected and an alarm signal generated. The usual forms of abuse are:

> Forcing the door
> Holding the door open
> Trial of personal codes with stolen card

The trial of codes usually causes an alarm signal to be generated after five false entries. None of these alarms may connect to a signalling system which calls the police.

Features suggested for the future are the ability to control facilities as well as access (such as the activation of photocopying machines and data terminals) and the combination with business routines so that the card could be used as a credit card.

7.6.13 Although installations of any size are easily justified, in terms of both security and cost the viability falls as the installation becomes smaller. There are many smaller premises with changing populations which would benefit greatly from the ability to maintain good access control at a single entrance for the current occupants alone; a card reading unit which could be programmed to reject cards declared void would be ideal, but the expense involved in such a single unit is usually prohibitive. One particular example of this type of premises is the smaller nurses' or students' hostel in inner urban areas: the occupants are prey to walk-in thieves and assault and they may only be in residence for periods of six months or so.

7.6.14 There are problems with electronic systems during power failures. Standby battery packs are available and should be installed but, again, this is difficult to achieve with smaller installations, and any standby power may be limited to retention of the programming data in the readers and may be insufficient for normal operation.

If the units become unlocked when power fails there is a loss of security during this time, as well as the possibility of tampering during normal operation. If they remain locked then access is impossible. The inclusion of a key-operated facility during power failure is a nonsense, as the whole purpose of the system will be negated. The only satisfactory solution is to man the entrance until power is restored.

7.6.15 Cardless electronic lock releases are available, which require only the entry of a memorised digital code. The basic weakness of such an arrangement is that with a code alone it is not possible to be sure that the code remains confidential: its illicit possession is undetectable. To counter this, the units are usually shielded so that overlooking during operation is inhibited, while the codes themselves are easily changed; but even so the degree of security must remain low. They are also relatively slow to use compared with a simple card in slot reader.

7.6.16 Signalling from readers to central processors or to alarm systems must be via secure separate cabling with the appropriate safeguard included in its installation. Much the same principles will be followed as with alarm wiring. Some access control systems—particularly those originating from the computer industry rather than the security industry—use data or telephone wiring to carry their signals, and this will not allow the installation to be fully secure.

7.6.17 Maintenance must be established and it will be necessary to allocate resources to it in a positive manner, especially with the more extensive installations. It will fall into several categories:

> Ironmongery maintenance involving electric releases, door closers and hinges
> Electronic maintenance of the card readers and processors
> Operational maintenance of the issue of cards, the hierarchy of access and the discipline of the users

The first two categories will normally be delegated to a security company, but the third does require a more active involvement for the management of the occupant organisation.

Repairs may be found to be needed frequently where readers are in public areas and subject to vandal attack. Card slots can be blocked by gum and other insertions, and digital panels damaged or defaced.

7.7   Phone entry systems

7.7.1 A telephone entry system is intended to restrict access to premises and allow limited personal verification of a visitor from a remote location. The installations provide access control on a simple (but useful) level. The degree of security provided is low because:

> Personal verification is incomplete

Entry, when allowed, is unsupervised

The discipline of use tends to decay

Abuse is common

7.7.1 The entry of regular occupants should normally be controlled by key, card or other conventional means, with the telephone restricted to visitors. This is because the process of entry is relatively time-consuming and cumbersome, so it is unsuited to mass habitual use.

Premises in multiple occupation benefit especially from these devices. Though the overall security is not high, neither are the main risks, so the communal areas in particular can be protected from the vandal and many of the opportunists. This level of crime reduction will make a significant difference to the quality of building which can be maintained and, even more importantly, to occupants' peace of mind.

7.7.3 Phone entry systems can be used in conjunction with visual inspection by TV, and several manufacturers include this facility with equipment. There must be a TV screen at each response point inside the building, and there must also be good lighting at the call point. If the layout of the entrance zone does not allow a good view of the whole of the adjacent area there is no point in including a television camera. As might be expected, the equipment is relatively expensive and in normal circumstances the money can be better spent on other forms of security.

7.7.4 The most useful application of phone entry systems is for multiple housing schemes in urban areas. Inevitably, these premises will incorporate communal areas—entrances, lifts, stairs and stores—and they are subject to vandalism. Once the property has been damaged the nuisance is likely to increase to intolerable proportions (see chapter 8), so free access to these communal areas cannot be allowed. In addition, single, nervous or elderly residents feel threatened by the presence of strangers in the building, and are greatly reassured if access is restricted.

There are many practical difficulties associated with such installations however, and the planning must be extremely careful if successful operation is to be achieved. The difficulties arise from three main areas of use and increase greatly with the size of the system:

The equipment is subject to vandalism

The operation decays as residents become lax

There are problems with deliveries and roundsmen

When fitting the equipment to existing premises the residents should be consulted fully and the reasons for installation explained. Where the premises are new, incoming residents must be given full details of the operational policy. In fact, the occupants will have to be trained in the use of the system and it may be necessary for security guards to be employed for a period after installation to monitor its operation.

7.7.5 When planning the system it is essential that the number of entrances is restricted: if there is more than one, success will be threatened, but account must be taken of existing or likely patterns of movement (e.g. from parking areas), as the installation has to be lived with. Multiple call panels can be fitted but the equipment must be able to discriminate and release only the door at which the call is made.

There is no theoretical technical limit to the number of dwellings served, and this number will in many cases be determined simply by the size of an existing block. In practical terms however, the very large systems are unlikely to be successful and an effective size seems to be 30–40 dwellings. The figures are rough guides and will be overshadowed by the attitudes of the residents, which are much more likely to determine success or failure.

7.7.6 The entrance must have a clear approach and be well lit by more than one fitting—visitors may feel uncomfortable standing outside a locked door—and tampering with the equipment or loitering must be discouraged. A canopy should provide shelter from the rain. If a draught lobby is included the entry system must control the *outer* door.

The doors themselves are still subject to attack and reference should be made to chapter 3 for recommendations on construction and glazing. As with card access systems, the lock and electrically released striking plate are potential weak points and should give protection equivalent to BS 3261. They will almost certainly require additional steel sheet cover. Exit should be easy, without any key operation, and the most suitable arrangement is a lever handle on the inside with a half spindle into the lock so that nothing appears on the outside. There will have to be some form of pull handle on the external face but it must be selected so that it does not act as an attachment point for towing or assist leverage. The common D-shaped handle is not suitable and pad designs are better. The handles should be bolted right through the door, with bolt heads inaccessible from the outside.

7.7.7 Door closing devices are absolutely essential to the operation of remote entry systems, as it is vital that the lock re-engages after the door has been opened. The closer must be carefully selected bearing in mind:

> The size and weight of the door
> The probable wind loading
> The strength of spring resistance on the latching mechanism
> The probable intensity of use
> The degree of exposure to the elements

It can be seen that for an external main entrance door the above factors will all tend to be high, so a durable heavy duty closing mechanism will be indicated. An inevitable disadvantage is the strength of the spring needed, which is quite likely to be difficult for old people and children to operate. To counter this, the size of the door should be kept to a minimum and the weight reduced as far as is consistent with security. Wind loading can also be reduced by the inclusion of a lobby inside, thus removing through draughts, but if any external shielding is considered, it must not provide concealment or obstruct the view from the entrance. The lighter domestic door closers are completely unsuitable. The device must have certain features:

Reliability

Adjustable closing force and speed

Separate adjustable latching force

Backcheck (to prevent strain from over-opening)

On no account should any form of hold-open be included. The most satisfactory closers for performance are hydraulic floor springs; they can however suffer from deterioration, as the box is partially exposed, so box cover plates and seals must be correctly specified. An alternative is the overhead concealed transom-mounted spring, provided that the timber or metal transom section is large enough to accept it. As a last resort, a heavy duty surface-mounted overhead hydraulic closer may be used, but only on smaller installations where the lightest traffic is expected. Not only are its mechanism and fixings of a lighter nature than the spring closers, but the exposed arm is vulnerable to both deliberate and accidental damage. Partially and fully concealed door-mounted closers are completely unsuitable, as they take up too much of the thickness of the door. Simple spring closers are cheap but allow the door to slam in a damaging and unacceptable way.

All door closers must be single-acting (like the doors) and hinge bolts should be fitted for additional security.

7.7.8 External call panels can be damaged by vandals. They should be kept as plain as possible, flush with the wall or slightly recessed, and the buttons should also be flush with the panel. Both should be stainless steel. Instructions for use must be clear and should be engraved on the panel itself. There should be no resident's names against each dwelling number, as a caller who addresses an occupant by name can easily sound plausible enough to be admitted; identification should be solely numerical. With the traditional one button per flat arrangement, there is a good chance that a nefarious caller will be able to gain admission by pressing the button of every flat: at least one occupant is likely to release the main door without bothering to use the telephone. A possible solution to this problem is the call panel which has only ten numbered buttons like a pocket calculator: only one dwelling can be selected at a time. A display indicates the number selected, though the novelty of this can invite attention and misuse by local children.

The apertures for loudspeaker and microphone need careful detailing to reduce the effect of liquid and mechanical attack. They should be cut into the front plate and backed both by an offset perforated plate and by mesh. The location should be such that any liquid introduced will not damage the circuitry.

7.7.9 The resident's individual unit should usually be sited in the wall close to the living area, but this will vary from one design to another. Extension bells or lights can be fitted, which may be appropriate for elderly, deaf or physically disabled occupants. Many designs use telephone handsets on wall-mounted cradles, but there is a risk that these many become accidentally dislodged, making the dwelling effectively inaccessible, so the wall-mounted microphone/speaker is more reliable in practice. Quality of speech reproduction is important in the acceptability of the installation to the occupants. One-way speech systems are not recommended.

7.7.10 In practice, the main areas of decay in the operation of phone entry systems are:

>Doors propped open by occupants
>Door closers malfunctioning
>Hinges breaking
>Uncontrolled secondary exists
>Badly fitted doors
>Admission of neighbours' visitors by residents
>Visitors walking in behind residents or admitted visitors
>Jammed release button on resident's units
>Power failure
>Proliferation of keys
>Nuisance calls
>Impractical delivery arrangements

7.7.11 Planning deliveries so that security is not compromised is a continuing problem, and various solutions have been tried, with varying success. It seems clear that there is no general rule for foolproof operation; and this.is another reason why the overall security of the installations can never be very high.

Some systems include a button marked Tradesmen on the call panel; this is ridiculous. It is also possible to include a time-clock so that the entrance is unlocked during the hours when tradesmen deliver, and though this is a possible solution the time bracket involved will be several hours (from, say, 6 am to 11 am) and it must be accepted that the deliberate intruder will know when this free access is available. On balance, therefore, a time clock is not recommended, but may become necessary as a lesser evil if the installation is otherwise unworkable.

Security can only be established if free access is denied to all but the regular occupants. Nobody should be allowed entry other than by an occupant and no special key switches should be installed.

Milk, post and newspapers are the main routine deliveries, and in practice it is usually found that one or more residents are willing to respond regularly to calls from these; such admission must still only be allowed if the caller can identify himself satisfactorily. Irregular deliveries are ignored and must first be accepted like any other visitor.

An alternative is the use of postal and goods delivery boxes so that tradesman do not need access to the building but can leave their goods securely from the outside. Although most types of box are designed for mail alone, some have facilities for other small deliveries and some also have a latching device to secure single insertions. Multiple units are very common elsewhere in Europe, and many different arrangements can be constructed, either as single-sided boxes for installation outside or as double-sided units mounted in a wall with access from both sides; these latter are restricted to mail and newspapers, fig 7.12.

Postal delivery boxes are particularly useful in blocks of flats. An incidental benefit is the removal of letterplates from the flat entrance doors, where they normally constitute both a weakness in security and a hazard in case of fire.

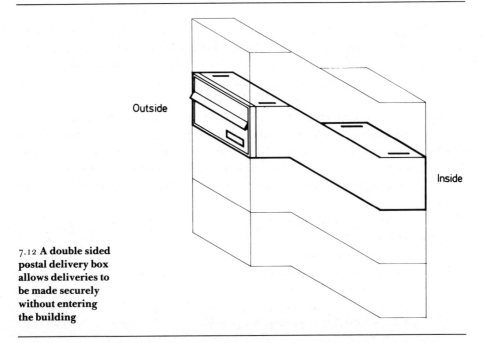

Outside

Inside

7.12 **A double sided postal delivery box allows deliveries to be made securely without entering the building**

7.7.12 The routine arrangements for refuse collection need consideration at the time the control of access is being set out. Refuse should not be collected from inside the secure area and in pratice this is not usually difficult to arrange.

7.7.13 Various complicated provisions are made for fire brigade access but these are almost always unnecessary and like all complications cause a reduction in the level of security. The fire brigade should be admitted like everyone else—by ringing the bell—but in practice it will usually be found that residents are waiting for them by the front door. In the event of failure, the brigade will force entry and the damage will be accepted as a cost of maintaining security. Ambulances and police will be admitted in the same way.

7.7.14 Power failure will leave the doors locked and the building secure. Residents' key access and free exit will be unaffected but visitors' access will be suspended and alarms for door hold-open time will not operate. This is preferable to a release of all the doors during a power cut. The emergency lighting system necessary for escape routes should extend to lighting the main entrance area.

7.8 Hotels

7.8.1 Special approaches to access control are called for by hotels and the way they work: although normally visitors to premises should not be given free authorised access by key or card, this is part of the essential nature of a hotel, so some measures must be introduced to compensate.

7.8.2 The possible complexity of the overall access hierarchy is well illustrated in the hotel key diagram in section 7.5. Until comparatively recently, a mechanical keying system was the only solution and while reasonable access control was provided for the rest of the hotel, the security of the keys to the guests' rooms was never certain; guests take keys with them—inadvertently or not—when they depart and in any case they are easily copied. Indeed, most hotel thieves are caught in possession of keys. Nowadays, electronic systems have been developed which overcome the key control problem and current major advances parallel to those in intruder detection now offer the hotel management many other facilities. Whatever method is used for guests' rooms, it must include a number of features as a minimum:

    Adequate constructional security
    Automatic latching
    Key operation from outside
    Keyless operation from inside
    Barring routine key operation (from inside)
    Invalidation of routine key (from outside)
    Emergency override of barring functions
    Adequate key differs
    Comprehensive suiting capability

7.8.3 Ordinary cylinder mortice locks can be fitted with removable cores to enable the control of keys to be sidestepped: for every 100 locks there will be, say, 120 cores and the spare 20 will be used as a rotating reserve so that lost keys cannot be re-used in the same room door.

7.8.4 Key-in-knobsets are the most popular equipment in this country for guestroom doors, mainly because of their versatility. The range of functions is illustrated in fig 7.13, and it can be seen that hotel bedrooms have been specifically kept in mind. These sets are comparatively cheap and easy to fit but their constructional security is very low, as not only are many rather flimsy, but all are vulnerable to being knocked off the door. Removable cores are not generally available.

7.13 **Some of the functions for locking knobsets**

A **Key and turnbutton**   F **Plain latch**
B **Single cylinder**   G **Double cylinder**
C **Key and pushbutton**   H **Wardrobe set**
D **Push button**   J **Cupboard set**
E **Communicating doorset**

7.8.5 Electronic systems nowadays often form part of an overall computerised hotel management/security/accounting complex, and more details are given in chapter 9. Most of the principles involved in room keying are common to all the designs, however, though there is no doubt that security is increased.

A single coaxial cable links all the rooms, including the electric lock on the door, to a central computer. The cabling should of course be routed properly in conduit like any other security wiring. At the reception desk is a device linked to the computer, which effectively makes keys for each guest on arrival, and invalidates them on leaving. The 'keys' may take various forms: cards, metal foil on cardboard or, more recently, notched plastic bars. The code is generated randomly by the computer and the room unit is altered simultaneously to suit, whilst retaining its submission to the submaster 'keys' held by chambermaids. If these latter are used, however, they cause a signal to be registered at the main console. Use of the coding device is itself authorised by insertion of a key. Some systems include a personal code which is printed and sealed unseen at the reception desk for use by the guest on a digital unit at the room door. Improper use of keys or trial codes register at reception. When a guest leaves, it is immaterial whether he takes his key or not, as a signal from the reception unit instructs the room not to open to it. The differs, being electronic codes, are practically infinite, so codes, once used, can be abandoned for ever. There are however drawbacks:

> The systems are comparatively unreliable and unfamiliar
> They are comparatively expensive
> Installation is more complicated
> Power failure creates problems
> Maintenance is high and specialised

The costs can often be justified by the inclusion of management facilities, though it is possible that these may obscure the access control function and thus compromise security.

7.8.5   The main access control to the hotel will benefit from surveillance, either directly by staff—as at the main entrance and reception area—or by television. TV cameras might be sited in the lobby, any rear entrances, the cellar door and in front of lifts. The most appropriate locations will depend upon the design and size of the hotel. Any infringement of access will require a response and this should be under the control of hotel security staff.

7.9   Means of escape

7.9.1   The conflict between means of escape and security has been mentioned several times in this book. Access control may be affected by the necessary provision of escape routes.

7.9.2   One of the first principles of access control is to reduce the number of points of access to a minimum—preferably a single entrance—whereas the principles of escape require at least two exits from each 'compartment' of a building. These emergency exits are potential weak points in security and must, as least, be alarmed. They should also be designed in such a way that they cannot be easily used as casual entrances, so no unlocking mechanism should be fitted to the outside.

7.9.3   Wherever possible the main controlled entrance should be used as one of the means of escape so that the total number is reduced. It may also be possible, subject to particular designs, to provide a secondary protected escape route leading to the lobby of the single entrance. The controlling authorities should be consulted about the detailed arrangements. Where access control systems are being fitted to existing buildings, all entrances which are designated as superfluous must be physically blocked up and not just locked.

7.10   Maintenance

7.10.1 It is important, particularly in the case of electronic access control systems, telephone entry systems, and hotel electronic systems, that a regular programme of maintenance should be set out in addition to the *ad hoc* procedures for repairs.

7.10.2 A maintenance contract should be entered into with the installing company and it is essential that this company maintains the whole of the system including:
Wiring
Card readers
Central control units
Call panels and units
Electrical lock releases
Locks
Door closers and hinges
Power supplies
Alarms
Card production
The user's maintenance should be limited to keeping proper records of the system, card issues, and operational disciplines.

7.10.3 Master keyed locks do not require the same kind of regular routine maintenance, as the hardware is more sturdy and simpler. Locks should not be oiled or greased, as this invites fluff and grit to accumulate in the mechanism; if the movement becomes stiff, graphite powder should be squirted in through the keyhole. Operational maintenance will again be required in the sense of key control and disciplines.

Checklist 7

Access control

Decay

> Define and recognise likelihood

Planning

> Examine movement/communication patterns
> Accept review phase necessary
> Make consequent organisational changes
> Select authority token (key/card/code/personal)
> Do not issue tokens to visitors

Locking

> Set out policy
> Only fit locks were necessary
> Avoid warded locks
> Select lock type (lever/butters/cylinder)

Keying

> Control key issue/possession
> Avoid labelling keys with location
> Change critical locks periodically

Master keying

> Design master keying system
> Exclude high security areas
> Exclude entrance doors
> Control issue of master keys

Electronic systems

> Ensure physical resistance is present
> Establish hierarchy of access and numbers of people
> Decide what other features are necessary
> Control issue of cards or codes
> Avoid punch cards
> Avoid labelling cards
> Consider consequences of power failure
> Allocate resources to maintenance

Phone entry systems

> Design entrance zone carefully for surveillance
> Include good lighting
> Consult and train occupants
> Restrict entrances
> Restrict number of tenancies to each system
> Ensure adequate physical resistance
> Specify reliable door closers
> Keep door size to minimum
> Do not use hold-open devices
> Keep call panels plain and flush
> Establish policy for deliveries
> Consider postal delivery boxes
> Consider consequences of power failure

Hotel systems

> Ensure adequate physical resistance
> Establish locking hierarchy
> Decide what management features are necessary in
>   the system
> Do not label room keys with hotel name

8 Vandalism and wastage

8.1 Definitions

8.1.1 Vandalism is a continuing problem which defies resolution. Much socio-logical study has been carried out in various countries, but few positive conclusions have been drawn. It certainly arouses feelings of outrage amongst its victims, and this may be part of the reasoning behind it. Certainly, there are many anomalies: why should one area be attacked, for example, when a similar one nearby is untouched?

8.1.2 Even the figures for analysis are difficult to compare because of the varying ways of defining vandalism used in compiling them. Firstly, a line must be drawn somewhere between vandalism and wear and tear, and this must be a matter of judgement. After this the definition may be expanded to include:
Arson
Flooding
Damage incidental to other crime
Quoted figures should therefore be read broadly, to give some idea of scale.

8.1.3 Further losses which are conveniently dealt with under the same heading are the wastage and spoiling of materials stored externally, and the general pilferage common on building sites.

8.2 Wastage

8.2.1 The word wastage is often used to cover vandalism, carelessness, bad stock-keeping and pilferage. If any degree of respect for the security system is to be developed it is essential that these causes of loss are firmly separated. This is a matter of management policy, and its absence will quickly create an atmosphere in which substantial losses are tolerated.

8.2.2 True wastage is the result of carelessness and bad stock-keeping. Some accountability for materials and goods must be held by those who take care of them, particularly where goods are not durable or require some action to protect them from the weather.

8.2.3 Pilfering has been mentioned elsewhere and the main defence is a determination that it will not be tolerated: organisations which turn a blind eye to pilfering cannot expect their property to be respected in any way.

8.3   Arson and flooding

8.3.1 The opportunities for arson are widespread. Though fires may be started accidentally during other acts of vandalism it is thought that this is comparatively rare, and that most criminal fires are started deliberately. Schools are common targets as they are unoccupied for long periods and familiar to the bulk of the vandal population. A second reason for arson is to cover a theft, so that it is unclear whether goods have been stolen or burned. Other less common motives are political action, insurance fraud and illegal demolition of listed buildings prior to redevelopment.

8.3.2 Flooding can also cause widespread damage and can spoil goods as effectively as a fire. It does not have the same psychological attraction for the culprit, however, and it is much more preventable: the main defence is to protect the sources of water.

8.4   The culprits

8.4.1 *Most vandals are not caught and so we do not really know who they are.* It is probable that most are young males and one theory holds that there is a peak age of about 10 at which the damge caused is associated with play because the sense of responsibility is not fully developed. In the middle teenage years other motives appear—pressure from peers in gangs for example—and the damage may be more serious. Increased responsibility in the late teens would seem to make vandalism less likely.

8.4.2 This theoretical pattern seems reasonable but it is difficult to back up with any real evidence, partly because of the reason given in 8.4.1 above, and partly because of the legal separation of offences by younger children. It is commonly held that there is a conviction peak of 14–18 years for vandalism, but the fig 8.1, which shows the numbers guilty or cautioned annually for criminal damage in England and Wales, does not give much support to this view.

8.4.3 It is also alleged that most offenders are local and that most offences occur between 1800 and 0200 hours, but once again this is an unreliable view and cannot be proved. The problem is not restricted to inner cities.

8.4.4 It is entirely possible that vandalism cannot be characterised by age or locality but is more deeply rooted, like theft, as a complex function of a society.

Certainly its occurrence varies dramatically from one country to another.

8.5   Damage

8.5.1 The total losses from criminal damage are loosely estimated to exceed £100 m per year in the UK, but there are many problems of definition and the figure may be greatly different.

8.5.2 On a smaller scale the estimates are probably more reliable. Hampshire County Council, faced with an annual cost of about £400 000 for the repair of county property in 1979, examined the buildings becoming most damaged: out of nearly 2 000 prosecutions the percentages of building types involved were:

Private houses	25
Shops	20
Commercial premises	19
Public buildings	19
Places of entertainment	10
Public houses	5
Churches	2
Caravans	1

There were 350 cases of arson with primary damage estimated at £1 000 000, an average of about £3 000 per occurrence.

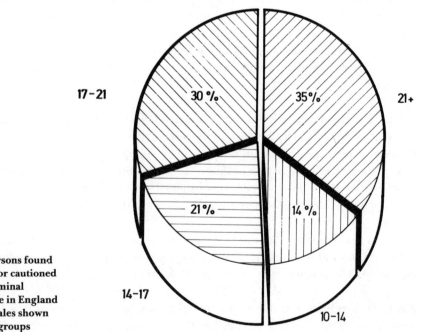

8.1 Persons found guilty or cautioned for criminal damage in England and Wales shown as age groups

8.5.3 The pattern of damage is sometimes consistent and has an air of tradition about it: London Transport, for example, know that they will lose about 30 000 light bulbs each year. In most cases, the damage is minor and it has been estimated that only 3 per cent of cases involve more than £20, though the average is about £150.

8.5.4 The consequential costs of the damage are usually ignored in the figures and so cannot be estimated. Other factors must also be taken into account when evaluating the true scale of the damage.

Anxiety can be created. Not only is there concern for the condition and care of an owner's property, but there is also an accompanying fear generated, particularly where the damage is continuous and widespread. Elderly residents of vandalised housing estates can feel real distress as they perceive a threat in this way. The general dissatisfaction with the reduced quality of the environment may be thought intolerable and these feelings can develop into rage if residents feel that they have been abandoned by an uncaring landlord.

Injuries can be caused as a result of vandalism. The destruction of lighting on footpaths and staircases is an obvious example where there is risk of accident, and broken glass is another common problem. Less obvious dangers arise when cover plates are removed from lampposts, meter cupboards and the like, exposing the live electrical parts. An employer or landlord has a duty to consider the safety of his employees or tenants.

Crime is related to vandalism, though the connection is not fully understood. It has been observed that a reduction in the level of vandalism in an area carries with it a reduction in other forms of crime.

8.6 Graffiti

8.6.1 Graffiti are common and widespread—more so since the availability of aerosol cans of spray paint. They are usually disfiguring and sometimes offensive.

8.6.2 The graffiti are often simply mischievous or daring, but many are political and are carried out to broadcast a particular message. In addition, there is the marking motive: see section 8.7.2.

8.6.3 Rough textured surfaces will resist lipsticks, crayons and brush applied paints. Smooth, hard surfaces are easier to clean with solvents but vulnerable to scratches and scores. Fairfaced concrete has an inhuman public building image and invites disfigurement from the beginning; it is also difficult to clean or repair. Ground level walls in public areas are favourite targets and one clear solution is to paint the surfaces and include a budget cost for frequent routine redecoration: this may be the only hope of keeping appearances respectable. Wallpaper and similar coverings are not suitable and should be avoided at all costs.

8.7   Motivation

8.7.1   A number of motives give rise to vandalism: some are traditional, part of a national character or of an age, but none are fully understood.

8.7.2   *Marking* has been mentioned above. Teenagers regularly congregate on unclaimed territory—empty sites, buildings, and playgrounds—they then assert their claim to the territory by vandalising and disfiguring it, thus expressing their control. As a means of social communication about territorial rights, the interpretation of marking by the culprits as well as those who observe them is well established. A non-destructive parallel is leaving a newspaper or book on a chair to retain its usage. Even the damage caused can be compared—in behavioural terms—with the increased noise made by regular customers in a public house as opposed to that made by strangers.

8.7.3   *Ownership* is a powerful concept. Much of the damage occuring is to public property which is perceived by the vandal to be ownerless or, at least, to belong to a body so diffuse or distant as to be unimportant.

The owner must be seen to have possession of the premises, his relationship must be obvious and his care continuous. It should be clear that he is ready to defend his possession, and if he is unable to project this image he can expect trespass, tentative damage and finally invasion and destruction. Little evidence is necessary before abandonment is perceived by the vandal.

The areas which appear to be in communal ownership should be reduced as far as possible. Especially vulnerable are play spaces, garages, tunnels, lavatories, lifts, planted areas and building sites. As far as possible these areas should be allocated clearly to the care of individuals or small groups. Planting in particular can easily be divided into plots which relate to occupational boundaries: it will be found that the image of the front garden is a defence in itself, whereas the landscaped communal area will be downtrodden and destroyed.

Common access routes should also be reduced. It may be easier or simpler to plan strategic pedestrian 'streets' through housing developments, but these are very bad ideas both for general security and vandalism. It appears that there is a critical density for pedestrian traffic and once this undefined level is exceeded the area is perceived as being in public ownership and damaged. Access corridors, balconies, lifts, subways and paths should be fragmented so that through-routes are avoided and each serves only a few premises.

8.7.4   *Triggers* are the mechanisms for the beginning of vandalism and the most frequent is the sight of previous damage. Although this may have been deliberate or accidental it lends the requisite air of abandonment to the property and can lead rapidly to extensive continuing attack. For example, London Transport (a well-known target) suffered some unexplained damage to a ceiling panel in a ticket hall; it was the first to be damaged for many years but, within the next three weeks, thirty more were lost.

Younger offenders are particularly influenced by the sight of previous damage and the most common incitement is the broken window. There also seems to be some mysterious way in which one building may be branded with vandalism so that, even when repairs are prompt, similar damage reoccurs quickly. This may relate to the extent of the original damage.

It is vitally important that a level of care and control is established for buildings from the outset. Empty new buildings are among those perceived as being ownerless and a pattern of vandalism, once begun, could be impossible to stop.

8.7.5 *Political* vandalism usually takes the form of graffiti, but there are other forms, such as digging up sports fields before international matches. Also in this category is the deliberate destruction carried out by occupants in an attempt to get themselves rehoused. There are several characteristics which set this type of vandalism apart: the attraction of the target is quite different for example, and the culprits are not necessarily in the same younger age group.

8.8   Defence

8.8.1 Property can and should be defended against vandalism. In practice, as the culprits are rarely caught, the normal legal procedures do not act as a realistic deterrent and defence falls into two categories:

    Reducing the attraction of the target
    Reducing the vulnerability of the target

8.8.2 The attraction of the target is affected most by the location and apparent ownership and the presence of prior damage as set out in sections 8.5–8.7. Positive planning will reduce these.

8.8.3 The second approach is a matter of detailed design: of ensuring that buildings, their contents and surroundings are sturdy enough to resist attack. At the extreme, the vandal resistant 'fortress' will develop, and though some buildings must be designed in this way—isolated sports pavilions are good examples—the result cannot usually be tolerated in the centre of a community. A school constructed in this way would carry a hostile image quite out of keeping with its function. Nevertheless, there are many principles to be followed in detailed design which are set out in the following sections and which will reduce the vulnerability.

8.8.4 Successful defence will involve an overall approach, with the fortress principle seen as a second line. Sporadic personal ideas and gimmicks are common enough in anti-vandal measures, but are no substitute for a considered professional solution. Perseverance wins.

8.9   Surveillance

8.9.1 Formal surveillance has mixed success. Patrols by police or security staff are important in the reduction of crime and can be effective in reducing the consequences of vandalism (by early detection of floods and fire, for instance) but have no great record to display of prevention. It is even suggested that the presence of patrols will increase the incidence of damage because the culprits (especially the younger ones) will be encouraged to display their daring: it may be seen as great fun to break a window so that a guard comes puffing round the corner.

8.9.2 The idea of the concierge has some value. Although they have never been customary in the UK, it is probable that the concierges in French apartment blocks are most effective against vandals.

8.10   Perimeter design

8.10.1 Consideration of details of the design should start at the boundary, figs 8.2, 8.3. Fences are vulnerable and it has been found that pvc coated chain link is unlikely to survive continuous attack. Metal angle fence posts are easily bent and concrete or even timber are more suitable. If chain link is used, the bottom links must be held down by gravel boards and a line wire must be strung 75 mm from the top but not through the highest links. Spiked palisading is much more resistant both to climbing and damage. Brick walls are expensive and unlikely to be used for barriers, except that lower walls can define boundaries and ownership. They are

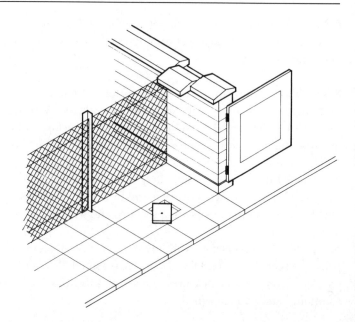

8.2 **External walls and fences: typical damage**

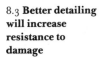

8.3 **Better detailing
will increase
resistance to
damage**

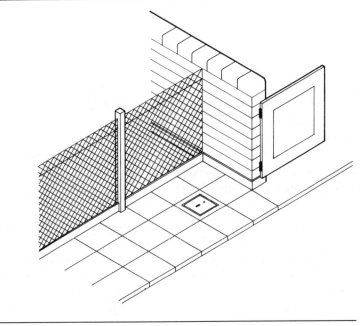

vulnerable to graffitti. Engineering brick dpcs are better than felt or slate as they
provide more bond, so the wall is not so easily pushed over. Bullnosed engineering
bricks should be used on copings rather than the precast type, which overhang and
can be levered off.

8.10.2 Gates which are locked for security tend to be sturdy enough to resist
attack. Those which are not locked are a greater problem: they can be swung on,
pulled too far and generally abused. Hinges must be designed with this in mind
and not be the lift-off type, and the gate itself should not encourage riding and be
stout enough for its purpose.

8.11   External areas

8.11.1 The layout of public external areas can be designed to minimise damage
and the first step is to avoid the pedestrian through-route. Areas which are
intended to be attractive are easily spoilt, especially in their infancy, and rarely is
there any money left in the budget for their re-establishment.

8.11.2 Planting should be carefully specified, and any tendency for short cuts
across beds can be deterred by the location of short prickly shrubs in the
appropriate places. These can also be sited to protect more delicate foliage. On a
similar principle, substantial fast-growing ground cover can be planted. Later,
when more attractive plants have matured, it can, if necessary, be removed.

Raised beds are helpful: the area is better defined and the cyclist is stopped, together with many of the casual short-cutting pedestrians. The height of bed plus planting should not however be above 1 m or attackers could lurk behind.

8.11.3 Young saplings planted near communal routes rarely survive, even when protected by tree guards: the worst location is at the junction of several footpaths, sited within a flush tree-grid. Money is better spent on fewer, more mature trees sited carefully away from the casual passer-by and possibly protected by other planting.

For general security of premises, trees should not give concealment and so any in critical locations should be species without any branches below 1.5 m (for their own protection it is better if there are no branches below 2.4 m).

8.11.4 Gravel paths and borders will constantly be disturbed and should never be used. Deterrent surfaces can be constructed using cobbles or large pebbles but these *must* be bedded into concrete for two thirds of their own depth. The use of such materials is not wise if it is thought that any rioting is possible, as there is a ready supply of missiles. The same applies to precast paving slabs, which are readily broken up for the same purpose. Tarmacadam paving is more suitable in such circumstances.

8.11.5 Gulley grids and access covers of all sorts are mischievously raised, removed or smashed. They should be the lockable types, requiring a special key to remove them.

8.12 Plant and machinery

8.12.1 The highest concentration of plant and machinery is found on building sites (see section 8.17) but there are also farm tractors and agricultural machinery to be considered, along with much specialised materials including industrial plant.

8.12.2 In fact, plant is surprisingly difficult to protect. The key principles which are usually quoted are:

Immobilisation
Securing in compounds
Marking
Alarms

Immobilisation to prevent vandals working the machinery is simple enough in mechanical terms, but in practice is often resisted by the management on the grounds that forgotten keys and the like cost too much lost time. Even so, it is surprising that so few pieces of mobile plant are fitted with steering locks. The problem goes further than damage to the plant itself because in the nature of the machinery it will almost certainly be capable of causing considerable damage to its surroundings, let alone the risk that it will be used for breaking into premises.

Securing the machinery in compounds is another excellent principle but can rarely be effective in practice, even if the space is available. Firstly, in many instances the machinery may be spread over a large area—motorway sites, new towns and farms for example—and secondly, not all will be mobile enough to be moved into compounds. Even if it is possible, the time and labour involved each day will create financial pressures leading to decay.

Marking plant and tools is valuable and worthy of much effort. Major items can be painted with specially formulated individual colours, each one unique to one organisation so that stolen items can be identified. Smaller items can also be marked by stamping, but difficulties arise with some power tools which can be damaged if marked in this way.

Alarms can be fitted to compounds, tool stores and individual items of plant. In some cases, it may be possible to link vehicle alarms to the main building intruder detection system. Otherwise, the alarms have limited value: they may be sufficient to scare vandals away but there is a good chance that they will be ignored.

8.12.3 Finally, the plant owner should take a responsible view about the possibility of injury caused to vandals by machinery and if its immobilisation is impossible, it should be left in a safe condition.

8.13 Lighting

8.3.1 Security lighting of external areas has been discussed in chapter 2 in the context of criminal intruders. A slightly different approach is required for the control of vandalism because although lighting is a proven deterrent:

> Vandals are not necessarily intruders; they are often legitimate occupants
> The lights themselves are targets for damage

8.13.2 The relatively high-intensity point sources used for outdoor security lighting are neither necessary nor desirable in public external areas, as the atmosphere created is that of the public owner once more, so that damage can be encouraged. Smaller, softer and more numerous lights are better, and if possible they should appear to be related to an individual property. As a general principle, single fittings are unsatisfactory, and multiple lights in the same area will provide a more constant level of protection.

8.13.3 Car parking areas are sometimes exceptions to the above, especially large level car parks outside stadiums, banqueting suites and the like, where large numbers of vehicles will be left for predictable periods. Access control is difficult and the nature of shadows cast is such that high-bay high intensity lighting provides a good solution. The more domestic parking areas which exist in housing schemes and shopping centres are better lit by the smaller types of street lighting columns.

8.13.4 Footpaths can usually be routed to take advantage of the available street lighting. Where this is insufficient it should be supplemented. Smaller street lighting columns are a possibility but they are vulnerable to missiles and airguns at high level and tampering with the access plates at low level. Lighting bollards are cheaper and there are several types which have been designed to be highly vandal-resistant, although ordinary tungsten lamps should be avoided. The light is pleasant and can be even more so if the bollards are sited within planted beds where they themselves are partially protected. They should be used in pairs.

Wherever possible, the footpath lighting should be combined with fittings associated with entrances, especially in housing developments. Even if the fittings by front doors are connected to the outdoor supplies, they 'belong' to a particular property: not only is this inherently safer, but broken fittings will be replaced more rapidly.

8.13.5 Entrances, lobbies, stairways and corridors must be lit. Though the method will depend on the building type, the principle of multiple fittings should not be forgotten.

8.14   The building envelope

8.14.1 Some of the principles of design of the building envelope coincide with those set out previously for security against intruders but there are differences as the object is to prevent damage, not intrusion alone.

8.14.2 Access to roofs should be inhibited, both from above (other roofs) and from the ground. The roofing material should not be fragile on low levels where bricks or other objects can be thrown up, and if access is possible, valuable materials such as lead and copper are inappropriate even for flashings. Rooflights must be securely fixed and made from impact-resistant plastics.

8.14.3 External walls will always be subject to graffiti. There are proprietary solutions which can be applied to masonry so that marks can be more easily removed with a special solvent.

Tile hanging and asbestos cement sheets are fragile and should not be used as cladding.

Any external rainwater pipes may be attacked or used for climbing. If it is absolutely necessary to site them outside they should not be pvc, and should be most securely fixed. Above a height of 2 m they can be coated with a non-drying anti-climb paint. Wrapping barbed wire around the pipes is not particularly effective.

Access panels for services should be steel and fixed with locks. External meter boxes are common targets, especially the communal ones controlling external lighting. The guards over domestic balanced gas are also vulnerable and the standard types are always too flimsy for use in exposed locations.

8.14.4 Windows are obvious attractions for the vandal. Their size and design is controlled by many factors which may not be compatible with resistance to damage. If possible, frame size and glass thickness should be limited in accordance with BSCP 153 and materials other than glass may be considered. Acrylic sheet should not be used: its flammability is not only unacceptable in most buildings for fire safety reasons, but it is also more vulnerable to vandalism for the same reason. Polycarbonates are tough and highly resistant to impact; although they provide a reasonable answer to the problem, they can be scratched, or disfigured by cigarette burns. They are expensive. There are also proprietary plastic sheets available with metal diamond mesh reinforcement for use where transparency is not important.

Glazing below normal sill height should be avoided, as should louvre blade windows below door head height.

8.14.5 External doors should always be solid (not hollow cored) and ordinary glazed panels at low level should not be included and, ideally, any glazing should be limited to 60 mm in one dimension, fig 8.4. Louvres, especially timber ones, must never be used. The ironmongery is traditionally at risk and it must be expected that any face-fixed items will be removed. Lever handles and pull handles are easier to attack than knobs; any closers fitted must always be on the inside and should have robust arms and a back-check facility.

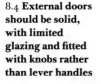

8.4 **External doors should be solid, with limited glazing and fitted with knobs rather than lever handles**

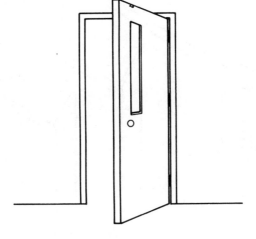

8.5 **More vulnerable details include plasterboard, lightweight wc partitions and top rails**

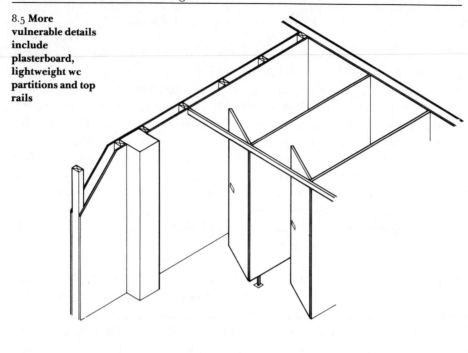

8.6 **Masonry partitions and the reduction of projections will reduce damage**

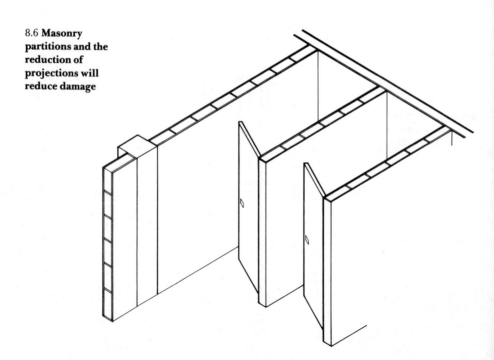

8.15   The building interior

8.15.1 Public buildings with uncontrolled access—railway stations, sports centres, and hospitals—suffer greatly from internal damage, whereas those in more private ownership, such as department stores, seem to escape the worst. Some schools are almost wrecked internally and the damage is done both inside and outside normal hours.

8.15.2 Partitions should be constructed from brick or blockwork and never from single skins of plasterboard on studs as holes are easily kicked in these. External corners and projections are also easily damaged by accident and protection to these will help to deter more deliberate damage, fig 8.5, 8.6

8.15.3 Doors should not be glazed below the mid-rail. The ironmongery is vulnerable, especially items which project, and screw fixings should be substantial and non-removable. Knobs are more resistant than lever handles.

8.15.4 Sanitary areas are the most traditional areas for internal vandalism and there are many points of detailed design to take into account:

WC cubicle systems must be tough and must not include a fascia rail as this will be swung on

Any plastic laminate cladding should be detailed without mitres: timber or metal lipping is tougher

An obscure glazed panel in the wc door will leave the occupant feeling more open to detection

Toilet roll holders bolted back to back will last longer

Hat-and-coat hooks and those which act as door stops will be pulled off. Simple coat hooks are better

Full wc seats are better than the split types and should be fixed with locknuts

Seat covers will be stood upon and are better omitted

The wc pan should be fixed down firmly, and as it is bound to get blocked, a rodding eye is needed to each

Cisterns are better concealed in ducts, and if this is impossible high level types are the next best. Exposed low level cisterns are unacceptable

Overflows must be arranged to discharge outside, not on the floor or under the seat

Slab urinals in ranges are resistant, but the single pod types will not survive. Sparge pipes should be concealed to prevent levering off

Pvc wastes are unacceptable on urinals and basins, as are bottle traps which are easily dismantled

Washbasins are often broken when stood upon and so should be supported on legs and not sited next to wc cubicles or below high level windows

Captive plugs in basins will last a little longer than chains

Overflows on basins are better omitted as they act as leverage points and are usually blocked

Blended hot water will increase the amenity as well as reducing the number of taps to be damaged. Non-concussive valves are preferable

Stopcocks are better kept out of public areas and should be key operated

Any drinking fountains are better stainless steel

Shower heads should be fixed as the adjustable types are easily removed

Services are better concealed generally but if pipes are exposed they must be supported at 450 mm centres with heavy duty clips fixed into the masonry (not the plaster) with proper expanding plugs

8.15.5 Floors in wet areas must be provided with drainage as they will be flooded sooner or later. Carpet tiles are easily lifted and are not suitable.

8.15.6 False ceilings at a reachable level are damaged if the tiles are brittle or, like metal, can be dented.

8.15.7 Engineering services which are damaged can become unsafe. Externally, stopcocks should be located in pits and exposed frost stats, oil tank gauges and the like should not be accessible. Surface mounted fans, convectors, and thermostats are best avoided and any grilles must be robust. Local fuseboards will be interfered with unless they are in locked cupboards. Fluorescent lights are better recessed, and their diffusers should be impact resistant. Fire hose reels of the automatic type are often run out and, even if they are pushed roughly back, the automatic valve may not reclose, but will leave the valve at the nozzle under pressure; flooding has been caused in this way and reels of the manual type are better.

8.16   Alarms

8.16.1 Normal intruder alarms will protect a building against internal vandalism during unoccupied hours. There are many cases however where the maintenance and operation of such systems is impractical. Experience with school building is a good example of the difficulties:

An intruder alarm sounding internally is ignored or broken and is of little value

An alarm sounding externally is often set off as part of the vandalism. It becomes such a nuisance to neighbours that it is deliberately broken to silence it.

Opening and closing routines on comprehensive detection systems for whole school buildings are difficult to operate

One solution which has enjoyed some success relies on the probability that vandals will be noisy: an acoustic detector registers noises on an accumulating basis (like a ratchet) and activates the alarm when a pre-set level has been reached.

8.17 Building sites

8.17.1 The changing temporary nature of the building site means that precautions against both vandalism and pilferage must develop and change accordingly. Sites are popular both with vandals and potential vandals who use them as adventure playgrounds. The losses from damage and pilfering cannot easily be separated and the additional problem of wastage complicates the issue. General carelessness and untidiness also make theft of materials very simple. The scale of this problem is not surprising, considering the size of the floating labour force and the fact that 22% have criminal records. Some 90% of all theft and wanton damage occurs during working hours.

8.17.2 Big buildings on small sites introduce problems of working space and storage which increase the risks of damage. It is also well known in housing developments that the problems increase as soon as occupation commences.

8.17.3 As with other areas of security, and vandalism in particular, the conspicuous display of an attitude of care is the first vital step; cleanliness and tidiness on site not only help to minimise damage and losses, but also enable them to be detected more quickly.

8.17.4 The personnel are important, and it is worth appointing a security officer or a security company to oversee the policies of loss control on site: they will be free of the overriding pressures of the construction programme and the technical problems which occupy the site management. If they are to have any value, the security staff must however be constructive and active, not merely the producers of lists of additional tasks for the site.

8.17.5 As for any other premises, formal closing routines must be established and operated. These need to take into account the presence of the various subcontractors on the site.

8.17.6 Subcontractors must be made aware of the site security disciplines. Sometimes, when allegations of loss or damage are made by subcontractors, subsequent investigations reveal them to be quite false; they are made to conceal poor progress and labour problems.

8.17.7 The sequence of work will be determined by operational requirements but there should be some thoughts of security when planning work. Advice is sometimes given to delay glazing until the end of the job but this is clearly against the major aim of making the building weathertight at the earliest to enable interior trades to commence. This point is usually marked boldly on contractors' programmes, but rarely is the building secure point similarly marked; yet beyond this is the only time when vulnerable fittings and materials have any protection against the intruder.

It is usually possible for whole sections of the job to be secured during working hours, as all areas are seldom being worked upon at the same time.

8.17.8   Private cars must never be allowed to park on the site.

8.17.9   Where there is a defined site perimeter it should be given adequate protection. Chain link fencing is expensive because it does not withstand the usual rigours of the site and will not be re-usable. Simple protection is afforded by 1.2 m high chestnut palings supported by 1.8 m high scaffold poles with barbed wire strung between. Ordinary hoardings from 19 mm ply or corrugated metal should be 2.4 m high and supported adequately, The top 300 mm can be coated with anti-climb paint. Gates must be of strength and construction equivalent to that of the perimeter barrier; they should be locked by a close-shackle padlock on the *inside* and *without* the use of chains.

8.17.10 Site lighting is an advantage and will probably be required for winter working in any case. Even so, the location of storage areas and site huts where they are illuminated by street lights will give added protection. Otherwise the general external areas should be constantly lit by multiple fittings. Building interiors should be deliberately unlit so that any lights seen will arouse suspicion.

8.17.11 Site storage policies should be established. Materials and site huts should never be stacked within 2 m of fences: a yellow line painted inside storage compounds may help to enforce this principle. A good site storekeeper is most valuable and should be a full-time job on all sites of any size. He should be responsible for booking tools in and out (every day) as well as issuing materials for use. The use of standard freight containers for site storage has met with some success as they are easily transportable, robust, securable, and even designed to stack up to six high.

8.17.12 Traditional site hut offices are not so easy to secure, as the normal door can only be fitted with a rim lock or padlock and usually fits badly within the framed opening.

8.17.13 Alarm systems on the perimeter are usually impractical. The construction of site huts makes the use of mechanical switches inappropriate but both the site accommodation and the incomplete building can be given some protection: the first by volumetric sensors (probably ultrasonic) and the second by acoustic sensors which are fixed to the concrete floors.

8.17.14 Fire fighting appliances must be carefully thought out. They are essential for the safety of the workforce and the building during occupied hours, especially in extension and alteration work, but if left in position they can wreak havoc in the hands of the vandal. There is a high probability of decay if the extinguishers are supposed to be deployed and collected each day.

8.17.15 The possibility of occupation by squatters as the building nears completion cannot be ignored. It is unlikely that the police will act to remove them and their trespass is a civil matter. Obviously, housing is more vulnerable than other building types in this way.

8.17.16 The protection of plant has been discussed in section 8.12 above.

8.17.17 Warnings, notices and rewards are effective in that they contribute to the display of care. Notices should be properly signwritten and out of reach, and the general view is that they should be as large as possible. Further notices can be delivered to local households offering specific rewards for the detection of vandalism. One national building contractor, faced with a site next to a school, offered a bribe in the form of sports equipment on the condition that his site remained undamaged. It has been said, however, that notices have little value, since much of the damage is caused by children who cannot yet read; this seems unlikely.

8.18 Social defences

8.18.1 These are outside the sphere of operational security and of any measures taken individually by the building owner. Examples of organised social defences are the education of children to the cost of damage in order to increase the sense of responsibility and the involvement of the police (in Los Angeles) in the active continuous management of a local sports complex. The effectiveness of these measures is not known but they are unlikely to be negative.

Checklist 8

Vandalism and wastage

Graffiti

 Paint surfaces
 Budget for redecoration

Damage generally

 Reduce evidence of communal ownership
 Express ownership
 Do not route paths through residential areas
 Avoid through-routes on access balconies etc
 Care for property
 Remove evidence of damage

Fences

 Avoid chain link and metal posts
 Hold lower edge down

Walls

 Avoid membrane dpcs
 Avoid copings
 Lock gates

External areas

 Avoid through routes
 Use strategic deterrent plant types
 Use raised beds
 Avoid isolated saplings
 Avoid loose gravel
 Use only lockable gully grids

Plant and machinery

> Immobilise
> Secure
> Mark
> Alarm where necessary

Lighting

> Avoid high intensity point sources
> Use multiple small, soft lights
> Use vandal-resistant bollards for footpaths (in pairs)
> Light entrance and corridors

Building envelope

> Inhibit access to roofs
> Avoid tile hanging/asbestos cement cladding
> Avoid external rainwater pipes or fix securely
> Avoid pvc rainwater pipes
> Avoid services access panels
> Avoid external meter boxes
> Avoid low level balanced flues
> Consider polycarbonate for vulnerable windows
> Avoid glazing below sill height
> Avoid panelled doors
> Limit door glazing to 60 mm in either dimension
> Avoid timber louvres
> Avoid lever and pull handles
> Avoid external door closers

Building interior

> Avoid plasterboard partitions
> Protect external corners
> Avoid door glazing: especially low level
> Detail sanitary areas with care (see text)
> Avoid surface fixed switches, thermostats, etc
> Use manual fire hose reels (not automatic)

Alarms

> Consider acoustic vandal alarm

Building sites

Keep clean and tidy
Appoint security officer
Establish closing routines
Brief subcontractors
Ban private cars
Protect perimeter where possible
Light external areas
Switch all lights *out* inside
Establish site storage discipline
Install fire fighting appliances
Set up warning and reward notices

9 Remote surveillance and environmental services

9.1 General trends

9.1.1 The general personal surveillance by patrol was covered in section 2.5. The limitations of coverage and cost of patrols together with the increased danger of assault has led to a greater reliance on remote surveillance of premises from a single point. Once the communications and technology for remote visual surveillance was developed, it was clear that other possibilities existed for their use, and many systems can now be extended to cover the housekeeping duties of monitoring the building environment and plant.

A word of warning: it is easy to be seduced by the available technology, but if high security is required, or even if security is an overriding consideration, the addition of extraneous facilities will probably cause an overall reduction in the level of security possible. The objectives, must, therefore, be clearly defined at the outset.

9.2 Camera surveillance

9.2.1 In the United States, by law, all banks must be fitted with photographic cameras which are capable of recording any attack. The films may be used in evidence or for detection, and there are recognised procedures for handling and developing them once an attack has taken place.

In the UK this is not common practice, though equipment is available. Cameras may be ciné, in which case they operate only when an alarm is activated, or still, when they either take continuous time-lapse film or respond to an alarm. The admissibility of the film in evidence is not established.

9.2.2 The more usual form of camera surveillance is the closed circuit television system. There is much value in the installation of such systems and there is no doubt that security manpower can be reduced considerably. Their effectiveness depends on several factors.

The traditional picture of a security guard sitting in front of a bank of tv screens is a poor one. If the pictures are continuous or seen repeatedly, the guard becomes bored quite quickly, and ineffective. It is possible (and highly recommended) to fit motion detectors in cameras, which respond to a sudden change in picture content so that the watcher automatically has his attention drawn. Alternatively, an intruder detection system can be arranged so that a camera is activated by an alarm signal in its field of vision. The cameras themselves can be arranged to pan, tilt, and zoom (at extra cost) and in some circumstances this can be automatic following an alarm activation.

9.2.3 Television cameras depend on light for detection, and in the past this has been a major drawback to their usefulness. Nowadays however, a variety of different tubes is available for low-light levels: silicon target cameras for example require less than 20 lux to operate, and there are expensive variants of military equipment which will work in starlight in conjunction with image intensifiers. Cameras sensitive to infra-red radiation work better at night (when the background is cold) than they do in the ambience of higher daytime radiation. Image definition is poor, though they are particularly useful for close-ups of vulnerable areas such as gates and for sectored perimeter detection. Bright light compensators will eliminate the possibility of blinding the tube by high intensity sources.

The cameras can all be confounded by fog. For use in other bad weather conditions they should be fitted with wipers and heaters. If washing equipment is included, a maintenance routine must be introduced to refill the washer fluid containers. Occasional access must be possible to all cameras and this raises questions of cost, safety and vandalism. Ideally, the cameras should be sited behind locked doors.

9.2.4 In all cases the picture must be useful: i.e. it must enable the watcher to see some specific action and not simply display a blurred image which does no more than create uncertainty.

9.2.5 Inside buildings, surveillance is easier: light levels are better, the cameras are not in a hostile environment, and access for maintenance is less of a problem.

9.2.6 Television cameras are often used in shops, both as deterrent to shoplifting and as an aid to detection. It is also possible to fit dummy cameras at less cost to increase the deterrent value; this principle is deprecated and should be firmly resisted: first of all it displays a weak attitude to security and diminishes respect, and secondly, though shoplifters may be fooled, the staff certainly are not, and know full well which are the dummy cameras. Shop cameras can be fitted with directional microphones as an aid to detection, though this may be resented by customers and is useless as evidence. Videotape recorders are more useful and are said often to lead to an admission of guilt by a thief; they are expensive but are becoming more widely used in the UK.

9.2.7 The power supplies to cameras should be treated as secure wiring in the same way as those to intruder alarm systems. No switching should be allowed.

9.2.8 Television surveillance of wage packeting is not recommended, as it is unlikely to be effective at the small scales involved.

9.2.9 Monitoring rooms should not be located in the public view. Central locations are acceptable but, in practice the manpower available will usually determine that they are sited near the point of entry to the building so that this can be overseen personally at the same time. Access to the rooms should be restricted.

A more recent development is the slow-scan television system whereby a picture is gradually built up over a period of up to a minute from data sent piecemeal over a telephone line. In this way pictures of building interiors can be displayed remotely in alarm company control rooms. The system is promising and has yet to be fully evaluated. As with all remote monitoring, however, should anything be amiss a visit to the premises will be necessary.

9.3   Combined systems

9.3.1 The increasing complexity of security installations and the sudden availability of high computing power at a practical level has brought security into a single concept of management with other aspects of the operation of the building. The two main branches of combined system which are developing seem to be:

> Security and environmental services
> Security and accountancy

9.3.2 A combined security/services system will be based on a micro or minicomputer and can monitor:

> Intruder alarms
> Access control systems
> Fire alarms
> Temperature sensors
> Ventilation systems
> Mechanical building plant
> Industrial plant and processes
> Refrigeration or freezers.

9.3.3 Security companies have long been involved in the monitoring of certain unmanned industrial processes as an adjunct to their normal patrols; paint and sweet manufacture are typical examples. They are now becoming interested in expanding this kind of service and including a response to all environmental alarms. The main reason is a need for this service declared by the customer, coupled with the present ability of microcomputer-based monitors. There is also a relationship seen between security in its broadest sense and the integrity of engineering services in the building. Computerised engineering services monitoring is well established and several systems are on the market. The combination with security is therefore happening from two directions, in that services monitoring companies are adding security to their systems, while at the same time, security companies are including services monitoring in theirs. There are some problems in both combinations: security companies do not generally have the experience or the technical expertise to monitor building services; on the other hand services monitoring companies do not have any security expertise and there is a genuine fear that they may misread the risks on the security front much more easily than the security companies may fail to employ engineers. Development is in its early stages, but theoretically at least, the security based systems seems to have the edge in that:

> Security companies have an established network of control rooms and communications
>
> Services monitoring is not configured on a secure basis
>
> Services personnel are not trained to react to emergency situations

In the event of an environmental alarm the security staff would summon the keyholder and/or a nominated specialist engineer. The opening and re-securing of the premises would automatically be taken care of.

9.3.4   A combined system must incorporate certain principles if it is to be secure. The software must include guarding procedures so that it cannot be examined, tampered with or altered. The building owner may be allowed to enter certain variables such as temperature limits which change from time to time, but for his own benefit he must not be allowed unlimited access.

All the communications and power wiring must be installed in a secure manner following procedures similar to those established for intruder detection installations: see chapter 6. The implementation of the system must be controlled by the security company. The systems are complex and therefore failure must be expected from time to time. Some suppliers take the view that operation should revert to a degraded mode in such circumstances, so that with suitable notification, some parameters are monitored whilst others are not. There are dangers in this approach, as holes in security are likely to develop and it is felt that, should any failure occur, it is better that the whole system should revert to a manual status so that its integrity is preserved.

9.3.5   One comprehensive system recently developed is designed to operate on two clearly defined levels, giving a depth of security and options of sophistication and expansion. At first level (level 1), dedicated single control units are linked to a maximum of eight card readers; up to eight of these single control units can, in turn, be linked to an identical unit for co-ordination. At this level the controllers may be programmed by the user with a hand-held programmer. The higher level in the hierarchy (level 2) is based on a general purpose microcomputer which provides logging, reporting, decision making and centralised control. All the data is encrypted for security. A variety of configurations can be established.

9.3.6 The market in these combined building management systems is rapidly expanding, particularly for smaller premises at the lower end of the market, and it is not clear how development will proceed. Certainly engineering maintenance can be included—pump bearings changed following notification of maximum hours run for example—but it should be possible to include work schedules for civil building maintenance as well. The possibilities are considerable and could cover:

Cleaning schedules

Repainting schedules based on weather records

Seasonal gardening schedules

Preventive maintenance

Such facilities would be most valuable for absentee landlords.

9.3.7 Combined security and accounting systems are particularly useful in hotels, where a constant series of charges must be debited to a guest's account, and stock control and ordering is similarly complex. The special problems of access control have been described in chapter 7 and the electronic systems mentioned are ideal for combination with accounting. A main computer holds details of:

Reservations

Room status

Guest billing

Stock control

Sales and management reports

It also monitors the status of fire and intruder alarms and generates keys for the access control system. In the bedrooms there will be facilities for:

Telephone calls

TV or film hire

Radio

Public address

Baby sitting

Wake-up calls

Message indicators

Environmental controls

Mini-bar

All these will be activated by the guest, with his key if necessary, and registered on the central system with appropriate charges debited automatically to his account. Air-conditioning to empty rooms can also be reduced automatically as an energy saving measure. Wiring is usually by a single coaxial cable forming a local network, though it is unlikely that high security will be possible in this way.

9.4   Control rooms

9.4.1 Security companies maintain central control rooms which are permanently staffed. Their main function is the reception of alarm signals from remote installations and the initiation of action in response. The rooms are high security areas and should be constructed accordingly. The operational policies and routines will vary from one company to another but will take into account the overriding need to preserve the integrity of the control room itself.

Checklist 9

Remote surveillance and environmental services

Cameras

Consider recording crime with still/cine camera

Avoid standard CCTV static surveillance

Consider movement detectors in TV cameras

Fit wiper/heater/washer to external cameras

Avoid dummy cameras

Protect camera power supplies and wiring

Restrict access to monitoring rooms

Combined systems

Ensure security of software

Protect power supplies and wiring

Consider additional facilities available

Control rooms

Check facilities and reference

10 Safes and strongrooms

10.1 History

10.1.1 In ancient times valuables were protected either by guarding them (an expensive, uncertain business) or by hiding them. All the protection offered by concealment is of course lost at a stroke when the goods are found, and so as soon as the technology became available containers of the highest possible strength were made to give as much physical protection as they could: to keep things safe.

Then, as now, the only predictable level of defence was *time*, in that all safes can be overcome eventually but the time taken to do so has a direct bearing on the likelihood of attack and the possibility of detection. In addition, the criminal must be forced to carry tools and to make a noise.

10.1.2 Up to the industrial revolution, safes were little more than reinforced cupboards and chests; construction was often timber banded with wrought iron and they were fitted with elaborate multi-point locks, but there was little key security. Although it was the best that could be done, little resistance was offered even to the tools of the day.

The industrial revolution brought with it new materials, new methods of manufacture and also a new spirit of acquisition: more people had more valuables to safeguard. Safes began to develop accordingly and their design and construction kept pace with two main factors:

> The ability to bend and join sheets of thick steel;
> The means of attack available.

This development continues to the present day.

10.1.3 Older safes can be identified by their appearance and be ascribed roughly to a particular period, as the means of construction is usually obvious. The main types are listed below and shown in fig 10.1.

Square body	1840–1880
Square body with bands	1850–1890
Recessed panel	1880–1900
Pillar banded	1880–1910
Four corner bent	1890–1914
Eight corner bent	1900–1920

Four corner bent banded 1900–1932
Twelve corner bent 1906 onwards

Nowadays all safes are made on the twelve corner bent principle and in effect the body of the safe can be regarded as a solid piece of metal with no single area weaker than another. Recent development has concentrated on the steels and other materials used to provide protection against specific attack, and on the detailed design of the door and locking mechanism.

10.1 **The development of safe construction**

A **Square cornered**   **to 1880**
B **Four-bend banded**   **to 1915**
C **Eight-bend**   **to 1920**
D **Twelve-bend**   **to present**
E **Modern composite construction**

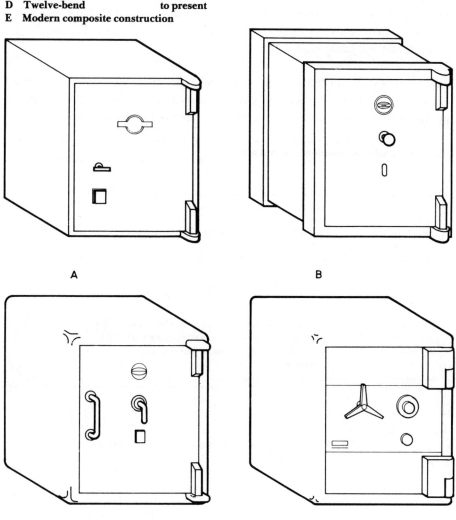

A

B

C
D

E

Safes have always been made of durable materials, however: it is part of their nature and they do not wear out. It is clear therefore that there will be many old safes still in use, and it must be understood that they will be attractive targets for the criminal and, with modern methods of attack, will offer little protection for the contents. The temptation to use an old safe must be resisted: it will give a false idea of security and is a grave false economy.

10.2 Contents

10.2.1 The selection of a safe is almost entirely governed by the nature of the contents: their value and their volume. As described in chapter 1, the question of value is not always a simple one to determine, but it is vital that the safe is not overloaded in security terms beyond its protective capabilities. Frequently the choice of safe will be determined by insurers.

10.2.2 As a very rough guide, the following types of construction are matched with both value of contents and safe cost. The list cannot be regarded too rigidly as the risk must vary with location and the costs differ between manufacturers:

Table 10.1. Safe construction, contents and cost

Cash contents £	Construction	Approximate cost £
150 or less	Wall safe	30–300
300–3000	Floor safe	75–500
500 or less	Drill resistant steel door with fully bent welded steel body	150–500
500–1000	As above with anti-explosive device in mechanism	350–700
1000–2000	As above with whole body drill resistant, anti-blowtorch door, and glass anti-explosive plate	500–1000
2500–4000	As above with anti-blowtorch alloy within door	800–2000
5000–7000	As above with anti-blowtorch alloy throughout	1000+
7000–10000	As above but heavier construction and copper sheet in door	2000+
10000 or more	Special construction	

10.3 Location

10.3.1 The location of a safe is important but it is often determined by the need for it to be close to the people who use it.

10.3.2 Wall safes should never be sited in the traditional places behind pictures or in built-in wardrobes as these are too well known. Their physical protection is so low however that concealment is important and a suitable place must be found in solid or cavity brickwork.

10.3.3 Floor safes are easier to conceal and can be sited below any suitable floor covering.

10.3.4 Conventional safes should be located in a conspicuous position where they can be seen by members of the public, police patrols or security staff from outside the building. This observation must obviously be maintained at night, so the safe should be illuminated by duplicate light fittings. If the safe is not obviously visible—in a shop window for example—then small observation windows or peepholes should be left in external walls or doors; mirrors can also help in some cases. Even where the safe is in such a visible position it may be possible for a criminal to penetrate the back by working through an opening made in the wall behind. This is especially easy where the safe is against a lightweight partition, and the proposed location should take this into account.

The police should be informed of the location of safes and any aids to observation, so that their patrols are more effective.

10.3.5 On a practical level, safes are heavy, and those of any size must usually be on the ground floor because of both the load bearing capacity of the building structure and the handling problems of installing it elsewhere. The route from the building entrance inwards should be checked to ensure that corridors and doors are wide enough. It may be necessary to have the safe delivered and installed at an early stage of construction; this is a good idea in that subsequent removal will be impractical, though for both physical protection and confidentiality it should be encased in a sealed cover until the building is occupied.

10.4 Fixing

10.4.1 The simplest way of stealing the contents of a safe is by bodily removal of the whole safe so that it can be opened at leisure. As a general rule, this must be considered possible for all safes weighing less than one tonne if they are at ground level and 0.6 tonnes at any other floor. These figures may require to be raised in industrial premises where mechanical handling equipment is available. The table gives indications of typical weights in tonnes for size:

Table 10.2. Weights of safes, in tonnes

Size (HWD)	6 mm body	10 mm body	13 mm body	25 mm body
600 × 450 × 450	0.20			
750 × 600 × 600	0.35	0.45	0.55	0.65
900 × 650 × 650	0.45	0.60	0.70	0.85
1050 × 650 × 650	0.55	0.70	0.80	1.00
1200 × 700 × 700	0.65	0.80	0.90	1.30
1350 × 750 × 700	0.75	0.90	1.00	1.65

Additional protection for the lighter models must be provide by some form of fixing or encasement.

10.4.2   Advice regarding fixing must be obtained from the safe manufacturer, as there are several forms of construction which will prevent either drilling the body or welding to it. Provision for fixing lugs is best made during manufacture. Where permitted, the base of the safe can be drilled and sleeved so that the whole can be located over studs cast into the concrete slab and nuts tightened down from inside the safe. Aternatively, steel channel sections can be welded to the base and then cast into a depression formed in the slab. The commonly used method of fitting straps around the body is not suitable as the straps are easily dealt with by hacksaw or flame cutting. Any lugs with exposed nuts are also clearly vulnerable.

The disadvantage of fixing a safe down is that it becomes a firmer object for attack, being conveniently held in place whilst ripping tools are applied. This is especially true of those with thinner bodies and they are probably better encased.

10.4.3   The only suitable encasing material is reinforced concrete; bricks should never be used, and mass concrete gives little protection. The casing gives additional protection to the weaker areas of the safe (particularly necessary on older models) as well as preventing physical removal. To prevent the safe from being pulled forward out of the casing it should also be anchored to the floor. The casing should be a minimum of 225 mm thick normal mix concrete on five sides, reinforced with 225 mm × 6 mm weldmesh or equivalent bars and the reinforcment should be attached to the safe body, where possible at 100 mm centres and by welding.

10.5   Forms of attack

10.5.1   Safes are defensive in their construction and their development has consisted of a series of steps, each one in response to a new form of successful attack. Safe-cracking is not a popular crime at present, perhaps because criminals see easier ways of stealing money. This has not always been so and there could well be a swing back at some future date. It should be remembered that the reputation of British safe-breakers is second to none. The main methods of attack are:

Key
Manipulation
Ripping
Cutting
Flame cutting
Explosives
Thermic lance
Acid

Key operation is speedy and clean, but the suspects will probably be limited. Key security and locking is dealt with in section 10.7. It should go without saying (but doesn't) that the safe key should not be left in a desk drawer.

Manipulation of key or combination locks is possible and the application of such skills is likely to be worthwhile. The internal mechanism of key locks can be examined through the keyhole by medical instruments such as endoscopes, and a hole can sometimes be drilled for the purpose beside combination locks. Some combination locks can be manipulated by feel, sound or even x-ray examination. Holes can be drilled in particular places for direct action on the bolt throwing mechanism.

Ripping is usually applied to older safes, especially to the backs, which tend to be thinner and can be torn off by the use of special power tools. It is quite easy but bulky equipment is needed and the operation can be noisy and lengthy.

Cutting with an electric trepanning device is quiet, but, again, bulky equipment is required and it will take some time. Attack may either be on the door, to cut out the lock, for example, or on the safe back to create a hole for removal of the contents.

Flame cutting with oxy-acetylene equipment is quiet and with older safes success is almost certain. The equipment is freely available and is often stolen nearby, though it is heavy and bulky. Modern safes are resistant to this form of attack. Oxy-arc cutting is a different matter and protection is much more difficult, though the equipment is less common. It cannot be used on concrete and so only the door of an encased safe will be vulnerable.

Explosive attack is quick and little equipment needs to be carried. Gelignite and detonators are much used in industry and are not difficult to obtain. There has been an increase in the use of plastic explosives, usually obtained from military sources, and there are always various more home-made explosives: a successful attack in Holland utilised ordinary town gas which was introduced through the keyhole until an explosive mixture formed with the air inside the safe: keyholes are weak points in explosive attacks. There is always some danger to the criminal however, and some risk of destroying or damaging the safe's contents. Modern safes have considerable resistance to explosive attack.

Thermic lances are bulky, require considerable operating space and create large quantities of smoke and fumes. Though they can open most safes, their operating temperature of over 2000°C will probably destroy the contents and so in most cases they are unlikely to be used.

Acid attack on the top of the safe or the door is effective. It is used elsewhere in Europe and is seen as a major threat to which there is no specific response. The quantities of acid required are manageable and the attack is quiet, though some time is needed and considerable fumes are generated.

10.6   Construction

10.6.1 The construction of the safe takes into account the methods of attack set out above. The case is fully welded and in a modern safe will have a steel thickness of about 25 mm minimum to inhibit straightforward ripping and cutting.

10.6.2 The door will be at least equivalent in strength, and, when the safe is closed it should to all intents and purposes form part of the whole shell. For this reason there will be a double rebate on the edge, protecting hardened bolts which shoot from all four edges into a reinforced surround. The only purpose of the hinge is to carry the door when open: it is redundant when shut and attack on this point will be fruitless.

10.6.3 Protection against flame-cutting is achieved by a combination of insulating fillers—some of which give off moisture when heated—and copper sheet behind the steel so that heat is conducted away too fast for the steel to melt. The fillers also protect the contents and are the reason why it may not be possible to weld fixing lugs to the case. Copper is expensive however, and aluminium may be used instead, but must be 25–50 mm thick.

10.6.4 Drilling in the vicinity of the lock is prevented by the inclusion of drill-resistant hardened steel plates. These tend to shatter under impact or explosion, however, and additional protection is obtained by the use of composite laminated panels. Even where the whole safe is drill-resistant, extra protection will usually be included over the lock.

10.6.5 A glass plate can be included within the door mechanism, with wires attached to the edges holding spring-loaded bolts withdrawn. If the plate shatters—as in an explosive or drilling attempt—the bolts are released and the door irrevocably locked. The connexions between plate and bolts should be arranged in a random way so that they cannot be predicted and neutralised by drilling in the appropriate places. Some vulnerability remains to side-blowing. The main weakness in explosive attack is often the keyhole, which can be offered some protection by an escutcheon lock or by the use of a keyless combination lock.

10.7   Locking

10.7.1 Lever locks on safes need only single-sided operation and so the limitations on differing described in chapter 7 are to some extent relieved. This is important because it is a basic principle of safe manufacture that a key should never be repeated so that each safe is sold with a unique pattern. In practice, copying must be rigidly resisted and the safe key should be kept by one person, not lodged in some place where it can be 'borrowed' for copying.

10.7.2 Keyless combination locks are commonly used on safes; the advantages are:

No keyhole is necessary

The combination can be changed at will

No key need be carried (or lost)

On the other hand, loss of secrecy is undetectable and it will be impossible to be certain of total security.

The lock operates through a rotating dial on the face of the door, inscribed with numbers (usually 1–100). Within the lock, a spindle turns a driving wheel which has a peg on its circumference; as the dial is turned to another position, a second tumbler is picked up and the peg on this picks up a third in turn; and so on. Each tumbler has a small notch on it and as each of these lines up, a continuous slot is formed allowing a fence to enter and the bolt mechanism to work.

The result of such ingenuity is a range of locks which manufacturers claim are unassailable and which criminals prove are not; certainly the simpler three-wheel combination locks can be opened by a skilled thief in a few minutes. To counter this threat, manipulation-resistant combination locks are available which do not allow the fence to contact the tumblers until the correct combination is set. A good quality lock would be expected to have four to six wheels.

Physical attacks on the lock may be made by removing the dial and driving spindle and tumblers backwards. To counter this, indirect drive locks move the dial aside so that the spindle is driven by a simple gear. The additional advantage is that the thief does not know exactly where the lock mechanism is in relation to the dial.

The combination might be learned by observation of the dial being operated and so a shielded dial is available to provide more confidentiality.

Clearly, knowledge of the combination should be restricted to the absolute minimum of people; should someone leave or the code be compromised, then it must be changed immediately. Routine changes should, in any case, be carried out, at, say, quarterly intervals. Whenever the code is changed it must be tried at least three times *with the door open* to ensure that no mistake in re-setting has been made: failure will reveal the value of this principle.

The combination chosen should not relate to telephone numbers, birth dates or the like, and should not be taped under chairs or written backwards under drawers.

10.7.3 Taking into consideration the characteristics of each type of lock, the best solution for high value safes is a dual control system with a keylock and a combination lock: one person holds the key and another the code, both having to be present each time the safe is opened.

10.8   Minor safes

10.8.1   Many of the constructional details above can only apply to the more complex high value safes. Other variations are:

Wall safes
Floor safes
Fire safes

10.8.2   Wall safes are not suitable for holding values of more than £150

10.8.3   Floor safes are inherently more difficult to attack and some are made with drill-resistant and anti-explosive doors. They are particularly useful as a type of night-safe in garages and cafes where cash can be inserted from time to time without opening the door, so protecting both the case and the staff from attack. It must be ensured that no one on the premises carries the keys.

10.8.4   Fire safes are intended to protect vital documents or electronic data from fire on the premises. Their integrity relies on a combination of thermal insulation and a substantial sealed construction which will not warp in the heat. Some fire safes look extremely resistant to attack but, in fact, their security protection is usually extremely limited. Documents may also be kept in fire resistant strongrooms but the same qualifications as to security apply. In both cases, the degree of fire resistance relates to a time of exposure in much the same way as other building components.

10.9   Standards

10.9.1   There is no British Standard for safes: the general view prevails that a standard form of construction by its existence would create an automatic loss of security. The Association of Burglary Insurance Surveyors do maintain certain standards of their own against which safes are assessed and graded.

10.9.2   Certain countries, particularly Sweden, France and USA, measure the performance of their safes against attack. The tests performed form a series and each one is a combination of limited time and a set of tools. The attackers are experts and are usually given full details of the design and construction of the safe before they start. The products are then graded according to their ability to withstand the attacks.

10.10   Strongrooms

10.10.1 Very high security for the most valuable articles: gems, bullion, money and works of art, is achieved only by the construction of fortress-like strongrooms deep within a protective structure.

10.10.2 The massive construction involved in a strongroom is such that it must usually be located at the lowest level of the building and, in fact, the ideal location for security is at basement level where the approaches can be more easily controlled. Strongrooms should never be on party walls.

It is relatively easy to take the decision to design the strongroom to the maximum resistance possible, and much of the detail in this chapter relates to such a concept. The more difficult decision relates to the lesser strengths because, clearly, there will be a difference between the criminal effort expended against contents of £100 000 compared with £5 m; strongrooms are extremely expensive and some reasonable relationship must be established between the value of the contents and the cost of construction. The traditional principle of construction relates the level of protection to the size of the room, on the basis that this would in turn relate to the value of the contents. Attacks on bank vaults have not supported this principle, and it seems that the risk is always high, irrespective of size.

10.11 Layout

10.11.1 There is no standard strongroom design for obvious reasons, though there are some sectional designs, intended primarily for installation in existing buildings. The planning of the room and any approach lobbies will vary from one situation to another. Different densities of defence may be established at various points depending on the attack most likely on any particular surface.

10.11.2 Internal fittings are important and may include:
    Safe deposit boxes
    Safes
    Booths for confidential work
    Fireproof cabinets
    Shelves
The provision of safes makes a considerable difference to the external envelope of the strongroom, as both the enclosing structure and the doors can be less substantial if the contents have the further level of protection offered by a safe.

10.12 Forms of attack

10.12.1 The biggest risks are those of hostage-taking and duress, and these can be applied either during the hours when the strongroom is in use or when it is shut. Violence and the threat of it are increasing as components of many crimes and as the technical problems of providing physical protection are solved, so the criminal attack will be transferred from property to people.

There are several ways of minimising this risk. First of all, doors fitted with timelocks reduce the period during which duress can be effective, which usually rules out all the closed hours. A further refinement of timelocking introduces an opening delay whereby, say, 30 minutes must elapse between operation of the main lock mechanism and withdrawal of the bolts. Alternatively, with lobby arrangements, the timelock on the inner door can be set later than the other one. These delays complicate the problems of duress for the criminal to the point where he may give up. The operation of an extra duress digit on combination locks can be made to set off a discreet alarm. Finally, turnstiles on the approach should be arranged so that no more than one person at a time can enter the strongroom.

10.12.2 Attacks on strongrooms and vaults are likely to be carried out by well-organised specialist teams of expert criminals. They may be prepared to take several years over both the planning and the attack itself, and it has been shown that they will use any tools or equipment which are available.

10.12.3 The structure is usually attacked by:
> Pneumatic or electric picks and drills
> Jacks
> Hydraulic bursting mechanisms
> Diamond tipped cutters
> Explosives
> Thermic lances
> Cutting torches

The door is usually attacked by:
> Explosives
> Thermic lances
> Combined oxy-arc burners and diamond tools

10.12.4 Specific defences are set out below but there are some general points to establish: many of the attacks require substantial electric power, for example, and this should not be made available within 30 m of the strongroom, at least during closed periods. One possible solution is to include circuit breakers within the floor distribution board to limit the power available on the floor to, say, 5 amps. This is not likely to cause great inconvenience to other users but will prevent the use of power tools.

Explosives are likely to need quantities of padding material to control and muffle the explosion and so, as a management policy, these should not be available in the vicinity of the strongroom.

In the same way as the protection of safes is arranged however, the aim should be to force the criminal:
> To take some time
> To carry equipment
> To make noise, dust and smoke

10.15.5 Other forms of attack which are possible but about which little is known include:

> Laser cutting
> Plasma-arc cutting
> Advanced high-frequency and electrical methods

10.13   Construction supervision

10.13.1 This must be carried out with great care and there are three main problems:

> Quality
> Interference
> Secrecy

Strongrooms are complicated in their construction and the quality of the end product can suffer through ignorance of the special attention needed for steel placement, concrete mix and consolidation, and the tolerances allowable around doors. Interference with the construction is quite possible, and subversive modifications must be watched for: the rearrangement of concrete mixes and reinforcement to leave weak spots for future attack are the most likely.

Secrecy must be preserved as far as possible so that details of the construction do not become available. Drawings should be kept safely in minimum numbers of copies, and should be removed from the site each night. Copies should be numbered and returned to the building owner on completion. They should not carry any name or address. Photography should not be allowed.

10.14   Walls, floor and roof

10.14.1 Strongrooms must *appear* strong, so that they inspire confidence and deter attack. Good quality durable finishes should be applied to the visible surfaces inside and out. Concealment of the structure is also a minor advantage. Of course, any such appearance must represent the truth, so the main structure must be massive enough to resist attack.

10.14.1 The main structure should be reinforced concrete and should be designed to remain intact should the rest of the building collapse upon it. The quality of the concrete is important, as a high compressive strength is an essential characteristic. High-strength attack-resistant concrete will be designed as a mix, but the approximate proportions will be (by volume):

> 2 parts Portland cement
> 3 parts sharp sand
> 1 part 6 mm basalt or granite chippings
> 5 parts 18 mm basalt or granite chippings

A low water/cement ratio is desirable, which can be achieved by the reduction of the very fine sand content and the use of an appropriate water reducing agent. A 28-day strength of 50–60 N/mm^2 is required.

10.14.3 Reinforcement of the concrete is complicated. Structural reinforcement will be calculated in the normal way, but is unlikely to provide enough resistance to attack by itself, and a higher concentration of steel, though preventing mechanical attack, will actually assist the passage of a thermic lance. The reinforcement of the concrete by special polymeric binding fibre is possible but special care is required during placement. Investigations are also being made into the use of glass fibre, but the more common solution is a mass of cut and twisted steel sheet (Tangbar) which binds the whole of the concrete together into a tough envelope but is not thick enough at any point to provide appreciable aid to the oxygen jet of the thermic lance, fig 10.2. The sheet is also relatively light so that the self-weight of the structure is not increased unnecessarily. Fig 10.3. shows the recommended spacing of the tangbars.

10.2 Tangbar strongroom reinforcement

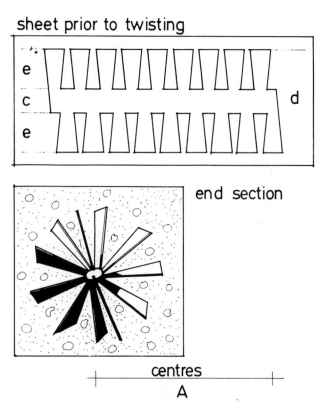

sheet prior to twisting

end section

centres
A

10.3 **Tangbar spacing**

d	c	e	A
77	17	30	77
125	31·5	46·75	104
167	31·5	67·75	136
200	31·5	84·25	165

With such a network of steel consolidation of the concrete is extremely difficult, but it is vital that proper compaction is achieved and the greatest possible care must be taken during pouring, with the rigorous use of vibration pokers.

10.14.4 Total thickness of external envelopes will vary according to the protection required, and will be determined by insurance companies, strong room specialists and national custom; variations in the latter are illustrated in table 10.3.

Table 10.3. Strongroom envelope thicknesses

Country	Standard thicknesses, mm
West Germany	600
	800
	1000
United States	300
	450
	700
	900
	1150
	1400
Holland	400 (minimum)
Switzerland	400 (minimum)
France	400 (minimum)
UK	800
	1000

Though it can be seen that very thick walls are quite common, a general rule during planning is that minimum wall thicknesses for high value strongrooms should be:

> 600 mm where contents are not in safes
> 400 mm where safes are installed

Those with walls below 300 mm should be regarded as 'secure rooms', giving protection roughly equivalent to a safe and suitable for archiving but not for high values. There should also be a consistency of protection between walls and doors, and the table gives matching thicknesses:

Walls	Doors
300	25 (thief resistant)
450	90–115
600	175–200
900	250+

Table 10.4. Strongroom wall and door thicknesses, mm

10.14.5 Explosive charges can be placed in such a way that pieces of concrete are forcefully projected from the inner face into the strongroom, and to prevent the walls from being weakened or breached in this way, the inner face can be lined with drill and torch resistant 5 mm steel sheet, fig 10.4.

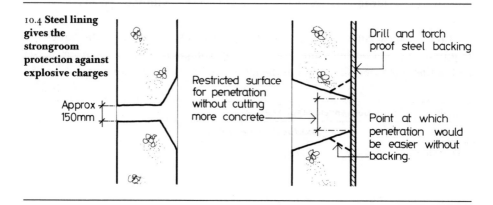

10.4 **Steel lining gives the strongroom protection against explosive charges**

Approx 150mm

Restricted surface for penetration without cutting more concrete

Drill and torch proof steel backing

Point at which penetration would be easier without backing.

10.15   Doors

10.15.1 For obvious reasons the details of door design are kept secret by the various manufacturers. In the more vulnerable installations the door will probably be purpose made and may combine a number of standard defensive features into an assembly which will protect against specific risks. Lamination will oblige the criminal to use a series of different methods to penetrate.

10.15.2 The larger doors will weigh several tonnes and will be carried on integral crane hinges, but there is a substantial load on frame, frame fixings and surround when the door is open. In addition, hydraulic equipment can exert forces of several tonnes inwards on the frame and this must also be taken into account. The weight will make the door difficult to move, and during working hours a light lockable gate should be provided to control access. The gate is often fitted within the main door opening but if it is possible to fit it as an outer lobby, then another barrier is created for the criminal, and another point for fitting an alarm.

10.15.3 If an attack is made on a door it is likely to activate defensive mechanisms which will make normal opening impossible. An emergency door should be provided for access in such cases and, clearly, it must be constructed to the same standard as the main door, though it need only be large enough to allow a man to crawl in. The emergency door should be completely separate from the main door and though it is sometimes used as the entrace for ventilation ducting it is better locked and the keys kept in a remote secure place.

10.16 Locking

10.16.1 There should always be at least two locks to a strong room and at least two people must be present to open the door. The main locks fitted are:

A combination lock: see 10.7.2

A key lock

There may also be a control lock, which secures the operating handle itself and can be used for minimal security during open hours; and a time lock which is inside the strongroom and determines irrevocably the earliest that the lock mechanism is allowed to operate. Time locks have two or three identical movements in case one fails and are particularly useful against the threat of duress or hostage-taking: see 10.12.1. The key lock can be in the form of a change key lock, which can be operated by a set of, say, 10 different keys, but can only be opened by the key which last locked it.

10.16.2 There must be some means of opening the main door from the inside: it has been known for the whole staff of a bank to be locked into a strongroom after a successful raid, and quite apart from the distress caused, an airtight room will eventually become dangerous. The device must be designed so that it cannot be tampered with to affect security.

10.17 Isolation

10.17.1 The best security is obtained by the complete separation of the strongroom enclosure from the rest of the building structure, and this should always be done in new buildings. The room will be surrounded by a void, as shown in fig 10.5, which will be monitored by alarm systems. The void should be visible but not normally accessible; its width is important and should be approximately 600 mm: this will give sufficient clearance for inspection but will not allow the criminal enough room to use thermic lances or bulky equipment. The void should be continued around the floor and roof.

10.18 Surveillance

10.18.1 Internal observation of the strongroom can only be carried out by TV cameras within, which will perform the dual role of surveillance and of confirming the cause of any alarm signal generated from the interior.

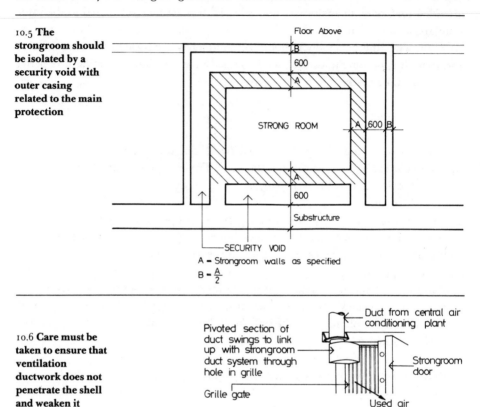

10.5 The strongroom should be isolated by a security void with outer casing related to the main protection

Floor Above

B
600
A

STRONG ROOM   A 600 B

A
600

Substructure

SECURITY VOID
A = Strongroom walls as specified
B = $\frac{A}{2}$

10.6 Care must be taken to ensure that ventilation ductwork does not penetrate the shell and weaken it

Duct from central air conditioning plant

Pivoted section of duct swings to link up with strongroom duct system through hole in grille

Strongroom door

Grille gate

Used air

10.18.2 Observation of the surrounding area and the security void can either be undertaken by camera or patrol. Mirrors at appropriate places in the void will allow a full view.

10.18.3 If full-time observation is not thought necessary, it should still be remembered that the criminal must be denied time to make his attempt, so the vault must be visited at weekends and holidays to ensure that no extended attack is being carried out at these vulnerable times.

10.19   Services

10.19.1 No additional openings for ventilation or services may be made in the strongroom walls. The only connexion which needs to penetrate the structure is that for alarm and surveillance wiring, and most manufacturers have a special detail fitting for these. Other wiring, for lighting and power, can be taken through the open door when the room is in use.

10.9.2 Mechanical ventilation is often required for rooms which are in use by the same personnel for hours at a time, but is less important where short visits are made to, say, safe deposit boxes. The ventilation for occupied rooms should provide 6–8 airchanges per hour, which can usually be achieved by ductwork which swings into the open doorway, fig 10.6. Serious errors have been made in the past, where large ducts have passed through the vault walls.

10.19.3 Care must be taken that power is not available to help the criminal: see 12.4., 10.12.4.

10.19.4 Lighting levels of the order of 200 lux should be available.

10.20 Alarms

10.20.1 Chapter 6 covered the principles of the various intruder detection systems available. Several of these will be used in combination for a strongroom on:
> The approaches
> The entrances
> The envelope
> The interior

10.20.2 The approaches should be covered by standard beam interruption or volumetric sensors.

10.20.2 The doors to the strongroom should be fitted with a complex of alarms:
> A duress code facility on the combination lock, enabling an operator deliberately to generate a silent signal whilst opening the door
> A monitor on the operation of the main lock
> Detectors for physical assault and monitoring of the various defensive bolt-throwing mechanisms.

10.20.3 The walls, floor and ceiling should be fitted with vibration detectors to sense physical assault.

10.20.4 The interior space can be fitted with volumetric detectors, but the other effects of intrusion are simpler and more reliably monitored, and so detectors will be fitted to sense:
> Noise
> Heat
> Light
> Smoke

Acoustic detection requires an ambient noise level below 40dBA if it is to function reliably. Further sensors may be fitted to the safes inside the strongroom.

10.20.5 Manual activation of the alarm should also be possible and some form of break-glass switch is suitable inside and outside the room.

10.21   Maintenance

10.21.1 Access to the strongroom during use will have to be severely restricted, and the initial finishes specified should be of the highest quality maintenance-free materials. Routine service access will thus be limited to light cleaning. Technical maintenance of the alarm systems and the door mechanisms will be necessary, however, and must be carried out under a service contract with the specialist installing company. There is a clear security risk arising from both the quality of the maintenance work and the possibility of illicit modifications. The most rigorous verification and identity procedures must be established and operated before anyone is allowed to work on door mechanisms and alarms.

10.22   Design life

10.22.1 The massive nature of the construction, and the fact that most of the work is well covered and concealed means that modifications to the strongroom are rarely possible. The attitude of design must therefore be similar to that adopted for building foundations, in that extra care is taken during both design and supervision stages to ensure that the solution is correct.

Checklist 10

Safes and strongrooms

Safes

Avoid old models

Match protection to contents

Locate wall safes carefully

Locate conventional safes conspicuously and
illuminate with multiple fittings

Consider bodily removal for small safes

Fix down in accordance with manufacturer's
guidance

Control key possession and location carefully

Ban key copying

Consider likely attacks

Avoid simple three wheel combination locks

Change combinations as routine

Strongrooms

Control approaches

Avoid party walls

Consider inclusion of safes to reduce overall risk

Protect by management against hostage-taking or
duress

Fit timelocks

Reduce numbers of occupants

Avoid electric power supplies nearby

Supervise construction and ensure confidentiality

Give appearance of strength

Ensure consistency between walls and doors

Fit escape mechanism

Isolate from main structure

247

Include security passage all round
Continue surveillance over weekends and holidays
Minimise penetration for services
Fit appropriate alarms
Control and oversee maintenance

11 Operation and maintenance

11.1 Positive operation

11.1.1 The establishment of defences against the elements of nature in the design of buildings is largely a static matter and is almost wholly in the control of the designer. Operational protection by the building occupant is minimal and is mostly confined to simple precautions against frost, unblocking gutters and the like.

This is not so with security defences: although many of the physical precautions are analogous with those constructed to combat the elements, security defences must have the dimension of *time* added, and they must be positively operated from day to day. The need for operational security introduces *people* into the matter, and inevitably the quality of operation will vary according to the skills and understanding of the personnel involved. In a security system, the greater the personal component, the greater the variation in quality. This must be taken into account when a system is established, but it must also be balanced against the greater flexibility which accompanies the personal component, and the fact that variation in security is not necessarily always a disadvantage: the creation of uncertainty in the mind of the attacker is in itself a form of defence.

11.2 Decay

11.2.1 Decay has been mentioned repeatedly in the preceding chapters of this book and there is no doubt that it is the most serious problem in the operation of security. It is almost exclusively a function of the human component of a security system but few installations are immune.

11.2.2 The provision of effective security is, paradoxically, the first step towards decay. This is because the effective system will not only repel successful attacks but will prevent the attacks being made; the illusion is thus created that the security is unnecessary, and decay will follow until the degree of security falls to the point at which an attack succeeds. In such cases, the immediate reaction is often to increase the security measures established, but in fact this is not usually necessary and all that may be required is the re-establishment of the intended level of protection.

A well publicised and classic example of this form of decay was the successful intrusion into the Queen's bedroom in Buckingham Palace in July 1982: there was little wrong with the *intended* security measures, but the decay of the operational element was widespread. In that case the immediate upgrading of physical measures was probably only necessary in response to publicity and the anticipation of imitative attacks.

11.2.3 The opportunist criminal wanders the world in search of low security measures; but there is also the more deliberate criminal, skilled, patient and vigilant, who will select a target and bide his time until the defences fall.

11.2.4 The avoidance of decay depends upon:
   System design: it must be tolerable
   Consistency: at all times, in all places and to all people
   Costs: they must be affordable

Tolerability of the security measures is mainly a social consideration, in that their need and their operation must be acceptable to staff, customers and delivery men as reasonable citizens. If this is not so the measures will at best be considered fair game for evasion, and at worst will lose custom or cause industrial disputes.

Consistency is a policy matter and the operation of the system must not depend on the chairman's liver or the impending visit from head office, nor must it be affected by the occasional panic or business pressures; it must apply throughout the premises, and no one can be exempt.

Costs are always difficult to substantiate, as it is never certain what losses might have been suffered if security had been absent. Often the best that can be said is that the costs must bear a reasonable relationship to the value of the property protected: see section 1.3 however, regarding the true costs of losses.

11.3   Procedures

11.3.1 It is important that the security operation is subject to the same management-by-objectives as the other management functions in the organisation. If this is not so, then it will not be appreciated for what it is, and it will not be long before the security effort will suffer from lack of top management support and finance.

11.3.2 The operation and staffing of the security organisation should be independent of the normal hierarchical line of responsibility within an organisation. If this is not so, the security will be comprised by the routine pressures arising from the normal course of business.

It must be remembered, however, that despite this essential independence, the function of security is secondary to the main purpose of any organisation, and it is there to *assist* management. The willing co-operation of many people is required, extending to peripheral bodies such as suppliers and customers, and external organisations such as neighbours, police, fire and ambulance services.

11.4 Personnel

11.4.1 Responsibilities must be clearly defined, not allowed to develop by default. Somebody must be allocated the task of studying the losses and security problems and initiating measures to be put into effect to correct the situation. It is essential that the person designated reports directly to the main policy-making body within the organisation: board of directors, council or whatever, and not upwards through the normal hierarchy. This principle is intended to prevent the matter of security becoming confused or complicated by other more immediate managerial demands; it also underlines the fact that the security disciplines must apply to everyone in the organisation.

Recruitment of security personnel, both at managerial and operational level, is a specialist subject outside the coverage of this book. The greatest care is necessary.

At some stage the decision must be taken as to whether operational security is dealt with as an internal matter, or whether all or part is subcontracted to a security company. The decision is often taken in ignorance and it is recommended that both options are examined most fully.

In-house security has attractions:

> It is within control all the time
> It appears to be more economical
> The personnel are loyal directly to the main organisation
> The personnel can carry out other tasks simultaneously

These are valid considerations, especially where the values, and the risks to be protected are low. Where more protection is required, however, they do not always stand up to scrutiny.

Control may be retained but, on the other hand it is unlikely to be exercised with the benefit of experience or expertise.

Costs will be high for full-time staff and they may not be needed on that basis; a more effective use of resources may be a part-time service from a security company. In addition, it is not easy to vary the cover provided by internal staff, whereas subcontracted personnel can be increased or laid off at will—perhaps brought in to cover some temporary risk.

Loyalty is a vital characteristic and should not be undervalued. Balanced against it, however, is the difficulty of familiarity and the enforcement of security disciplines by full-time colleagues in a working environment.

Other tasks can be carried out by the security staff but the limitations set out in 11.3.2 must be observed. It may be useful to include the monitoring of plant and industrial processes but, as described in chapter 9, these can also be carried out by security companies in many cases.

It should not be thought that the duties of enforcing security can be effectively performed as a sideline to, say, building maintenance or portering.

11.5   Updating

11.5.1 Whatever security measures are established initially, it must not be expected that they will last for ever. In fact it is most unlikely that the first solution will be absolutely correct, and there must be a built-in review after, say, six months.

11.5.2 Apart from this first review it will be necessary to instigate a routine of inspection and analysis. Updating the system may be needed because of changes in:

Technology
Methods of attack
Operations
Society

Technology changes all the time and its effects can be seen in the products used in security protection—electronics in particular—but the technology of attack will also change.

Methods of attack change for other reasons as well; some simply because of a new idea or fashion, and some as a result of weakness perceived in new security techniques or equipment. The anticipation of new attacks is extremely difficult because most of the thinking in security is defensive; the majority of protective methods have come into being as reactions to earlier attacks rather than as anticipations of new ones. This principle is so deeply instilled into security planning that the initiative will probably always remain with the criminal. As a general rule, however, every security system should be presented to an 'odd-man', who knows nothing of its intended working but will apply his imagination to defeating it.

Operations peripheral to the security measures are subject to frequent change: the main business of the organisation concerned is unlikely to remain static, and new machinery and methods, new premises or alterations to the management structure will all have their effect on the original security plan.

Society evolves and mutates. Crimes which were rare in the UK a decade ago, such as mugging, now cause concern in some areas, whereas others such as safebreaking are on the decline at the moment. Fashion, history, the climate of society and the quality of policing all play a part, but the most tangible factor is probably economic: some crimes are worth committing while others are not, and the current attraction and value of certain categories of goods make them especially vulnerable.

11.6 Drills

11.6.1 Breaches of security, whether they be shoplifting, burglary, vandalism or terrorism, are almost certain to precipitate a crisis. In such a situation it is impossible to restore security or even to protect the premises or their occupants unless crisis has been anticipated and a contingency plan is available. This is not a difficult matter to arrange and a competent management should not require much advice to enable plans to be registered. They should cover:

Declaration of emergency
Individual responsibilities
Communications
Individual duties
Restoration of normality
Review

11.6.2 If such plans are to be reliable, it is essential that they are tested and in exactly the same way as fire precautions; drills must be arranged so that the occupants go through a simulation of the events of the crisis.

11.6.3 Tenants, employees and security staff should all know what is expected of them. They may be required to:

Go to a place of safety
Apprehend a suspected criminal
Raise the alarm
Take notes
Register their own whereabouts
Assist with a search
Wait for instructions

The most important drills concern personal safety and are those which detail methods of evacuation and search.

11.7 Maintenance

11.7.1 The security hardware must obviously be properly maintained but sometimes this is carried out as an isolated routine, and in this way weaknesses can appear. The selection of the hardware in the first place was not carried out without consideration of its context, the building fabric, and maintenance should likewise be kept in context; the well-maintained lock is of no use if the door frame is rotten.

11.7.2 There is also a risk that the installation, particularly alarm wiring, may be damaged in the normal use of the building.

11.7.3 Any building alterations must be carried out in parallel with a full reassessment of the security plan.

11.8 Records

11.8.1 Records of the security system must be kept, so that there is a reasonable base for updating and assessment of its efficacy. In some cases such as intruder alarm systems, there is a clear procedure laid down in a British Standard; in others, such as master-key systems, there are well-tried habits in the lock industry which help. In the main, however, it will be the building occupant who must develop and maintain records of his security installations.

11.8.2 The records must be confidential, with access severely restricted. Ideally, they should not be kept on the premises, and if records are kept elsewhere, the location of the premises in question should not be obvious.

11.9 Cash-in-transit

11.9.1 Cash is at its most vulnerable while being moved from one place to another. This principle applies both inside and outside buildings.

11.9.2 The precautions taken will vary according to the amount of cash, the time in transit and the nature of the route. It is almost entirely an operational matter with little relationship to the physical nature of the building, and is fairly regarded as a specialist subject in its own right. Ideally, the matter should be delegated to a security company, especially if vehicular transport is involved.

11.10 Security companies

11.10.1 Specialist firms cover all aspects of security and the industry is growing. As with any industry which is developing rapidly however, the quality of service, the reputability and capability varies enormously from one firm to another. The concept of security is nebulous enough by itself without introducing the uncertainty of a contractor who cannot provide it at all.

11.10.2 Selection of a security company must follow certain guidelines. First, the company should be able to undertake as many aspects of the security installation as possible, including:

> Consultancy advice
> Hardware
> Access control
> Intruder detection
> Response to alarms

Patrols and staffing

Cash protection

Maintenance

Secondly, the company should have the following qualifications:

Membership of the British Security Industry Association (and other trade
bodies where appropriate, such as NSCIA)

Proven standard operational procedures

Its own staff training programme

Excellent references

A professional attitude

11.11   Costs

11.11.1 It is, of course, impossible to give generalised guidance on the costs of
security installations. However, the costs must relate to the values being protected
and the risks. They must also be financially acceptable to the organisation; if they
are not, the pressures for modfication will be so great that the system will probably
fall into a degraded state in which it will not be effective, and none of the money
will be spent usefully.

Checklist 11

Operation and maintenance

Decay

Consider and plan for decay
Ensure security is tolerable
Apply principles throughout

Procedures

Manage security in parallel with other functions
Update regularly

Personnel

Define responsibilities
Take care with recruitment
Decide whether personnel are in-house or contract
Recognise security as a separate function
Hold drills for crisis procedures
Publish procedures

Maintenance

Ensure comparability with building maintenance
Keep records

Security companies

Check references and qualifications

Index